Effective Grouping for Literacy Instruction

Greta K. Nagel
California State University, Long Beach

Allyn and Bacon

Boston • London • Toronto • Sydney • Tokyo • Singapore

To the memory of
William Johannes Kallio,
my dad

Series Editor: Aurora Martinez Ramos
Series Editorial Assistant: Patrice Mailloux
Marketing Managers: Brad Parkins and Kathleen Morgan

Library of Congress Cataloging-in-Publication Data
Nagel, Greta K.
    Effective grouping for literacy instruction / Greta K. Nagel.
      p. cm.
    Includes bibliographical references and index.
    ISBN 0-205-30920-8
    1. Group work in education. 2. Language arts. 3. Reading. I. Title.
LB1032.N34 2001
371.39′5—dc21

                            00-062064

Printed in the United States of America

10 9 8 7 6 5 4 3 2 1   04 03 02 01 00

Contents

Section 3   Creating a KPA Community

▶

Preface

In their efforts to promote effective learning in groups, educators need appropriate criteria to plan groupings well and to analyze their successes and failures. Views provided by the Knowledge, Power, and Affection (KPA) model can inform educators' decision making about forming groups and setting tasks, especially in literacy classrooms in which notions of ability have influenced group membership, instructional time, and teacher-student behaviors for decades. Well-designed and well-guided groups, including whole-class groups, can reach their goals and get along.

Teachers lead busy lives, interacting with many different sets of people at work, at home, and in their communities. Readers from the field of education will nod their heads in agreement that, in the course of just 1 week, they participate in dozens of groups. At school alone, they have faculty teams and committees, partnerships with aides and parent helpers, team teaching, as well as roles within various student groups, classroom subgroupings, and clubs—in addition to their whole-class group. Some of these groups "work," and some do not.

In one teacher's life, faculty book club discussions might be gratifying, and the school leadership committee seems to be accomplishing great things, but the grade-level team does not seem to get along—ever. The morning ESL group may be making fine progress, and the student council is reaching many of its goals, but this year's sixth graders are earning their ongoing reputation as "the class from hell." And, to top it all, the new teacher's aide is simply not a team player. Similar complex scenarios are repeated across hundreds of thousands of lives with millions of groups involving educators who often conclude that they work with difficult people.

Teachers certainly have many questions about classroom groups, especially as they plan various activities for literacy instruction. Heading a long list of queries are "What is the best way to assign students to groups?" "When is it appropriate to do whole-class lessons?" "How big should groups be?" "How can I teach skills in groups?" "How will I manage many different groups at the same time?" and "Why is a class of twenty better than a class with thirty-two?"

Students, like their teachers, are members of many groups. They, too, discover that some groups work well for them, but others do not get along. For example, strong students who participate in group work often complain that they "have to do all the work." They say that some group members "do not even know what to do." Other students complain that some of their classmates cannot get along, or it is boring to be in the same group all the time. Parents describe scheduling nightmares as they attempt to host their son's or daughter's homework group projects, noting that some students seem to "get away with doing nothing." Furthermore, some families are disturbed by the way an entire class group may be going, with tales of rowdy behavior or atmospheres of disrespect in their children's classrooms.

In the meantime, teachers may be tempted to lay blame on one or two individuals, or they may even conclude that classroom group work will never work. Feelings of powerlessness are not surprising. They live in a society in which one of the most important groups is marriage, and yet nearly 50% of those relationships end in divorce. Many individuals are clueless about the dynamics of groups, much less how to improve them.

This book is based on four key perspectives that I embrace after 30 years of working in diverse classrooms. My first is that the work of educators is, indeed, "social" work. Teachers are the ones who, in their important spheres of influence, can establish and guide groups of students into successful relations. The acquisition and retention of knowledge is dependent on varied and positive group dynamics. Teachers who, in teacher's lounge conversations, exclaim, "I'm not a social worker!" or who express the desire to "just teach" miss this very important point. It is they who can combat racism, sexism, and classism through their own examples and talk as well as through their daily and long-term plans and actions that involve children.

Second, learning to work productively with groups must be a cornerstone of educational practice in a democracy. A constant challenge for educators is the dichotomy of addressing individual needs while serving the common good. Teachers must connect with each student's capabilities while connecting the whole class to core knowledge and shared ideals. Effective use of instructional groups is the only way to accomplish both liberty and equality in classrooms of diverse learners.

Third, educators, particularly those in literacy, must get off the historical/political "grouping pendulum." Inspired by policies at local, state, and national levels and promoted by site administrators, this phenomenon has meant that teachers over time flip-flop from whole-class instruction to ability groups and back, ignoring many other necessary and valuable formats. The pendulum of grouping practices is as political and pernicious as the phon-ics/whole-language pendulum (or any other of several that plague educational practice across the curriculum). Not only does it create practitioner unrest, but it also interferes with the academic and social progress of schoolchildren.

Finally, as I hope to show by examples, reports of research, and narrative vignettes, teachers can find wise social solutions when they understand, and use, judicious balance in promoting a multiplicity of groups. Their students will achieve more if they have opportunities to work in many different types of group settings with many types of books and materials. In a democracy devoted to promoting equity, placing children in static low groups that are labeled by euphemistic names such as Orange Group, Robins, or any other ongoing title is unacceptable.

As I will explain in this volume, many researchers have written about three key needs that interact for each member of a successful group. They have used a variety of words for three ideas that have prevailed through the decades. For purposes here, the terms that seem to express the basic needs most clearly are (a) *knowledge*, (b) *power*, and (c) *affection*. Individuals reach satisfaction in group relations only when they feel useful for the knowledge (skills, talents, information) they bring to the group, when they have a sense of power (influence, say-so, choice) within the group, and when they possess a feeling of affection (being listened to, cared for, respected) by other group members. If groups are to reach their goals, members must be dedicated to the group. Sticking together and sticking it out are critical. Groups are then able to experience community and maintain cohesion.

The purpose of this book is to assist teachers and teacher educators as they reflect on the effectiveness of various types of groups and group activities in promoting literacy learning. I hope it will be a useful tool for thinking and planning. It will focus on situations within classrooms in which literacy is taught because of the influential roles played by reading, writing, speaking, and listening activities in K–8 education. Nevertheless, the ideas in this vol-ume are easy to apply to instruction in all areas of the curriculum. Although these chapters are focused on classroom practice and not school restructuring, schools do change when teachers decide to teach in certain ways. In addition, the impact of the work of informed, committed literacy teachers can also be felt in greater arenas of influence. Although this is not a book of broad-scale social change, attributes of the larger community can follow when the expectations of well-informed parents and children are clear, focused, and communicated.

I believe that the theoretical model of KPA can serve as a useful tool for making decisions, but I also hope that readers will find practical ideas and perspectives in vignettes that I have gathered during 20 years of observations in schools and from a variety of studies that, over the years, have examined literacy groups in kindergarten through eighth grade settings. Findings from 50 years of research in group effects and group dynamics will form the central section of the book and support other chapters. Respected writers and researchers such as Elizabeth Cohen, D. W. and R. T. Johnson, and R. A. and D. A. Schmuck, as well as Rebecca Barr, Robert Slavin, William Glasser, and Spencer Kagan, are just some of the individuals who have provided fine insights into ways to analyze group interactions, design group strategies, and guide groups. Others, such as Jeannie Oakes, have helped create the big picture of societal implications for grouping decisions or have brought us into the teaching/learning process through perspectives of action research.

In Section I, "Learning about Knowledge, Power, and Affection," the chapters explain the three concepts that work together to build positive sociopsychological dynamics for "good" groups. The explanations include classroom scenarios in which various teachers' assignments and classroom conditions support positive group dynamics. Examples of less effective situations are depicted to provide contrast and promote understanding. Some ideas are also supported by reports of related studies.

In Section II, "A Look at the Research," the chapters focus on the key studies that not only inform the notion of the KPA model but provide the context within which grouping decisions must be made. In Section III, "Creating a KPA Community," chapters describe teaching tips for building KPA through classroom decision making about groups, as well as provide answers to teachers' specific questions. In Section IV, a series of charts, diagrams, and lists can help readers to apply concepts of KPA and to share their knowledge with others. Finally, in Section V, a glossary can help readers to review and assess their understandings of key terms.

If classroom groups are to succeed, educators must know how to plan. Teachers not only want to design group configurations and activities in appropriate ways, but they want effective ways to assess successes and failures. In addition, the KPA model holds value beyond the realms of literacy groups, classrooms, or schools. Students are growing up in a world that is pondering its diversity and its relationship-related problems such as attachment-deprived children, alienated adolescents, pregnant teens, high divorce rates, and lonely elders. Application of the KPA model can make a big difference for students *and* teachers. They will be able to enhance group work in school and build better relationships in their lives outside school. Groups that are truly "good" must provide for the complex sociopsychological needs of individuals as they reach their varied goals.

Teachers possess the power to create conditions that can help students learn a great deal—or keep them from learning much at all. Teaching is the intentional act of creating those conditions, and good teaching requires that we understand the inner sources of both the intent and the act.

—P. Palmer

Acknowledgments

I am grateful for the insights and support of many people who helped me in different ways during the last ten years while the ideas for this book percolated through many thoughts and conversations. I would like to express my affection and thanks to several wonderful people, including the following individuals:

To Jim Flood and Diane Lapp, Mary Poplin, Natalie Kuhlman, and Joe Weeres, my doctoral advisers and my dissertation committee, for helping me think and write as I first examined KPA.

To Hilda Sramek, Ella Burnett, Deborah Hamm, Felipe Golez, and John Sikula for their ideas and comments about early pieces of this manuscript and to Carole Cox and MaryEllen Vogt for their insights about writing books.

To Joy and Jon Anderson, Mary Jaedtke, Laura Kaulfuss, Karla Kaulfuss, Lisa Frantzis, Jean Houck, Kathy Cohn, Steve Turley, Candace Kaye, Cathy DuCharme, Pat Irot, Ellen and Dave Nichols, Marilyn and Mike Meeker, Harold Horn, and Virginia Horn, in memoriam, for their interest in and support of my writing and my ways of thinking.

To Donna Jaecker, Angela Vasquez, and Christy Lunceford, for their enthusiasm about and their support of my work.

To Sue Abel, Helen Brown, Peggy Caron, Sue Cody, Nancy Henderson, Wendy Lloyd-Davies, Lew Kerns, Fred Lentz, Bev Maeda, Nancy Moore, Marion Nordberg, Layna Rushing, Andrea Street, Marsha Thicksten, Sofia VenderKooy, and many other educators I cannot name here, who have worked diligently to empower students as learners and have allowed me to share in their pursuits through the years.

To my reviewers, who have provided wonderfully helpful comments and suggestions to help me clarify this work and strive to communicate to a wide audience: Deborah Diffily, Texas Wesleyan University; Lorraine Gerstl;

Eileen Madaus, Newton Public Schools; and Nancy Peterson, Utah Valley State College.

To my editor Arnis Burvikovs, who has been a friendly, insightful, and patient guide.

And special gratitude to my husband Glenn, my daughter Christina, and my son Paul for their patience when I toil at the computer, for their love, and for their special insights and perspectives about life and school.

▶ 1

The Search for Successful Groups

*Organization is nothing but getting things into connection
with one another, so that they work easily, flexibly, and
fully.—JOHN DEWEY*

This volume is about classroom groups of all sorts—whole-class, half-class, small and very small, including partners, as well as variations that are teacher-led or student-led and more. To be classified as a group, a relationship must consist of two or more people who meet face-to-face with a purpose over time. Any group may be thought of as a network of social and psychological relationships (Bonner, 1959). In good groups, members meet their purposes and manage their relationships. As portrayed in the chart shown in Appendix A, many grouping arrangements that involve literacy learners are possible. Teachers of literacy have a responsibility to engage students and promote their growth in reading, writing, speaking, and listening. How they do that involves many kinds of stories, but all of the tales include groups. This chapter will set the stage for future chapters by providing a brief overview of the history of grouping in education and by explaining some of the key concepts that relate to group dynamics and "getting along."

GROUPS FOR A DEMOCRACY

In spite of the difficulties that often arise when people work together in groups, such interactions are essential within a democratic society. The history of education, however, cannot tell many stories of instructional groups with heterogeneous memberships across social classes, ethnic groups, and genders until recent times. Although students have studied in groups within various cultures for thousands of years, group memberships were limited to only select rosters of individuals, usually male and usually of an upper class in the particular society. For example, Socrates conducted dialogues with small groups of boys; for centuries, Chinese scholars gathered in similar groups. Most instructional groups were alike in gender and composition— (i.e., male and aristocratic) right up to the 19th century, varying only for anomalies such as the women who trained to be geisha in Japan or courtesans in France.

Changes occurred with the unfolding of American history, but, nevertheless, at no time has public education offered equal access to all children. In the Massachusetts Bay Colony in 1642, reading instruction was made available to white males only (Monaghan, 1989). Girls were never included in reading instruction until the late 1700s. African Americans were never included until the antebellum years of the late 1800s. As Salvino (1989) points out, American public education has promoted paradoxes ever since, overtly supporting "equal education for all" but covertly endorsing various forms of stratification and discrimination.

Thomas Jefferson brought forth a bill that proposed "to diffuse knowledge more generally through the mass of the people" to lay the groundwork for republican government and eliminate the aristocratic domination (Hirsch, 1996). Although Jefferson's vision for education in the new democracy in the colonies was groundbreaking in its conception, it took time for his inspiration to come anywhere close to reality in the new society.

In the early 1800s, public schools began to play an important role in preparing students of varied backgrounds and genders to participate in democracy, emphasizing the importance of discussion, debate, and decision making. Horace Mann argued that all children would benefit from a common school that prepared them with the knowledge and skills to become economically independent and free.

With the onset of the Industrial Revolution in the late 1800s, the new emphasis was on schooling as a way to promote unity and respect for authority. Classroom groups were designed to be similar in size so as to fit in "factory model" schools and instruction within intimate groups. Nevertheless, it was not until the turn of the 20th century that school contexts for groups with nonselective memberships were formed, although when all children were finally allowed to go to school, the schools they attended were often different for children of varied races, economic levels, and ethnic groups. In situations in which varied groups of children did attend the same schools, they were grouped and tracked into separate classrooms and/or into separate groups within classrooms.

John Dewey (1915/1966) advocated that schools model aspects of democratic living and realistic problem solving. As grouping experts point out, Dewey inspired the current tradition of thinking about the social aspects of learning in the 20th century (Schmuck & Schmuck, 1979, 1988). Dewey's notions for democratic organization have influenced many schools and many movements. He encouraged others to see education as an opportunity for learners to solve problems of both a personal and social nature, using collected knowledge in an active way.

GROUPINGS FOR LITERACY INSTRUCTION

Although the research about ability grouping will be explored more thoroughly in Chapter 8, a mention of it here seems necessary. Perceptions of "ability" have been pivotal to many grouping controversies and dilemmas. In her reviews of grouping practices for reading instruction, R. Barr (1989, 1995) notes that ability-based reading groups have been popular since the advent of IQ tests and standardized achievement tests during World War I. A 1913 teacher's manual suggested that different groups be formed for "those who progress rapidly" and those who are "slow and need more assistance." The practice of ability grouping was seen as reasonable and convenient, and it began to be popular in the 1920s. Researchers of the 1920s, 1930s, and 1940s said that ability groups benefited slow pupils, had the next greatest benefit for average children, and were the least helpful for bright children (Otto, 1950).

Historically, teachers have grouped children in many varieties of ways, but in times during which ability groups and the use of basal reading texts were most prominent, the times and opportunities for other types of groupings were infrequent. Ability groups drove the classroom management of the reading time and often controlled the structure of the school day for teachers who felt compelled to forego other activities to "get in all their reading groups" each day. Ability grouping has been a common procedure up through the present, used in many districts, schools, and classrooms to accommodate individual differences in learning rates (Good & Stipek, 1983).

Research collected within the last four decades, however, has prompted the rethinking of grouping practices. Ever since Eash's (1961) summary on the negative effects of ability grouping, others have concurred that ability groups depress academic achievement for students in average and low groups. Children in "low" groups do not receive the same quality of instruction, nor do they enjoy access to the same curriculum (e.g., Allington, 1983). In addition, children who have been assigned to low groups in kindergarten and first grade end up remaining in low groups and tracks throughout their entire school careers (e.g., Burns & Mason, 1998; Hallinan, 1984).

Arguments in favor of meeting children's needs better in homogeneous ability groups have been frequent and strong within various communities.

Since the 1960s, one strong group of advocates includes parents and teachers of gifted children, who believe that gifted children need qualitatively different education in settings that are segregated from slower-learning students (O'Neil, 1990). In exact opposition to conclusions about grouping in the first half of the century, research of the second half of the 20th century seemed to support the view that ability groups provide advantages to the members of the highest groups, not the other way around.

In the field of literacy instruction within the United States, the use of groups has been a focus of practitioners for decades, but popular perspectives about group size and membership have changed along the way. When basal reader use became widespread in the 1940s and 1950s, teachers latched on to the idea that the grade-level readers would work for all. They did "work"— but only for some children. Some children did not keep up. Some children were bored. In subsequent years, teachers learned to form varied classroom reading groups. Student placements were based on the practicality of ability groups, and three groups emerged as the favored number of groups to be manageable in most classroom time frames. The groups worked—for the high groups, at least. However, the lower groups did not encourage progress in reading and thinking to the extent that low-group students remained in low groups and became school dropouts over time. The 1970s era of open classrooms reminded educators that children could read and write well in individualized and heterogeneous settings. The system worked well—for the responsible children, at least. Unfortunately, public school adaptations of the British Infant School methodology in the United States often experienced off-task behaviors of children and suffered the discontent of parents and school boards.

Another era of ability grouping encouraged precise "scientific" placements into as many reading groups as deemed necessary. Students' scores on basal reading tests determined which level was best and to which group a student would be assigned for the school year. A room with five reading groups came to be perceived as better analyzed and more beneficial to the students. "Diagnosis" on sequences of skills was deemed important, although in reality such profiles did little to determine group formations or activities. Indeed, the top groups did well—again.

The advent of whole language philosophy along with literature-based classrooms in the 1980s reminded teachers to facilitate authentic learning opportunities in literacy and provide equal access to literature and the core curriculum. However, some schools (and some publishers), in turn, perpetuated mistaken notions that whole-group instruction was the way to go for whole language. The turn to whole-group reading practices meant that some children simply did not have the opportunity to interact with texts that were truly readable for them. The benefits of practice in fluent reading and instruction in appropriate materials were lost for many. Poor readers were often asked to navigate in materials that were inappropriate for them to handle and failed to help them benefit from the use of multiple cueing systems. Thus, students were destined to experience "Matthew effects" (e.g., Stanovich, 1986) whereby the "rich" readers got richer and the "poor" readers got poorer. Good readers could read and grow in fluency and vocabulary, but poor readers could seldom glean enough from their experiences to make appropriate progress.

As teachers learned to better understand their students through conscientious assessments, they came to see the values of flexible groups and independent reading (e.g., Flood, Lapp, Flood, & Nagel, 1992). At the same time, political mandates have begun to guide policy for reading instruction in many geographic regions. The ensuing emphases on skills and test results have prompted school principals and other instructional leaders to depend on ability groups once again. Not only are schools and districts promoting such groups for within-class instruction, but they are also returning to tracking formats that cross classes and grade levels. They hope to improve performance by having children of like ability read in materials at "scientifically" designated levels. Such practices are occurring in the context of ongoing research and publications that key into harmful attributes of tracking and ability grouping for students (e.g., R. Barr, 1995).

The time line shown in Figure 1–1 provides an overview of the key historical points related to groupings.

A Time Line of Key Historical Points

Worldwide Background

500 B.C.	Ancient Greece: small interactive groups, aristocratic boys Ancient Egypt: children of the elite educated
100 A.D.	Male, upper-class groups of scholars in various parts of the world such as China, Japan, France
Middle Ages	Literacy achieved by selected elite only

U.S. History

1642	Massachusetts Bay Colony All parents required to see that their children learn to read

(Continues)

FIGURE 1–1   Literacy Grouping

U.S. History	
1647	First public schools New England Grammar schools—literacy education for white males only Elementary schools—open to all children
Colonial Days	Wealthy children to "dame" schools in private homes Poor children serving as apprentices: • boys to crafts, trades, professions, reading, writing • girls to household tasks, cooking, sewing, spinning, weaving
1740s	Time of great awakening—interest in "common man," democracy
1770s	Thomas Jefferson's vision: diffuse knowledge more generally
Late 1700s	Girls first receive reading instruction
Early 1800s	Education regularized with Lancasterian schools Introduction of standardized textbooks Start of state public school systems One-room country schools open to all
1830s	Horace Mann promotion of a "common school" for all
1847	First graded schools, Boston "Factory model schools" with the start of the Industrial Revolution; children sorted into grades
1860s	First tracking within grades, St. Louis
1875	African Americans' participation in reading education
1900	Introduction of graded readers, such as the McGuffey readers Schools with nonselective memberships, but classes tracked and grouped; Mexican Americans and Native Americans included Progressive educator emphasis on child-centered learning (discussion, creative activities, trips) to prepare children for life in a democracy
1910s	Advent of IQ and achievement tests; U.S. educators pioneering reading groups arranged by ability *within* classrooms

FIGURE 1–1   (*Continued*)

U.S. History	
1920s	Ability groups thought to benefit *slow* pupils but disadvantage students in *top* groups
1940s	Widespread use of basals; grade-level readers for all students in majority of schools
1954	School desegregation by court order, *Brown v. Board of Education*
1960s	Ability groups dominating educational practice (despite conclusions of researchers that ability groups benefit *top* pupils but disadvantage students in *low* groups).
1980s	Whole-language movement, many educators misinterpreting philosophy to mean *whole-class* instruction
1990s to Present	Some literacy educators adopt flexible grouping practices. Nevertheless, ability grouping remains a prominent, if not dominant, practice

FIGURE 1–1   (*Continued*)

As the following chapters will support, educators must solve the social and academic puzzles presented by various grouping arrangements. An important part of finding solutions will be to glean insights from group dynamics research. For example, few educators would discount the value of small-group work as an ideal. The rationale and techniques have been spelled out well in many excellent volumes during the last two decades. Teachers in most schools have many understandings. Nevertheless, knowing about something and being able to do something are two different things. Many individuals have not overcome the frustrations of getting group work to work.

GROUPS THAT GET ALONG

The category of "gets along with others" has been an attribute evaluated on public school report cards for many decades. Although "gets along" has often meant "obeys the teacher," some teachers have also devoted class time to teaching the skills involved with getting along and have devised meaningful assessments of their students as helpful, desirable classmates and citizens. At the start of a new century, many schools are involved with various forms of conflict management programs, including peer mediation strategies and efforts at peace building. Efforts, however, are typically focused on behavior as children play in the schoolyard. Less attention seems to be paid to the more subtle, and yet more influential, status games that are played within the various instructional groups inside the classroom walls, including the class as a whole. The memberships and dynamics of classroom reading groups, in particular, can determine success or failure for children at the moment, during the school year, and for years to come.

Most people seem to know when groups are going well, for not only do tasks get done but the group "gets along." A group is able to keep going, maintaining its membership and focus over time, when the members have positive morale. Such a group is said to be *cohesive*. It has esprit de corps and the involvement of each member. Nevertheless, these group attributes can develop only when the individual group members all have feelings of usefulness, say-so, and belonging. As presented in the next chapter, these feelings can be designated by the terms *knowledge, power,* and *affection*. The three attributes form a useful set of lenses for the examination of group dynamics. Getting along with peers is one critical aspect of getting along in the classroom. The nature of student-to-student interactions can be affected by many variables, including the number of students who work together each day. Getting along with the teacher is another major part of classroom dynamics. The quality of teacher–student relations can impact the quality of learning. Getting along with parents plays an additional influential part, impacting classroom success for the student—and for the teacher.

Some classrooms are characterized by minimal changes in grouping throughout the day and a focus on the whole class, but others are characterized by changing patterns of flexible groupings. This book draws on a variety of observed group situations. A number of vignettes are from notes I gathered while conducting literacy studies across 27 classrooms in six districts as well as from videotapes and field notes made while I was "living" in six elementary classrooms for 6 months. Others are from situations recorded in narratives that I have written as a clinical supervisor during the past 2 decades. I have seen that, although students' assigned group tasks usually (but not always) get done, the quality of the work accomplished and maintenance of the group itself were dependent on the talk and actions of social interrelationships. Each student's needs are extremely important and must be met. The next chapter will describe those major requirements.

> *When the world saw failure, you, Teacher, saw light.*
> *Because of you that light shall never flicker, and I am now*
> *motivated to light the dying embers of others who too, have*
> *been tagged and labeled.—MARVA COLLINS (1992, p. 206)*

▶ 2

What Is KPA?

> *Many people feel empty and don't know why they feel
> empty. The reason is we are all social animals and we must
> live and interact and work together in community to be-
> come fulfilled.—ROBERT BELLAH ET AL.*
> *Habits of the Heart*

This chapter will provide an overview of *knowledge, power, and affection* (KPA), the model that provides the central theme for this book. I will describe why I selected these three particular terms as well as suggest some of their impli- cations for success in groups. I want readers to begin conceptualizing KPA, both as an organizing acronym for developing successful group work in the classroom and also as a way to analyze and enhance relationships of all sorts.

If an artist were to paint a picture of positive group dynamics, it would be a portrait of community. Red, yellow, and blue would be knowledge, power, and affection, for they are the primary colors that can blend in a vari- ety of ways to create group success and maintenance. They are the sociopsy- chological needs that are met by good groups and that effective teachers consider in their planning. Each group, like an individual painting, has its own detail and character, whether it is a class or a partnership.

The ideas that comprise the KPA model are not new. During the past five decades, these same three big notions have appeared in several key places within writing related to group dynamics and personal motivation. Various authors have used different terms, but they all stress the importance of the same three traits in order for groups to be successful for all members (Back,1951; Borich & Tombari, 1995; Coleman & Bexton, 1975; Connell & Wellborn, 1991; Deci & Ryan, 1990; Kolb, Rubin, & McIntyre, 1979; Schmuck & Schmuck, 1988). The three sociopsychological *needs* of individuals relate to their motivation for joining and staying in group relationships.

The relationship among K, P, and A is not sequential, although some individuals may have a preference to stress one over the other in their personal philosophies. All three attributes are important, and each interacts with the other two. On the other hand, although the three traits have the greatest impact when they work together, each one represents an idea that also holds singular prominence. The order of presentation for this book—K first, then P, then A—is arbitrary and rather simple: KPA simply sounds better to my ear than APK or PAK or other configurations.

Also, I have opted to use the acronym KPA rather than the full terms (knowledge, power, and affection) because most such combinations of letters in the literacy world seem to represent strategies, such as KWL (Ogle, 1986) or CSR (Klingner & Vaughan, 1999), and simply because I hope that the acronym form will be more memorable. I hope that educators will, indeed, use the model in their day-to-day thinking and planning.

In addition, K, P, and A are not only indicators of group success but also prime qualities of personal motivation. For many decades, starting with the work of noted social psychologist Gordon Allport (1937), incompetence, powerlessness, and rejection have been seen as blocks to motivation for individuals. Those three blocks are the opposites of K, P, and A. Teachers will recognize these traits in their struggling students who are at risk of falling behind and dropping out. Incompetence, powerlessness, and/or rejection are reasons that propel younger children to disengage from classroom tasks and older students to stay away from their classrooms and leave school. They are attributes of students who are subjected to groups that do not work for them.

KPA is not just for students who are in trouble, however. Many students who look just fine "on paper" in terms of decent grades, high test scores, and living on "the right side of the tracks" are often just going through the motions of school. Teachers frequently hear parents or colleagues lament the unused potential of certain students. In an era when teachers are fighting illiteracy, they must also work to remedy "aliteracy"—the condition in which individuals *can* read but do not choose to. Students who simply do not participate in much reading or writing are aliterate, and their condition is problematic for schools as well as for society. Inspiring engagement with literacy is a challenge for educators that can be won with applications of KPA teaching. Also, as explained further in Chapter 7, esprit de corps, morale, and self-involvement are three attributes of positive groups that play overlapping roles with knowledge, power, and affection for members of groups. They develop as a result of KPA, and they serve with KPA as indicators of group health.

I believe that a firm understanding of the KPA model will help teachers to go beyond fads and pendulums to see the primacy of good group work to effective education. It is not merely something "nice" teachers can do if they attend the right workshop or training session. I hope to make clear something that is vexing and complicated.

Because groups are *social* networks of *psychological* relationships (Bonner, 1959), the framework for much of the thinking presented in this book is sociopsychological. The umbrella of key ideas comes from research and writing in social psychology that are connected with ideas from the field of literacy education. However, I also incorporate views from a wide variety of disciplines that lend additional, multiple perspectives. I do not want to perpetuate the syndrome of "The Blind Men and the Elephant," sharing a few insights that tell only a limited story and get at only part of the truth. Therefore, I will share information from multiple literatures, including ideas from anthropology, sociology, linguistics, philosophy, and psychology. Findings from neuroscience inform quantitative and qualitative studies of classroom life. In addition, I believe that perspectives from transformative research and writing must spread to become part of the explicit discussion in public school settings. Educators in all contexts must examine and untangle issues of race, class, culture, and gender. Ideas from critical and feminist perspectives bring to light many key social dilemmas and help shed light on their possible solutions. We must not hide from controversy. We must continue to abolish foolish segregations of scholars and practitioners from one another.

Recently, educational researchers have described learning as *situated* (e.g., Lave, 1988). It occurs in social contexts (situations) through social practices. People come to "know" their worlds because of their experiences. The subjectivity of researchers can shape the work they do and its outcomes (e.g., Alvermann & Dillon, 1991). Thinking is best developed when several perspectives are explored. One perspective tells us that grounding a notion in a wide range of disciplines is the key to research in the 21st century (Kirshner & Whitson, 1997). In facing the new millennium, I agree. Our communities of educators would be wise to integrate knowledge from the following four areas: (a) the impact of cultural environments and interpersonal relationships on learning, (b) the effects of culture and social processes on the development of cognitive/intellectual ability, (c) the roles of motivation and effort in developing ability, and (d) the power of caring relationships and high expectations in fostering student resilience (Williams, 1999) . I believe that the KPA framework provides a useful, comprehensive tool for such exploration in, and integration of, multiple resources.

Literacy instruction is complex, involving important decisions to be made many times a day—some instantaneous, some processed over time, all affecting the lives of children. When the classroom door closes, each teacher must navigate through an incredible variety of issues and viewpoints to come up with appropriate applications in their work. For example, a fifth-grade teacher may start the year with a new set of textbooks for her new set of students. Both teacher and students are eager to enjoy the pages of the colorful new books, only to discover that just a few students can actually read the paragraphs. Teachers incorporate several ways of knowing in facing the multiple sets of dualities that come their ways. Their decisions are seldom made on the basis of only one clear-cut belief.

At any given moment in a teacher's thinking, words and concepts from a wide variety of sources make their appearances. Philosophers past and present may line up behind psychologists and sociologists to have their say. Then come the voices of officials from the state legislatures and departments of education. Books, newspapers, magazines, journals, and curriculum guides make their appearances, along with the principal's newsletters and memos. All blend with the voices of culture and class within the college-educated minds of the individuals who teach. They do not all sing the same tune.

In preparing this book, I have come to see that only a complex probe would shed appropriate light on grouping practices. Some individuals mistrust research as being manipulative, "able to prove *any*thing," because of the limited stances that many studies take. Therefore, when I talk about KPA as a sociopsychological model with sociocultural perspectives and sociocognitive, sociopolitical, and socioemotional attributes, I am actually leaving out a lot. The reality is that educators are informed by data from the realms of neuroscience, sociolinguistics, "romantic" literature in education, and more. Perhaps most fitting for some of the ideas in this book will be concepts that derive from the work of ecological psychologists. The references in this volume serve as only small testimony to the many types of investigations that seek to better understand the intricacies of learning in social contexts. This book will present probes into many paradigms, but it does not begin to explore their complexities. Many books—certainly thicker books—can take teachers and scholars on those journeys. I think of myself as a new learner poking around in many types of scholarly and practical works during the years of thinking and preparing for this book. This volume is intended to be taken off the shelf and become a well-used companion for others like me who believe that *eclectic* is not a bad word for those who are searching for the truth.

KNOWLEDGE

The first trait, K (knowledge), refers to an individual's ability to do the tasks before him or her. It also refers to that person's expertise, such as leadership, that can support the group's activities or help everyone learn. It is not IQ. Ideally, no task to be performed within a group should be impossible for the designated member of a group. The work must not be too hard, nor should a task be boring because it is too easy. Various writers use other synonyms for knowledge: Coleman and Bexton and Kolb, Rubin, and McIntyre refer to this attribute as *achievement*, whereas Borich and Tombari, Connell and Wellborn, and Deci and Ryan refer to *competence*. Murray (1938) and Allport (1937), on the other hand, refer to the converse idea: *incompetence* is one of three major qualities that block motivation. Individuals will stick with a group, maintaining their membership, if they believe that their efforts, past or present, are important to the group's success.

Students perceive that they possess knowledge within the group context when they see that they have the information, resources, or skills that are respected by the group and useful to the group's purpose(s). Because all groups are heterogeneous in many ways, the abilities and potential contributions of various group members do not need to be identical in order to be equitable. Children come to school with great stores of experiences, general knowledge, and vocabulary that spring from different cultural and linguistic contexts and meet different perceptions of being necessary for school. Good teaching respects each student's prior knowledge. Group activities that are well designed must allow children to draw from their existing knowledge bases and build on those concepts to achieve "school" concepts and language. Ideas for planning and teaching address the notion of knowledge in Chapters 3 and 11.

POWER

In successful groups, members also possess P (power), having a say about some aspect of their work and the ability to make choices that affect the outcomes of the group's work. The term selected to represent this notion by Coleman, Bexton and Kolb, Rubin and McIntyre is also *power*, whereas Borich and Tombari refer to *influence*, and Deci and Ryan discuss a sense of *control* over the environment. Connell and Wellborn explore *autonomy*. Authors Allport and Murray speak of *powerlessness* as a blockade to motivation. If individuals have been able to help shape the course of their group's work toward meaningful goals, they will support their group's efforts and maintain focus over time.

Power means being included in decision making, even when it is not the quickest or most expedient way to reach a conclusion. Just as adults have various levels of input, students may offer opinions, give suggestions, make choices, or cast votes. They also have some latitude in choosing where to work, on what to work, and/or with whom to work. Teachers may frame some selections for their students, but their choices should be real. If the teacher asks, "Would you like to read a story about an airplane, or do you prefer this story about a horse?" or "Shall we write and put together a newspaper or make a bulletin board display?" the students' decision should prevail. The individual should be exercising higher levels of thinking, justifying decisions, as his or her decisions are made. Each group member should have a clear responsibility, but members may also have more than one designated task or play more than one role. Even the youngest children are capable of performing multiple tasks. Concepts and teaching ideas about power are further explored in Chapters 4 and 12.

AFFECTION

Group members experience A (affection) when they feel respected, when their needs to feel appreciated are met, and when they have the caring support of other group members. Affection is the presence of positive affect. In classrooms, both students and teachers have this need; they fulfill this requirement for one another. Without affection, feelings are unsafe and taking risks becomes impossible. Coleman and Bexton and Kolb, Rubin, and McIntyre refer to this as trait as *affiliation*, but it is known as *acceptance* to Borich and Tombari and as *belonging* to Deci and Ryan. Connell and Wellborn use the term *relatedness*. According to Allport and Murray, it is known as *rejection* in an environment that blocks motivation. Individuals work in groups with greater ease when the social "lubricants" of positive morale and esprit de corps are accomplished.

Members of successful groups perceive that other group members have positive feelings toward them. It is not optimal merely to be "tolerated." In the eyes of the beholder, a sense of caring and belonging is best. Adults and children alike can understand what it means to be "nice." Educational caring is not identical to care in friendships or family. There is no need for excessive affection or a need for "friends forever." A sense of feeling welcome can serve well.

The interactions of affection are noted in many places. As one spokesperson for neuroscience puts it, "Our emotional system drives our attentional system, which drives learning and memory and everything else that we do. It is biologically impossible to learn and remember anything that we don't pay attention to" (Sylwester from D'Arcangelo, 1998, p. 25). Emotion is not just for recess or art class.

Because various individuals have unique conceptions of what constitutes caring, teachers need to recognize that their caring acts will often vary with the student. Chapters 5 and 13 will elaborate on the individuality of symbols of affection within classroom cultures.

THE KPA MODEL

As shown in Figure 2–1 and again in Appendix B, KPA is not just a collection of three separate principles. Knowledge, power, and affection interact to form

The KPA Model

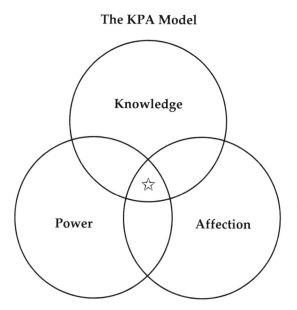

FIGURE 2–1   The KPA Model. A triad model of sociopsychological needs.

a key that can help understand the sociopsychological needs of individuals in group work. Although the attributes can certainly be thought of as separate entities, all three parts of the key are necessary to open the lock of successful group dynamics. The intersection of the three entwined set circles, marked with a star, signifies the very best in group dynamics, when all three attributes are acting together for each individual group member. The KPA triad applies to all classroom group relationships. It serves as a model for the success of the teacher in relationship with her or his students, but it also helps to plan for the whole-class group and holds meaning for interactions with families.

Interactions of K, P, and A

The three components of the KPA model inform and affect one another. It has often been said that knowledge is power. Foucalt (1980) is one of many thinkers who have stressed the importance of this idea over time since Thomas Hobbes in his 1651 work *Leviathan* or earlier. Cohen (1986), in her influential writing on group work, reminds us that status within a group is closely linked to the importance of the knowledge that an individual brings to the group. As Heath (1983) and others (Weinstein, 1991) have determined, teachers are much more prone to accept the words and stories of some children over others. In studies of children's narrative styles for sharing, the focused stories of white children driving toward a punch line were preferred by teachers, especially in contrast to the many-part narratives that were linked together in implicit, rather than explicit ways, by black students. Many educators are well aware of the cultural bias of IQ tests and other standardized tests. More and more, we will see ways in which *some* knowledge is power; some is not. Certain kinds of knowledge automatically imbue their holders with authority in school contexts. Teachers who endeavor to support their children will find ways to respect more types of knowledge as they bring children into learning together.

Knowledge can also inspire affection. Improvement of academic skills can have reciprocal effects on social competence. For example, one study involved four groups of acting-out, disruptive, struggling fourth graders who could not read. One group was assigned to extra academic tutoring, one to social skills training, one to combined academic and social skills training, and one group served as a no-treatment control group. Results revealed that both groups of students who improved their reading (those who received tutoring and those who had combined training) also enjoyed improved status and long-lasting effects. They began to be accepted by their classes and were fitting in as they went on with their educations. Students who were taught social skills only did not improve in their reading, and their social improvements soon faded. The effects of their training soon diminished in the face of their ongoing lack of expertise in reading (Coie & Krehbiel, 1984).

Situations that promote a sense of power also help students to gain a sense of self-efficacy (Bandura, 1977). That feeling of "I think I can," in turn, promotes achievement. Noddings (1985) explains that from a connectionist perspective, power and freedom promote an ethic of caring and lead to increased sense of social responsibility. Power also involves being listened to, and Karl Menninger (2000), a well-known American psychiatrist, remind us that listening is a creative force, a thing both magnetic and strange. We move toward the friends who listen to us, and we want to sit "in their radius." Being listened to helps us unfold and expand (Ueland, 1999).

Affection enhances understanding and reinforces retention in learning situations. As indicated earlier, it does not substitute for learning in status determinations, but it can make a difference in the quality of learning. The best learners are not anxious. They experience stress, but it is eu-stress ("good" stress), not "bad" stress that results in a fight-or-flight response. When a classroom group eliminates anxiety, it enhances the brain's acceptance and retention of new ideas. According to Vygotsky (1962), every idea in the mind carries an affective attitude "toward the bit of reality present at the time." When students are engaged, they will learn and retain when the work gives them a sense of meaning and has something to offer in their everyday life. A relaxed, happy child can express him- or herself. A child who is feeling good—neither anxious nor bored—is the child who has a clear road to achieving cognitive growth (Csikszentmihalyi, 1990).

Studies of the way the brain works tell us that achieving greater number of connections among nerve cells builds intelligence (Tomlinson & Kalbfleisch, 1998). Enriched environments promote such growth in nerve cells. Neuroscientists advocate insisting that children talk to one another to promote learning. In addition, three principles that come from modern brain research indicate that a differentiated classroom environment at the start of the 21st century is also a KPA context. Notions from decades ago have now been supported by the work of neuroscientists.

- To learn, students must experience appropriate levels of challenge. (Knowledge)
- Each brain needs to make its own meaning of ideas and skills. (Power)
- Learning environments must feel emotionally safe for learning to take place. (Affection)

Sociocultural research also advises educators to have students talk with one another. We have learned that the richest conversations occur in settings where students are able to problem-solve and interact with manipulatives, as well as talk with one another. For example, beginning second-language learners who work together to stick labels on objects around the room will benefit more than students who recite answers from their classroom seats. When students are acquiring language, the affective filter (Krashen & Terrell, 1983) can be a help or a hindrance, depending on whether it is low or high. Several key ideas help to compose the filter: (a) Students generally do better if their motivation is high, (b) language acquisition is helped by high levels of self-confidence and positive self-image, (c) low levels of anxiety, of either a personal or academic nature, can facilitate language acquisition.

Noddings (1986) explains that from the perspective of an ethic or metaphor of caring, it is the person before the teacher who becomes of central concern. This view does not mean a lack of concern for teaching skills or for academic rigor or excellence, but it does mean that skills are taught, for example, as a result of concern for the person. That is, the "one is undertaken in light of the other." An ethic of caring will promote thinking about the effect of learning opportunities on the person who is being taught as well as on the classroom community.

COHESIVENESS; COMMUNITY

Group success is often referred to as *cohesiveness*, and it is indicated by loyalty, ongoing membership, closeness, and trust. Group members are attracted to the group, and the members are accepted by one another. When the involvement of each member is valued and his or her needs are met, the group has reached a state of *community.*

Any group gains in overall cohesiveness and attractiveness if it incorporates one or more of the following three bases: common interests, prestige, and status of other group members that is somehow attractive. To build a spirit of cooperation, teachers can use their influence to encourage intragroup cooperation as well as intergroup community. The influence of the teacher has been shown in many ways, both through experiments that have been conducted in controlled situations and through teachers' and students' accounts from experience. Group dynamics work has shown that teachers' words could be used to enhance the status of selected individuals in their classrooms (Sharan & Sharan, 1976). Many teachers are familiar with the ways in which students will rush to read books that they have recommended. Their words can create "halo" effects around individuals as well. Following the models set by their teachers, students can also help build KPA. Teachers who share their thinking about wanting to include all students can influence their students to do the same.

One of the greatest difficulties for group work in areas of literacy instruction is the student who simply does not do his or her part. Therefore, two prominent themes will appear throughout the various sections of this book. One is that motivation is important to the success of any group. The other is that students and teachers must avoid—or resolve—conflict in their classroom settings. When conflicts occur in groups, they tend to spring from one of three main categories: indecision about goals, different opinions about procedures, or difficult interpersonal relations (Borich & Tombari, 1995). Therefore, discussion of group goals will comprise a large part of this book's sections on knowledge; talk about procedures relate mainly to concepts of power; ideas about interpersonal relations will be a significant part of affection.

As I hope this book will show, KPA is really an explicit way to describe community in a literacy classroom. As *Merriam-Webster's Collegiate Dictionary* (1993) portrays, a *community* consists of socially interdependent people who participate in discussion and decision making and who define and promote shared practices.

Effective teachers understand that the notions of K, P, and A are based on the needs perceived by each individual group member, not by what the teacher believes or by outside attributions of others. They design group opportunities that exercise all three areas. They can assess their classroom group compositions or activities only if they possess the empathy to look at events and circumstances through the attributes and eyes of their students as well as their parents. Several thoughtful educators, in reflecting on the well-known work of Benjamin Bloom's taxonomy, think that, beyond evaluation and synthesis, the highest level of thinking for an individual would probably be empathy (e.g., Shulman, 1989). I would also be sympathetic to that ideal. It takes analytical thinking of the highest order to provide KPA.

The next three chapters will provide further insights as to the factors involved with knowledge, power, and affection and circumstances that do or do not promote each attribute. Later on, three additional chapters will take a look at classroom ideas and activities that can help fulfill student needs for KPA and, in so doing, "grow community."

> *All studies grow out of relations in the one*
> *great common world.—JOHN DEWEY*

▶ 3

Circumstances That Promote Knowledge

*To know that we know what we know, and that we do not
know what we do not know, that is true knowledge.*
—HENRY THOREAU (QUOTING CONFUCIUS)

What is *knowledge*? It is the demonstration of expertise that is respected by the group and useful to the group's purpose(s). It is the possession of information or access to informational resources. It is the broadening of concepts and perspectives through images and reasoning.

Teachers work with diverse groups of learners in today's school settings. Because their students arrive with many types and levels of expertise, they struggle to decide what to do to meet their needs. One award-winning teacher, attempting to accommodate the wide range of abilities in her third-grade classroom, asked:

> *How can I keep Gabriel, a very bright student who always manages to fin-*
> *ish his work before the rest of his classmates, occupied for the last ten min-*
> *utes while the rest of the class is still working and I'm still teaching a reading*
> *group? How can I continue to challenge and stimulate students who are at*
> *third-grade reading, writing, and math levels while allowing students who*
> *are at pre-primer to second-grade levels to keep their pace?* (Ly, 1998, p. 56)

She would empathize with Sophia, a respected first-grade teacher whose class includes many children who are new, Spanish-speaking immigrants. Sophia discussed her dilemma with grouping in her classroom:

How do you deal with all these different levels that you have? I have every-thing from someone who can't distinguish between letters and numbers to those who are starting to read. And, regardless of where they are, you know that by April or May, whenever you have the [standardized] tests, they need to have reviewed all of the curriculum so that they have a fair chance. You know very well that not all of them are ready for that test, but you have to just make sure that you've covered the knowledge. (Nagel, 1992, p. 129)

The reality for teachers is that their children possess different incoming types of performance in reading, writing, speaking, and listening. Studies that explore language use in children's early home life show that some families, particularly those that are Euro-American, use modes of talk and exposure to books in ways that correlate directly with school usage. Other families nurture their children in ways that are not as culturally compatible with the discourse expectations of classrooms (e.g., Au, 1980; Heath, 1983). Aspects of early education correlate with students' later levels of success in school and indicate that something as rudimentary as alphabet knowledge ties to a child's future literacy performance (Adams, 1990).

At the same time, teachers know that they must not overlook skills development, but they do not want to withhold other challenges from children who have already mastered basic skills. Many kindergartners, for example, come to school knowing how to read. Teachers want to provide interesting learning opportunities for all of their students. They want them all to communicate effectively. Students, as senders and receivers of ideas, need to "get" what is going on. Educators want every child to feel appreciated for what he or she *does* know and accepted as someone who *will* learn. So, what is a teacher to do?

This chapter will examine knowledge as it relates to literacy groups in classrooms. The attributes of group activities, group members, and their interactions create the context. Contexts for learning affect the discourse of students and teachers. The discourse affects the cognitive outcomes for each student. The types of discourse make a difference in what types of knowledge are gained and retained. Because the topic of knowledge building is complex, the pages that follow are many. The various sections will discuss the following as related to groups: (a) talk, (b) goals and expectations, (c) preparation and assessment, (d) roles and tasks, (e) membership, (f) motivation, (g) time, and (h) remembering. Group dynamics, ability, and size are additional important factors that will be mentioned in this chapter, but they are addressed more specifically in the research summaries of Chapters 7, 8, and 9.

SOME CONSIDERATIONS

Although classroom work incorporates and promotes many types of literacy, reading plays a major role in placement procedures and perceptions. Therefore, it will receive a large share of attention in these pages. One common solution to the ability dilemma is to teach everyone as if they are the same through whole-class instruction. Such instruction is driven by thoughts of providing equal opportunity and access for all children. All classmates, for example, should enjoy core pieces of literature at each grade level. Although whole-class groups do work for some purposes, they are not effective for the development of specific skills beyond the stage of being introduced (Cohen, 1984). Because children are different from one another, they come away either needing more lessons or not.

When whole language was initiated, it was guided by individuals with varying degrees of expertise in the philosophy. In many situations, whole language came to be equated, mistakenly, with whole-group instruction. One teacher's reaction was strong:

> *Tell me that this new approach isn't a plot to keep our kids from achieving.*
> *What I'm seeing with this new reading series is* awful. *Kids are being placed*
> *in materials that they don't know how to read. They don't know the vocab-*
> *ulary. They have no fluency. They know they don't know it, and their class-*
> *mates know they don't know it. I thought that putting everyone in the same*
> *book at the same time was wrong. Where did diagnosis go? What can we do?*
> *What should I be telling the teachers I work with?* (N. Stevens, October,
> 20, 1989, personal communication)

As most educators know, the whole-group perception was incorrect. Whole group instruction does seem to be effective in some cultures, such as in Japan or Korea, but it goes on in contexts where accommodations outside the long school day are made to support students who need special tutoring and extra classes (R. Barr, 1995). However, in North American society, teaching to the whole-class group as a dominant practice usually means that some students do not succeed.

Another typical classroom procedure is to establish several "ability" groups. Such groups seem to make organizational sense, and they meet teachers' beliefs that they are providing instruction appropriate for individual students' needs. Teachers use leveled materials (often part of a commercial, basal series) to do reading and associated activities in one of several (usually three) groups. Group placements are based on performance assessments such as the basal readers' tests, usually combined with group placement data from previous teachers. Teachers enjoy the orderliness of assigning students to groups that rotate with the clock. The process allows a teacher to meet with each group separately while other groups do seatwork. Unfortunately, studies have shown that such group placements reflect inappropriate matches and are ill suited to meeting the needs of students (e.g., Cook-Gumperz, Simons, & Gumperz, 1981; Hiebert, 1983; Shake & Allington, 1985). Furthermore, a placement in a low group provides a qualitatively different experience that discourages, rather than encourages, sustained reading and thinking. Comparison charts of attributes of high and low groups appear as Appendix D. The charts represent a synthesis of research presented in Chapter 8. As that chapter will explain, many states have advocated an end to ability groups because of the inconsistent expectations and inadequate literacy learning opportunities that take place for students who are not the "high group" kids.

> *During April of her first-grade year, a little girl dropped by to visit her kindergarten teacher from the year before. Her former teacher inquired, "Maria, what do you learn in first grade?"*
>
> *"Well," she responded, "if you're in the Yellow Group you don't learn much, but if you're in the Orange Group you learn all kinds of things . . . and I'm in the Orange Group."* (Nagel, 1992, p. 23)

For sure, the social context has a great impact on a student's growth in literacy knowledge (e.g., Weinstein, 1991). Outcomes relate to the quality of the interactions, regardless of the size or type of group. Large groups and small groups all have their place, and, led by teachers or students, each type can be effective for various purposes. Typically, teachers are nervous about peer-led groups and want to make sure that they are productive. However, tape-recorded conversations analyzed through years of research projects seem to assure that such groups hold fine potential for focused discussion and dialogue (Cohen, 1994). When norms are clear and students are engaged, their participation promotes and reinforces various types of knowledge (Farnham-Diggory, 1994). New knowledge (cognitive outcomes) may be *declarative* (facts) or *procedural* (skills) as well as *conceptual* (big ideas), *analogical* (images), or *logical* (valid reasoning). All "knowledges" are part of effective reading, writing, speaking, and listening; they can be introduced in large groups but are usually best developed in smaller settings. As with two pools containing identical amounts of water, the wider circle will be shallow, and the narrow circle promotes depth.

The cognitive outcomes of a literacy group vary with written or oral discourse. The discourse is influenced by the individuals' preparation, the group members, their tasks, and their roles. I have selected the fountain in Figure 3.1 to represent the basic configuration of the situation. Although it lacks the dynamic interplay of all the elements that occur constantly in real life, the fountain seems at least to hint at the motion, recycling, and fluidity of the circumstances.

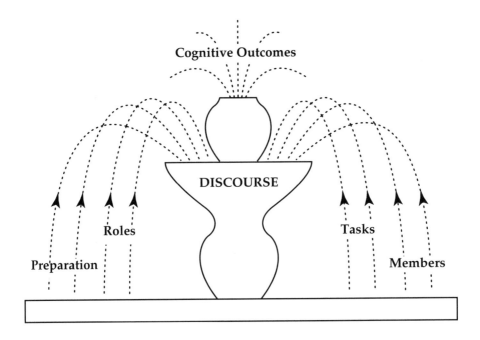

FIGURE 3.1   The Fountain of Knowledge

If a student plays a role in one group, it does not mean that he or she will persist in that function with other groupings or even in the same group as it continues. An individual experiences the change of going from leader to recorder to encourager, and the group experiences change according to the individuals in the various roles. In school contexts, changes from class to class, subject to subject, or topic to topic can also make a difference because of the changes in students' preparation (backgrounding). The other members of a group also affect who says and does what, by both their status and disposition. A person who is prepared to provide a wealth of information and inspiration in one context will hold a different place in another group with different membership and other tasks to perform. Students who talk confidently within some groups are silent in others.

TALK

The type and amount of talk that members contribute within any group will depend on their personal perceptions of how much they know and of what the other members think of them and what they know. Preparedness allows students to fulfill roles and complete tasks. A sense of trust toward other members allows students to relax in the face of status differences.

In a review of studies of small-group learning, searching for conditions that promote productive groups, Cohen (1994) describes how interactions relate to outcomes. Different kinds of discourse within groups produce different kinds of learning. When there is an open exchange and elaborated discussion, conceptual learning is more likely to take place for participants. Desirable interactions foster productivity.

Forming good groups requires careful "kidwatching" (Goodman, 1985) as a prerequisite. Such watching must include focusing, listening, and record keeping. "Good" groups are designed by teachers who know their children in many ways. To do their analysis, teachers work with intimate groups. Many teachers miss the opportunity to use small, teacher-led discussion groups, but their potential must not be overlooked. Behavior in such a group setting tells more about the child as a group member than any individual assessment. The small-group setting provides each child an audience with the teacher and an appreciative audience for the positive relationship that can exist between teacher and child.

Compared to working with the whole-class group, gathering in small groups also helps students, for the group size encourages self-expression from students who would otherwise not have appropriate (too aggressive, too shy) voices in the larger setting. What appears to be true, however, is that when teachers work with small groups, they engage in behaviors that resemble assessment and evaluation more than discussion. The teacher's presence in a group may serve to diminish, rather than encourage, student talk. Small groups with peer leadership, on the other hand, tend to promote more open exchange and elaborated discussion. Students engage in more kinds of discourse and more of it.

Students need a reason to interact, for simply doing "collaborative seatwork" may help students complete their assignments but not attain concepts. One finding that sheds light on how to sustain discussion in group work comes from the work of a project in Great Britain called Oracle II. It states that children will continue to discuss and problem-solve when they are dealing with tangible and/or authentic opportunities (Galton & Williamson, 1992). The insight is not new, perhaps, just as many positive practices and concepts are not. According to Dewey (1915/1966), "There is all the difference in the world between having something to say and having to say something. The child who has a variety of materials and facts wants to talk about them, and his language becomes more refined and full, because it is controlled and informed by realities" (p. 56). But having something to say is only a part of the situation. Discussions and interactions are all affected by the nature of the tasks to be performed. The things that groups do are related to what they are supposed to accomplish.

Beyer (1987) refers to 10 skills that require critical thinking and are important to the success of discussions and dialogues. Participants want to

1. distinguish between verifiable facts and value-based claims,
2. distinguish relevant from irrelevant information or reasons,
3. determine the factual accuracy of statements,
4. determine the credibility of sources,
5. identify ambiguous claims or arguments,
6. identify unstated assumptions,
7. detect bias,
8. identify logical fallacies,
9. recognize logical inconsistencies, and
10. determine the strength of an argument or claim.

Developing these skills can begin when students are able to distinguish between true and false notions. Teachers who work with gifted and talented students are, undoubtedly, familiar with dimensions of critical thinking. All students, however, will benefit if prepared for their roles as decision makers in a democratic society.

When children do cooperative work, their speaking and listening provide feedback and reinforcement for one another. Teachers are familiar with students who seek truth: "That's not true. Did you make that up?" "Who says?" "That doesn't make sense." "My dad says that isn't true." "It isn't really like that in New York." The more educators design talk times to promote critical thinking, the more success students will have. Individuals who participate in debate also develop advantages in other arenas in which speaking and writing clearly are required.

Most educators seem to have had experience with Bloom's taxonomy (Bloom, Engelhart, Furst, Hill, & Krathwohl, 1978). Its levels of educational objectives include knowledge, comprehension, application, analysis, synthesis, and evaluation. I share them here to remind readers that discussions can always go "beyond Beyer" to incorporate synthesis through creative connections. In his later years, Bloom expressed that synthesis was often beyond evaluation. Discussions that lead to the synthesis of new ideas—solutions, inventions, new ways of doing things—can be expected to be successful.

GOALS AND EXPECTATIONS

Over the years, as methods of literacy instruction come in and out of popularity, teachers and researchers agree that no one approach can do it all. Effective teachers draw on multiple techniques and activities, but their decisions play across understandings of where it is all going. Answering questions of "So what? Who cares? Does it matter?" are necessary for effective planning. Ideas that spring from the literature of strategic planning certainly apply to instructional decision making. At the broadest level, (a), plans spring from a consistent *vision*. Once that is established, the construction of groups with appropriate memberships and activities relates to intended accomplishments at three other levels: (b) broad *goals for instruction*, (c) *group-specific goals*, and (d) *goals of individual members*.

I use the term *goals* as having meanings that vary with its qualifiers. Educators want to have a sense of where they want to be, what their optimal outcomes will look like. For decades, people have found Mager's (1970) work to be useful in analyzing goals and objectives. His terms are appropriately applied within plans for instruction in the behaviorist mode. *Objectives* must describe observable behaviors in specific terminology: students write, draw, tell, underline, outline, and so forth, to prove they have learned something. I decided that it would be inappropriate to focus on Mager's language when so much of what we accomplish in literacy comes through constructivist learning opportunities. Students also write, draw, tell, underline, outline, and so forth, as *ways* of learning. Goals not only relate to how individuals' behaviors change. They also relate to broader or more abstract outcomes that are represented by complexes of behaviors. Teachers will acknowledge that some goals are maxi- and some are mini-; some are never fully reached but are faithfully held; and some goals are never thought about at the outset of lessons but are, nevertheless, reached by learners.

Level 1: Visionary Goals

Curriculum planning answers questions as to what is important to learn and to what extent it should be learned. However, conflicts in how to teach and how to group in school settings can spring from the varied belief systems of the individual teachers themselves. Teachers "come from within" to do their complex work. Those who believe that the goals of their instruction are limited to knowledge/skills acquisition are, understandably, puzzled by other possible views.

Disagreements between and among educators, parents, and politicians usually spring from their differing broad visions for education (Lankshear & O'Connor, 1999). Three main visions tend to compete:

- *Operational*: Education prepares students to become effective workers (reading articles, reports; writing letters, reports, invoices, bills).
- *Critical:* Education prepares students to participate in a democratic society (recognize alternatives and innovate, improve, and make judgments
- *Cultural*: Education prepares students to get along and enjoy daily life.

Literacy can change with the situation. My response, as with so many other arenas of dualistic, "this or that" thinking in education, is that we cannot succeed unless we do it all. My vision for literacy has been to support democratic participation, which includes workplace and daily life literacies. It is for learning why and how things are in the world around us, for analyzing the past and projecting the future, and for recreation. It is also a ticket to esteem, to further education and to occupations that have status (Nagel, 1991).

Teaching practices need to be tested against the accepted vision to check for consistency of classroom practice and lack of hypocrisy. Whatever the vision, it must belong to the individuals involved, although the language and inspiration may come from many places.

Level 2: Broad Goals for Instruction

Working from a vision is wise, but groups need more than that. Their success is dependent on knowing their purpose at a more specific level. Several goal frameworks have been shown to be helpful in educational planning, but I believe that the four goals of education as depicted in *Models of Teaching* by Joyce and Weil (1992) are familiar and encompass what many others have proposed. The authors declare, "Teaching is the process of building communities of learners who use their skills to educate themselves." (p. 1) Models of teaching are really models of learning. Their work honors the thinking of John Dewey (1916), who promoted teaching as the establishment of environments in which students can interact, and Herb Thelen (1967), who believed that education in a democratic society should teach democratic process. Their framework presents four dimensions for teaching and learning:

1. In the *behavioral systems* family, models of direct instruction help students to reach sequenced, organized behavioral objectives.
2. The *social interaction* family of models is intended to expand students' ability to relate productively to one another.
3. Models in the *information-processing* family seek to master information, retaining it, organizing it, and applying it as well as developing hypotheses and making inferences.
4. The *personal* family helps students to develop themselves as flexible and original through creative expression.

Other insightful goal frameworks have been published in relation to education and used by many within a variety of educational contexts. For example, Johnson and Johnson (1972) work with three goal structures: individualistic, competitive (ability-focused), cooperative (task-based). Specific to literacy instruction (e.g., Mosenthal, 1987) are the following: academic (reproduction of linguistic stimuli), utilitarian (real-world survival skills), romantic (understandings of self and others), cognitive-developmental (problem solving), and emancipatory (elimination of socioeconomic discrimination). Several are well known and applicable to thinking, including Bloom's taxonomy, which was mentioned earlier. It acknowledges the increasing complexity of thought related to (a) knowledge, (b) comprehension, (c) application, (d) analysis, (e) or (f) evaluation, (f) or (e) synthesis.

Good goals for instruction are to be enacted across the curriculum throughout the grades. In a well-integrated school program, all teachers plan instruction to enact all goals. Behavioral goals are not limited to math or reading. Social interaction goals or personal goals are not just for health class or social studies. Information processing is not just for science. Personal goals are not just for physical education. Typical classrooms devote 2 or more hours each day to literacy development. Effective teachers will see the value of incorporating multiple tasks to achieve one or more of the four broad goals. Much of education's pendulum swinging could turn to balance if teachers' visions were broad in focus. In addition, many lessons serve multiple goals. For students to be motivated, the goals for groups to get together must be understood and compelling (Ford, 1992). Teachers may often keep goals at an implicit level, missing the opportunity to inform and motivate students through explicit explanation of the goals being sought or requests for student input about goals. Goals are for sharing.

Behavioral Goals

Teachers are very comfortable with the notion that students must acquire and retain information as well as grow in ability. No matter what the particular literacy focus, students are engaged in learning "stuff" and acquiring "how-to" abilities. As mentioned earlier in this chapter, psychologists refer to one as *declarative* and the other as *procedural* knowledge. As a result, students can recall, summarize, use rules, and master skills and concepts. They understand and apply. In reading lessons, the "rapid reproduction of linguistic stimuli" is one primary target (Mosenthal, 1987). The teacher (or other provider) serves as an information giver or trainer. Programmed instruction through computerized materials, tapes, or books is also a typical means used to reach the skills goal. Teachers seek many objectives within the category of behavioral goals and are indeed looking to alter behaviors. It is common to think of "behavior" in a disciplinary sense, but readers will recognize that its meaning is far broader here.

Direct instruction may take place in a model that serves that purpose only, or it may be embedded in another educational experience. The point is that the learner's behavior is to be altered in some way, and teaching for transfer or retention is stressed. Modeling is desirable for incorporation into the instruction. Students are expected to recall key ideas, apply rules, and master skills and demonstrate their acquisition through independent performance.

Teachers design instruction to build fluency in oral and silent reading and to write with accuracy and fluency. Not only do they want to develop students' skills of recall, comprehension, summarizing, but they want them to apply various understandings, including rules. Students need a variety of practical literacy skills to deal with tasks in the workplace, such as knowing how to fill out forms, write reports and letters, and prepare documents. School must help students fulfill responsibilities associated with citizenship and adult living such as reading newspapers, drivers' handbooks, or voters' booklets. They need to learn to read charts and tables and deal with a variety of nonfiction genres. They also need to read recipes or interpret directions for sewing a dress or putting together a bicycle or a bookcase.

Groups that are established for the acquisition of information can be of all sizes, but one key group member tends to be the information giver, usually the teacher or an appropriate substitute. Plans for direct instruction include many variations, but one well-known model is that of Madeline Hunter (1982). Sometimes known as the Hunter model, the seven-step lesson plan incorporates the notion that teachers (a) build anticipation and (b) set an objective for the lesson, helping establish motivation and reason for learning and connect to students' prior knowledge needed for the new lesson. Then, in the (c) input step, new information is presented and (d) modeled. The teacher (e) checks for understanding next, followed by the students' (f) practicing under the guidance of the teacher. Then students (g) practice independently. An example of a lesson that incorporates this model appears as Appendix E.

In reaching this goal and in working within this family, the greatest grouping struggles occur for teachers. Teaching to the whole class works, but for only some of the time or for only some of the students. The teacher who uses direct instruction often lectures through a series of lessons that are graduated in difficulty over time. Direct instruction works when the level of skill to be attained or knowledge to be acquired is within reach of all students. Only rarely does that occur, for classrooms serve students with capabilities that extend over many grade levels. It is not unusual for a fifth-grade class to have members reading at the second-grade level or the eighth-grade level or any grade in between.

The acquisition of skills and information is not limited to behavioral techniques, however. For example, the work of William Nagy, Steve Krashen, and others demonstrates that students do learn the meanings of vocabulary words in indirect ways from various reading contexts.

Social Interaction Goals

As students speak, listen, or respond to others through reading and writing, they form bonds of knowing, shared influence, and caring between and among various individuals. Literacy activities that permit students to interact can help them adapt to one another's personalities, ages, genders, characters, and cultures. Reaching social goals promotes understandings of self and others through developing such qualities as originality, elaboration, and flexibility. Each individual's perspectives serve as lenses through which he or she comes to develop understandings. Positive social encounters of a personal nature can begin to eliminate socioeconomic discrimination and level the playing field.

However, sitting in groups does not mean that children interact, for there are at least three levels of interdependence: pooled, sequential, and reciprocal (Thompson, 1967; see also Appendix F). Teachers know that sometimes groups merely provide convenient seating arrangements for independent work. Several students may just sit near one another to produce different products. For example, six students may write separate stories or fill out identical worksheets.

> In *pooled* interdependence, the group has a joint outcome, but members fulfill different tasks. For example, students may prepare a presentation about Benjamin Franklin, but one person might tell about his childhood, one might tell about his political career, and another might tell about his inventions. Students cooperate to prepare but are conceptually independent.
>
> In *sequential* interdependence, students have a joint outcome but fulfill tasks that link in order of time (writing, illustrating, and presenting a story). The students have separate tasks but must cooperate and communicate in order to accomplish their goal.
>
> In *reciprocal* interdependence, students have a joint outcome and share most of the tasks for an assignment, problem-solving as they go. This represents true collaboration.

Some activities may, of course, require a combination of interdependence types. Students might collaborate to write the introduction and closing to a written work and may work in pooled ways to complete the internal sections.

As these three categories indicate, teachers do not promote interactions unless they promote certain types of activities and groups. Students truly discussing and collaborating is rare; they engage in cooperative or collaborative groups combined for only 9% of their time in class.

Of all the broad literacy goals, teachers often overlook social goals. Although they would agree that social outcomes are important, and they may see these as goals of their program in general, the ways in which they serve as goals of literacy instruction are not always recognized.

Information-Processing Goals

To reach those goals, literacy is used to inform, annotate, and assist the identification of questions and problems that confront individuals and groups of people. Problem solving depends on strategies of information processing. Literacy is a tool for critical thinking, using information from other contexts in time and space to deal with new situations, and students are called on to develop advanced levels of thinking through analysis, evaluation, and synthesis.

Problem solving can be related to literature or real life. Students may search for evidence, find proof, explore relationships, and identify main ideas. They may also engage in activities that use literacy as a tool, such as conduction explorations in science (How long does it take the seed to sprout?), carrying out demographic studies (What are the ways by which students travel to school?), or finding solutions to predicaments that occur in the school setting (How can we avoid the long wait in the lunch line?). These activities can promote further dialogue, reading, and writing.

Throughout the world, many scholars and teachers are interested in the work of Brazilian educator Paulo Freire (1993). His work through critical pedagogy made clear how important dialogue is to education. He believed that students need to read and write about what truly concerns them to be able to make changes in their world. His process of "problem posing" had its origins in adult education but now involves students of many ages. A teacher would first assess what truly concerns the students and begin to look at their experiences and concerns through stories, pictures, or poetry. Then, collaboratively, students and teacher would focus on a problem and meet in discussion circles to narrow down a problem that will engage them in further reading and writing, finally engaging in social action.

Similarities can be found in a model for decision making promoted by Wales, Nardi, and Stager (1986). They present a four-step process in which participants determine a goal, generate ideas, prepare a plan, and take action. Within each step are three procedures: (a) analysis (identifying problems), (b) synthesis (generating options), and (c) evaluation (select one from the options) at each level. Decision making is critical thinking. It is integral to problem solving.

How individuals speak and listen to one another makes a difference in the quality of learning. Cherniss (1998) reminds educators that well-handled conversations can become skilled discussions or true dialogues. There is a difference. Discussions lead to decisions, so the goals of discussion must be clarified. Dialogues, on the other hand, lead to collective meaning making and shared understandings. Both require many of the same capabilities. Both can occur in the same context.

As individuals learn to discuss, they also learn skills that require critical thinking. Among them are the ability to distinguish facts from opinions, see what information is relevant or nonrelevant, and determine what sources of information are believable, as well as detect bias (Beyer, 1987).

Personal Goals

When the goal is personal, the emphasis is on promoting better understanding of self, taking responsibility to become stronger, more creative, and sensitive. Taking responsibility for one's own destiny is another way of saying that one has an internal locus of control rather than external. Terms familiar to many educators are *self-actualization* and *self-esteem*. Teaching to this goal is nondirective and facilitative and is sometimes called part of the counseling model. The strategies can involve one or more of several lenses: cultural, spiritual, rational, autobiographical, or artistic. Individuals may work toward personal goals throughout their lives, but the path can begin with the wise guidance of sensitive teachers.

Level 3: Group-Specific Goals

Every group within the whole-class group also has its own goal(s). For example, when a class decides to write and perform a play for their parents, each group may carry out tasks to fulfill specific goals. Although the whole class is preparing a play for performance, one group may prepare scripts while another does costumes and others do staging, music, and acting. The composition and size of any group do relate to expectations for their work. Group goals connect to the tasks to be accomplished.

Level 4: Goals of Individual Members

Good groups must have group goals, but their members must also have explicit goals related to their work. Effective teachers not only recognize that students have a variety of learning attributes but that, as instructors, they have distinct styles and preferred approaches to instruction. Member goals can be set in collaboration with the teacher. Together, they can establish specialized outcomes within group learning situations. Good goal setting with individual students can influence the ongoing dynamics of the class.

When individual member goals are task related and nonthreatening, as opposed to competitive with normative grades, students develop intrinsic motivation. Task-focused goals allow students to be aware of their accomplishments and to see that their success is related to exerting effort. The tasks to be performed also include the functions that come with the roles that individual students are to play within their groups. When we are explicit about roles and tasks, we can better see how learning opportunities align with our desired outcomes. The way to learn the Mexican Hat Dance is not to sit still and listen, yet we make similar mistakes in matching practice to outcomes.

Teachers often set the purposes for lessons to link the content of a lesson with what they perceive are students' member goals. For instance, before reading a contemporary adventure story, one teacher explains, "You will want to read this with care because, just like this family, you may find yourself stranded in the desert after your car breaks down." Sometimes designated as the "anticipatory set," the talk or activity that precedes instruction can activate personal goal setting.

PREPARATION AND ASSESSMENT

Making sure that students have the necessary background for learning experiences is necessary to assure comprehensible lessons. Several factors contribute to being prepared. In addition, one form of preparation is to know in advance what sorts of assessments will be used to gauge successful learning.

Prior Knowledge

According to Dewey (1900/1966), the schoolchild is already intensely active, and the question of education is the question of "taking hold of his [*sic*] activities, of giving them direction" (p. 36). He explains that the greatest asset in the student's possession is his "own direct and personal experience." Teachers must assess levels of prior knowledge to teach well. To provide for learning of specific skills, the lesson design must also provide instruction that is neither too hard so as to be impossible to understand nor too easy and, therefore, uninteresting. The teacher's task is not to make everyone the same but rather to help each student grow as much as possible. When teachers tap into their students' prior knowledge, the process is part of the "anticipatory set." When children have little experience to tap into, a teacher can provide the necessary opportunity, or *backgrounding*.

Backgrounding

What children know before they begin to explore a particular concept or acquire a certain skill is extremely important to the speed and depth of learning. Children who have done the activities that are written about in their readings can read difficult materials with greater fluency and comprehension than comparable passages about unfamiliar topics. When students come to a learning opportunity without the necessary prior knowledge to make new connections, someone must take the responsibility to provide necessary information or insights.

Such a burden falls on the teacher, of course. Teachers who claim to teach reading all morning and forego teaching science or social studies "because there isn't enough time" are sacrificing their students' performance on a great number of tests of reading. Confident comprehension of many nonfiction passages depends on students' past experiences. Their levels of background-ing are critical to their success.

The work of Lev Vygotsky (1978) is also important to understand learn-ing in groups. Vygotsky depicted learning as proceeding along a pathway of social interaction to internalized independent functioning. Knowledge is first acquired through social interaction with a mediator, then internalized, and then carried out independently. A teacher or tutor guides and supports the learner, mostly through social dialogue, from activity that is at first regulated by others to self-regulated performance. The area within which such growth can take place is called the *zone of proximal development* (ZPD). When instruc-tion is adjusted properly to a student's needs, it is operating within that in-dividual's ZPD. Learning awakens a variety of developmental processes that are able to operate only when the child is interacting with people in his or her environment and in cooperation with peers. Once these processes are internalized they become part of the child's developmental achievement (Vygotsky, 1978).

Whether the projected lesson involves direct instruction or student con-struction of knowledge, it is inefficient to operate outside any one student's zone of proximal development. If the student does not hold prerequisite no-tions, the new skills and content simply will not be learned. Teachers who know their students can help clarify the points at which connections can be made. In the very best such *scaffolding*, teachers use multiple links to help join new knowledge to old understandings.

Scaffolding is not a rigid frame. It is the "hand up" that any student could use to get from one place to another. It is, perhaps, like midair refueling. Careful planning and positioning make it work. In "Scaffolded Reading Ex-periences for Inclusive Classes," Graves, Graves, and Braaten (1994) describe scaffolding as a flexible framework that helps students get the most from a variety of literacy experiences. In addition, teachers can best scaffold and monitor their students at work when they know them well. Ongoing analytic assessment practices that were once an expectation only for special education students have become a mandate for all in many school settings. Knowing the multiple aspects of students' intelligences—their interests and talents, their likes and dislikes, their characters and personalities—can assist educators in seeing how narrow the focus on characteristics of intellectual ability have been.

Backgrounding is not, however, the exclusive domain of the teacher. Stu-dents can prepare for lessons in many ways through efforts of their own. A boy who knew his class was going to study California missions persuaded his family to take a vacation to visit two missions near Santa Barbara. A student who reads homework materials with care is doing personal backgrounding. Parents are certainly backgrounding agents as well. By reading school newsletters, surveying textbooks, reading books about their child's grade level, or asking questions of teachers and fellow parents, they can get a good sense of the kinds of lessons that will be coming their child's way. Parents who seek out library books or purchase special magazine subscriptions for their children will help them gain deeper understandings.

Assessment

Although books can be—and many have been—written on the topic of examining the quality of student learning, the purpose of addressing it here is to acknowledge its importance rather than engage in a full-blown explanation of it. The term *assessment* is derived from linguistic roots that express it as "sitting beside." It can gain meaning as a friendly, guiding process rather than a scheme for judgmental ranking and sorting. Teachers need to have facility with gathering varied types of assessment data, and then they must develop the ability to analyze the collected data to select lesson context that "works." Teachers seldom have the money or power to obtain and align materials with needs and goals in prescriptive ways. They must, therefore, have well-developed skills of materials analysis and management. Savvy teachers know what to omit from, or add to, texts, kits, and curricula that are already in place. Finding just the right reading passage or tape at the proper time requires good organization on the teacher's part.

Assessment of group work, as mentioned elsewhere, needs to be done on a variety of levels. Each group member should have an opportunity to be evaluated as an individual as well as receive a group grade for the group's efforts. Classes can also evaluate their progress in handling small group work. Rubrics (scoring guidelines) that are established ahead of time, preferably with student input, set expectations for the quality of the cognitive outcomes but, also can apply to other aspects of the group work. Playing the role, doing the task, participating in the discussion or dialogue, and being a supportive group member are all important to promoting cognitive growth.

ROLES AND TASKS

Beyond philosophy; beyond curriculum . . . the context makes a difference, and the literacy task can be a strong predictor of motivation. Group roles and tasks should acknowledge the expertise of students if they are to be engaged. Discussions and interactions are all affected by task instructions, student preparation, and the nature of the teacher's role (Cohen, 1994). Teachers with insight know that if a student serves a function in one group, it does not mean that he or she will persist in that role within other groupings. The person who can provide a wealth of information in one context may hold a different place in another group that has other members and other tasks to perform. In a group of three students who are writing a book on whales together, one student's ability to draw complements another group member's ability to write and yet another student's sense of how to edit writing and organize time and tasks.

Differentiation of Opportunities and Responses

Teachers can deal with individual differences in the classroom, yet still attend to the need for students to have central, unifying experiences. One way is to examine the ways in which to frame tasks as learning opportunities and organize the responses to them. One approach that many teachers use is to provide the same learning opportunity for students but allow for different responses. Children often all listen to a story, read a book, hear a recording, view a film, listen to a guest speaker, have a hands-on experience, engage in a physical activity, or go on a field trip. They then respond in different ways, working with other individuals according to their expertise and interest. Their responses may, at times, be self-selected. At other times, teachers would design those responses to be in keeping with the children's specific needs. Working with one or two people in an oral presentation, a retelling, a dramatization, a discussion, a written piece, notes, or a creation would all be possible and suitable. Then, within the response, specific skill and practice tasks can be incorporated. For example, if all the children have been listening to *Charlotte's Web* being read aloud, some students might do a dramatized comparison/contrast to another children's novel, whereas for others it may be more appropriate to do a small-group retelling, and others would practice writing the dialogue with quotation marks. Response tasks may be assigned with various levels of complexity and abstraction, with differences within the tasks to allow the activity to reinforce a sense of competence in the various learners.

The other way to meet differences is to have different opportunities but the same response. Many literature circles are brought together to discuss specific concepts, but the group members can talk about separate books from their self-selected readings. High-level concepts can be developed around each person's comfortable content. Self-selected content adds interest to many literacy activities and enhances the opportunity for success. The focus can be on achieving competence because the raw materials for thinking are familiar (Pogrow, 1990). Children can create a flowchart about storybook characters before they can begin to do the same task related to a novel. Analyzing a problem in his or her own life must make sense before analyzing the problem of a Shakespearean character.

The important thing for literacy teachers to remember is that analyses of standardized test results show that the clearest correlations for success in test performance are not to skill-based practice. Rather, the greater the amounts of wide reading and writing and discussing that students do, the higher their scores will be (NAEP, 1996; Reeves, 1999). We must remember to extend the opportunity to all students for those types of activities that have always characterized work in high groups.

MEMBERSHIP

A classroom group may consist of a teacher with one or more students or peers with each other. In either case, the "more knowledgeable other" influences students' learning. The membership roster of any "good" group must have at least one person whose knowledge aligns well with the task. Other members have status of various sorts, promoted by various influences, as explained in Chapter 7 on group dynamics. The "Who's Who" list in group work is not merely a roster of smart students. Perceptions about groups held by the students themselves, reported in the work of Erlbaum, Schumm, and Vaughn (1997), reveal that upper elementary-grade students love mixed-ability groups, especially pairs. The students in the Erlbaum et al. study not only preferred mixed-ability groups to same-ability groups but also liked whole-class instruction better than same-ability grouping or working alone. Student commentaries indicated that they were comfortable being in situations in which they knew the most and could teach others. They also found it helpful to work with students who could help them with ideas that were difficult for them to understand or tasks that they needed assistance in performing.

That cross-age tutoring is such a success for students should come as not surprise. Furthermore, contexts that seek "teaching and being taught" group opportunities for students will offset the difficulty experienced by "middle" students who do not often get to teach or be taught. The differences in ages provides a visible, acceptable differentiation of status. Group members who are hard workers and do their parts get the job done. The realities of working together in proximity allow students to overcome stereotypes and grow in trust and respect.

MOTIVATION

The complex interactions among cognition, metacognition, and motivation promote the construction of meaning (Turner, 1995). Social guidance and cooperation are fundamental to motivation, and motivation plays a key role in promoting and energizing strategic activity. As social and linguistic diversity increases in society, educators note how we can help transform education: we must find ways to get, and keep, students engaged (Poplin, 1992). Students who are motivated can be very energetic and focused.

As just described, motivation is, however, largely dependent on the context (Jensen, 1998). Tasks that are motivating promote learning and inspire the use of coping strategies, persistence in the face of difficulties, and control to stay on task (Turner, 1995). Such unwavering persistence is glorified in some cultures, probably to the advantage of their students. Natives of Finland call it *sisu*. The Japanese call it *gaman*. Both nations have high success rates on international measures of academic success that can be attributed to a complex of factors that, undoubtedly, includes strong perseverance.

In a study of tutoring completed by Derry and Potts (1998, p. 87), individual tutors noted the following behavioral evidence of students' motivation levels. I share their findings in the following chart as a way to provide insight about motivation in groups of all sorts. The kinds of behaviors shown can be observed in whole-class settings, as well as with teachers and students in small-group settings and in groups of student peers.

Low-Motivation Students	*High-Motivation Students*
Do not question	Ask questions, explore ideas
Make no suggestions or comments	Make comments, suggestions
Are distracted	Attend to the task
Blame the system	Praise the system; adapt to it
Act frustrated	Resolve frustrations
Have difficulties	Do extra work; express interest
Are impulsive	Are reflective, thoughtful
Ignore leader	Cooperate
Do no extra work	Go beyond
Display negative affect	Display positive affect

Tutor/leaders' responses to low motivation: Encourage taking more time; avoid theory; discourage criticism; avoid humor; explain; vary the activity; personalize the lesson and tasks; shorten lessons; reinforce success; acknowledge frustrations; encourage and reinforce thinking aloud, use questions designed to draw in reluctant students

Tutor/leaders' responses to high motivation: Elaborate theory; provide encouragement; interact with light banter, humor; reinforce success and interest; answer all questions

What appears to be the case is that motivation in groups is a two-way street. Students with low motivation are treated with care, but they receive less complex instruction and end up being handled with less warmth. Highly motivated group members respond well to the leader and, in turn, get a positive response. The "rich get richer" phenomenon occurs in many ways within educational contexts.

Another dimension relating to unmotivated students is the difference in behaviors that may be called *approach* (displaying effort, persistence, engagement, choice, performance) and *avoidant* (avoiding risk taking, resisting seeking help, withdrawing effort, giving up). Beyond that, some students practice *learned helplessness* and *self-handicapping strategies* as an attempt to manipulate others' perceptions. As a way to avoid appearing incompetent, they use their negative behaviors as excuses. Some students fool around the night before a test or put off doing their schoolwork. They are too involved in other activities, their mother does not care; their friends and family keep them from paying attention or doing their homework (Urdan, Midgley, & Anderman, 1998). Self-handicapping occurs with boys slightly more than girls, and low-performing students tend to use these excuses more than others.

As mentioned earlier, a task-based goal structure is less likely to promote self-handicapping as compared to an ability goal structure that is ability focused and promotes competition. Studies done of parent belief systems and expectations shed light on this dimension. Asian American parents, for example, believe it is not ability that leads to success but place more emphasis on the role of effort (Ogaki & Frensch, 1998).

Relationships in classroom groups can create intellectual opportunities and prime each student's intrinsic motivation. They can also present barricades to learning and promote emotional problems. As Borich and Tombari (1995, p. 268) propose, effective learning can be enhanced or stifled depending on whether a student feels comfortable in the presence of others. In a positive climate, students' drives to influence others, achieve, and be accepted can arise. These drives can produce greater levels of achievement and promote learner satisfaction. If frustrated, they can lead to despair, listlessness, and conflict.

Gathering in small groups helps students, for, in contrast to working in the whole-class group, the group size encourages self-expression from students who would otherwise not have appropriate (too aggressive, too shy) voices in the larger setting. Such groups offer advantages for provocative thinking and full student participation in speaking and listening. The large group may be efficient, but it should be used only when teachers want to convey the same message to all students and the content is such that all are ready to receive it. When educators want to encourage self-expression and literary analysis, they must downsize their groupings.

TIME

Classroom schedules are often very hectic. Teachers lament that they do not have enough time to do everything. What often happens is that the time that is available does not always focus on the things that will really make a difference in learning. Students may, indeed, be spending their time on task, but if the task is not meaningful, motivating, and appropriate to the goal, it is time wasted. Discussions that are focused make a difference, although a bit of "birdwalking" by teachers or students serves social goals and should be encouraged. Students care about having enough time as well. One student comments: "My favorite part about Sycamore is that they let us move at our own pace; . . . [we] feel less pressured and feel better about the assignment" (Oldfather & Thomas, 1991, p. 118).

Teachers are wise to look closely at the tasks that go on in relationship to time taken. Lesson plans and surface appearances are often far away from the realities of what individual students do and say. Students spend approximately two-thirds of their reading times independent of the teacher and engaged in nonreading or indirect reading activities (Allington & McGill-Franzen, 1989). When students are being instructed directly by the teacher, they spend about 70% of their time passively watching and listening, not reading and not interacting (Simmins, Fuchs, Fuchs, Mathes, & Hodge, 1995). Analyses of activity segments in classrooms show that students doing seatwork (individual tasks, worksheets) takes up a majority of time in a typical classroom day and that student true engagement time is low compared to times when students work with others (Weinstein, 1991).

Any kind of group, regardless of the configuration (including tutorial, cooperative, and whole-class), must seek to look at time as an important investment for each participant. The time teachers and tutors spend in training and planning at the front end of a task is sometimes cut short, devastating the effectiveness of the group and wasting the entire time expenditure. Time spent in helping students remember their learnings is often overlooked, thereby eliminating the value of the time spent in the learning task. Knowledge saved is knowledge learned. With that in mind, planning for groups must integrate thoughts about memorability.

REMEMBERING

Effective group processes help students retain, not just acquire, new learnings. Remembering is important, for the learnings from today become the prior knowledge for tomorrow. As just discussed, the amount of meaningful time spent on tasks makes a difference. Not only does it offer opportunity for deeper exploration, but it also promotes greater retention. Students who are empowered with knowledge of their own learning styles, dominant modalities, and strengths among the multiple intelligences will have greater opportunities to use personal techniques that make a difference. Teachers and students will want to look at memory enhancers such as ways to provide a low-stress environment and mnemonic devices. Furthermore, no analysis of meaningful time for building knowledge would be complete without considerations of time devoted to practice and to other projects that occur in the home environment.

Considerations of Learner Style

Teachers who recognize their students' preferences in terms of preferred and ingrained attributes can help them grow. It will be outside the scope of this particular book to explore the fascinating attributes of styles and approaches, but qualities such as impulsivity or reflectivity can affect a learner's progress and impact classroom relationships (Leaver, 1997). Upper-grade teachers can teach note-taking skills for students who need the visual and kinesthetic interaction as well as briefer formats for those who can listen and retain. Practice with charts and notecards as opposed to recitation and recordings appeals to students with different strengths. Learning in social or independent ways may relate to temperament. Ways to enhance personal retention include enabling students to draw pictures, use actions, touch materials, make recordings, take photos, and learn things in different ways in different contexts.

Low-Stress Environment

Helping students lower anxiety is critical for learning. They do not want to fail. Literature about instruction for students learning English as a second language emphasizes "lowering the affective filter" and engaging in conversations within natural settings (Krashen, 1982). Also, to prepare the brain for learning, attention, memory, and test performance, we need to think about how to make a difference. Before students engage in academic memory techniques, they need to be informed about proper nutrition and exercise. Neuroscientists also share ideas that educators can pass on to their students. Calmness can make a difference in readiness to learn (e.g., Sprenger, 1999). Teachers may employ such techniques as music or silence, role-playing or movement activities, and storytelling or guided imagery to bring about an atmosphere of relaxation. Meditation and prayer are also effective, but everyone must respect policies as well as consider students' individualized thoughts that vary with their varied religious and ethnic backgrounds. Those who at first do not feel comfortable dealing with teaching concepts outside their usual domain may choose to turn to other resources such as books or guest speakers.

Homework

If schoolwork needs to be motivating, homework needs to be even more motivating because of the constant competition of outside contexts. Teachers are all too familiar with the stories of children who hurry from sports to lessons to religious and family events. Some children may scribble answers and fall into bed late at night. Others simply do not do their assignments. Unfortunately, the term *homework* is full of negative connotations for many. Students who go home to stressful environments are seldom able to complete homework assignments there with ease. If we were able to look into the afternoon and evening lives of students, opportunities for sustained and coordinated time for a calm review of the day's learning and a thorough preparation for the next day(s) would be the exception, not the rule.

Perhaps *outside study* would be better terminology. The work is frequently done at libraries and other centers away from home, including on the benches at sports events. Whereas some research studies tell us that homework does not make a difference in many academic endeavors, other reports tell us that homework is a discriminating factor for excellence. Current assessments tell us that the relationship between homework and achievement is, at best, weak (Cooper, 1989). However, too much assigned work is unfamiliar, uninteresting, and unsatisfying. Students are often given monumental tasks that require persistence and organization, and they need help to grow in those areas. Helping parents help their children with homework can make a difference. Parents do care and are interested in having the proper tools. Homework is a part of most school-based parenting programs. We also see differences in homework habits because of parents' ethnic and cultural backgrounds. The expectations of an immigrant parent from Taiwan could be very different from someone who does not come from a background that included a seven o'clock to six o'clock school day plus two hours of homework after dinner.

KNOWLEDGE MINIVIGNETTES

Students will grow in knowledge best within group contexts for which they are prepared and in which they are well supported to deal with appropriate tasks.

- The Title I program provides in-class support services through the work of a specialist teacher who plans with the classroom teacher each week. The support teacher knows that students have been reading and writing about animals in this class. She elicits those ideas and refers to their projects as bases for lessons in comprehension skill development.
- The multiage class has small-group book discussions that are open to anyone who has read the book. Group members know the rules: Respect each others' reactions. The leader records responses on the group feedback sheet. Each student has a chance to ask questions. All students are expected to contribute.
- A student research team designated to study canines has four members: two students have dogs at home, another person has read a book

on dog care, and one other helps at a veterinarian's office on Saturdays. Their teacher has provided a small tub of books of various degrees of difficulty about dogs gathered from the local public library.

- The teacher asks everyone in the class to draw and write about one favorite aspect of a tidepool. Their class was on a field trip there the day before.
- After hearing more than 14 fiction and nonfiction books read aloud about bears and learning two bear songs, students bring toy bears to school one day. Their teacher asks them to write imaginary adventure stories about the bears that they have brought to visit the classroom. Then they all go outside to march in the parade of the teddy bears.

On the other hand, some groups may have valuable tasks to do, and the teacher may have "taught" something, but the groups do not have K:

- A student teacher assigns the whole class to write limericks. She recites an example, then points out the rhyme pattern. Half of the class members have never heard of nor seen a limerick. Some children learned about limericks last year in third grade. Several students finish quickly and begin to recite their creations out loud, but some pout and fold their arms, grumbling, "I can't do this."
- Students are assigned partners to study vocabulary flash cards, but some students already know all of the words that are supposed to be mastered, while others know only one or two of the selected words. The students who know the words are told that they should pair up with other students and "be the teachers."
- During September in a fifth-grade class, a randomly selected group of four students is sent off to the library to produce a one-page research report on the Continental Congress. One student finds an appropriate volume and copies the information. The other three members look at books and talk about the television show they had all seen the night before.
- A second-grade class has a spelling test with 12 words each week. Five children get all the words right every time. Their pretest early in the week showed only one or two words that needed practice. On the other hand, four classmates always miss most of the words on the pretest, and then they miss large numbers of words on the final spelling test as well.

Children can learn from experiences that connect and build on their knowledge in groups that vary in size and composition, doing activities that relate to all aspects of instruction. With thoughtful teacher planning, classroom learning opportunities can be structured to respect the knowledge that students have and provide knowledge that they will see as worth remembering.

As teachers, we can improve our thinking and planning by making explicit our own visions and goals and share those with others. Why we do so much of what we do should link to what we stand for. Educators who have earned their credentials during the recent decade are familiar with the process of writing personal philosophies. The process of clarifying personal philosophy can certainly extend beyond the realm of academic exercise to become part of the ongoing planning process.

> *Knowledge comes, but wisdom lingers.*
> *—ALFRED, LORD TENNYSON*

► 4

Circumstances That Promote Power

Not student-centered, not teacher-centered, but . . .
"subject-centered."—PARKER PALMER, 1998

. . . concerned with both and their effect upon one another.
—HUGH BONNER 1959

What is *power*? It means the opportunity to make decisions and have influence. It means having choice as well as a voice. It means having rights and responsibilities along with a vote. It means social justice. It means being listened to.

Many words relate to power in society. Individuals may have authority, potency, leadership, dominance, prominence, eminence, status, visibility, or influence. They are words easily associated with kings and queens, presidents and mayors. They have been connected with principals and teachers. They could, in many situations, be words that apply to students. The location of classroom power is revealed when we ask, "Who tells us where we are going? Who sets the procedures? How will we know whether we're going in the right direction?" Dozens of activities occur in the daily life of a typical classroom, but the person who chooses the topics for study, the learning activities, the assessment procedures, the physical organization of the environment, and the organization of groups is usually the teacher. The person who chooses the methods for taking turns, the modes of discourse to use, the times when to notice rules being broken and the consequences selected, as well as the criteria for grades and what grades are given is usually the teacher. The person who sets the level of civility and the emotional context is usually the teacher.

Teachers reading the prior three questions as they relate to power in their schools and districts might answer by saying, "The district . . . state standards . . . The legislature . . . my principal." The political disempowerment of teachers is certainly a real phenomenon, and it is prominent in many teachers' perceptions. When teachers' practices are not consistent with their beliefs, statements such as "My principal wouldn't like that. . . . We aren't allowed to do that. . . . We have to follow . . ." are common responses to questions such as "Why don't you . . . ?" Even when the classroom door closes, when issues of power could be between teachers and students, external forces and past experiences always influence teachers' (and students') thinking. Disempowered teachers do not empower students when they do things only because they have to. Teachers who operate out of fear are not effective. Acts and words that are hypocritical do not create difference. On the other hand, working with students out of beliefs and principles will. Children of all ages respond to authenticity. When teachers decide on the best ways to support student learning, they must often, as Cochran-Smith and Lytle (1993) indicate, learn to teach against the grain. Their power is demonstrated by directing their own lives and influencing the lives of their students (Joe, 1993).

When students hold referent power, they are sought after as classroom group members. To be trusted comes to those who are fair and care about their classmates. It is the sort of power that promotes being liked in addition to being respected, and because the powerful individual is listening, she or he is listened to.

In the best of groups, teachers and students are not bullies (too strong). Neither are they doormats (too weak). They share power in various ways that are assertive (just right). Teachers may also think about their styles as authoritarian, laissez-faire, or democratic. However, *power* is a psychological concept. It is bestowed by others as they interact in groups. Therefore, one individual's concept of being "just right" may or may not match the visions of other group members. People who earn power in the most appropriate ways must be very good listeners (e.g., Peters, managing by walking around) and need to use great empathy in their decision making. In other words, the best leaders will hold referent power in addition to other types.

Palmer (1998) adds meaning to the three style categories in his analysis of how teachers handle truth. A classroom might seem like a dictatorship if truth is seen as "something handed down from authorities on high." If truth is "determined by personal whim, it will look like an anarchy. If truth emerges from a complex process of mutual inquiry, the classroom will look like a "resourceful, interdependent community" (p. 51).

This chapter explores the ways in which teachers use their authority to inspire that of their students in ways that promote literacy. It indicates types of power and addresses status as a phenomenon of classroom group life. Then it will talk about what teachers might do to promote voice, choice, votes, as well as clarify rights, responsibilities, and social justice for their students. It suggests that students examine issues of social justice from school settings to the community and into the world around them. It also encourages teachers and their students to use literacy as a way to find answers to their questions and find the questions they want to ask. Specific literacy activities that may build students' and teachers' senses of power appear in Chapter 12.

FIVE TYPES OF LEADER POWER

All groups have leaders, even groups that are called "leaderless." Sometimes the leader is identified by a title, such as leader or chair or president. Sometimes the leader is simply someone who influences the group, despite lack of a title. One system of classification identifies five types of social power for leaders or authorities (French & Raven from Borich & Tombari, 1995):

- expert,
- referent,
- legitimate,
- reward, and
- coercive.

These "powers" may be those of the teacher or may be attributed to any members within classroom groups.

Expert Power

When individuals hold expert power, they are knowledgeable and enthusiastic. A person who enjoys knowing things can engage in dialogue and discussion. Quite often, people who talk a great deal in groups are identified as leaders early on. Other group members may believe, at the outset at least, that the individual knows what he or she is talking about. Talking eases the social discomfort of silence, so people are usually grateful to have a talker in the group. It takes time for other characteristics of integrity and leadership to emerge. In view of this phenomenon, groups should not usually select leaders until groups have had opportunities to get to know each other.

When teachers give students opportunities to share their expertise, they are empowering them. From Sharing Time in kindergarten to upper-grade jigsaw projects, the person who knows is the person in power. Students may use expert power in many ways. Some of the ideas presented here may seem new, but most classrooms already provide similar opportunities that can be expanded. The greatest adjustment in empowering students comes in changing teachers' thinking. Teachers have, traditionally, "worked too hard" in their classrooms. As soon as they entrust their students with certain duties, their jobs become less. Students possess a great deal of informational and procedural knowledge that can be shared with others. With the proper context—group, task, assigned role, support—it can be done well, and perhaps better than if the teacher her- or himself had done it.

Referent Power

Individuals who hold referent power can be both respected and liked because they are trustworthy, concerned, and fair. Their leadership is characterized by warmth and competence. As Delpit (1995) reminds us, teachers who are considered "nice" by showing warmth, friendliness, and concern to students must also hold challenging standards for their students. They need to provide instruction that not only honors process but also coaches skills explicitly, honoring product. Otherwise, this power can turn into oppression, victimizing children who will not succeed. "I didn't feel she was teaching us anything. She wanted us to correct each other's papers and we were there to learn from her" (p. 31). Turning to direct instruction as the mode is not the solution. Rather, positive changes will come from minilessons or conferences with the teacher. The teacher who listens will be the one who best holds this form of power.

Legitimate Power

Legitimate power is bestowed by title, rank. This category is typically that of teachers, principals, presidents, or judges. It comes with the title and is usually deserved until the trust is broken. For sure, teachers hold authority in their classroom settings—even when they are physically absent from the scene. Their authority comes with the title, at least at the outset of any given new year. Most teachers are able to share positive tales of children's wonderful respectful and engaged behavior on the first day at school.

As time goes by, however, such authority is not always sustained, especially within some contexts in the United States. Automatic honored status is not automatically bestowed as it is in some cultures, notably Japan. As a matter of fact, although teachers do maintain levels of legitimate power by virtue of their job titles, many factors can serve to diminish it. Students come with preconceived notions that derive from attitudes within the surrounding school community and the greater cultural community.

In addition, any teacher's agenda is only one of many in a given classroom (Manke, 1997). No teacher is ever totally in control because of the independent wills of their students. Burdened by a sense of responsibility, a variety of external dictates to enact, and many variables to control, teachers struggle to control it all. They can easily become overwhelmed. As a result, many resort to extremes. Teachers may shield themselves with authoritarian rigidity or retreat behind a cloud of laissez-faire laxity. Understanding power, as well as how to share it and how to promote it, can help teachers form groups and design activities in which they and their students can prosper.

This automatic power may be conferred on students when they assume designated roles with meaningful titles in the classroom. Educators have a great amount of experience with individual line leaders, special monitors, and class officers. What they do not have, at least not in most K–8 settings, are roles that can enhance identification and responsibility in areas of literacy. Leaders are needed for libraries, book clubs, and literature circle functions. Students can be tutors and teachers and hold roles in dramatic productions and clubs. The weekly newspaper needs editors and reporters." If individuals with linguistic intelligence often become professional writers, actors, announcers, journalists, storytellers, teachers, poets, critics, and editors, then students can begin to discover their expertise by playing those roles. Regardless of each student's level of performance, he or she will have an opportunity to become engaged, trusted, and responsible.

Reward Power

When the authority comes through reward power, the individual has the ability to reward those they lead. Bosses and teachers bestow favors and evaluations. They give awards and rewards. They have the capacity, through words and actions, to enhance the power of others. Parents are well known for their use of gifts and allowances. Good grades and approval of the teacher are not always sought after in some contexts.

Another way to interpret reward power is the ability to provide access to status. It is not desirable, it cannot substitute for referent and expert power, but it does happen. Some students may respond to someone with a cool car or stylish clothes. Relationships that incorporate this type of power are, however, on shaky ground.

Student reward power is seldom a formal part of classroom life, yet the potential certainly does exist. "Bosses" in any setting are familiar with the power that comes with rewarding others. If children are to grow in power, they must have something to offer.

Coercive Power

Coercive power, on the other hand, comes when someone has the authority to assign consequences of a negative nature. Teachers and parents are familiar with this form from their own early experiences with paddles and spankings.

All powers may be used with effect. All may be misused. Coercive power can appear in schools and classrooms in the form of grades (possibly bad), tests (possibly failed) and, for teachers, standardized test scores (possibly embarrassing). This type of power is entwined with individual and cultural values, for, although all students fear failure, some students fear it in more overt ways than others. One student may come from a family that sees low grades as shameful to the whole family. Another may have a parent who claims that any negative comment from the teacher goes double at home.

Summary of Leader Powers

Empowerment is highly dependent on the social context and the ability of the individual student to operate within it. Noted educator Paulo Freire would have us find ways to avoid constant use of "banking education" through which teachers "deposit" knowledge into students for withdrawal at some later time. His work has inspired many other educators who see that students can take on important roles in the classroom. Learners' involvement can help develop their confidence and motivation to succeed in academic ways (Nieto, 1996). Students can serve as teachers, for they know about many topics and know how to communicate with peers. They can think and solve problems, they can talk, and they can listen—not just to the teacher but also to one another. An encouraging and supportive political context can promote self-expression and critical thought when students engage in interpretive discussions (Lewis, 1998). They can choose what to learn and how to learn in the right situation (Ladson-Billings, 1994).

Power comes from multiple sources in classrooms. When literacy is the focus, the powerful students are usually the ones who read the best. Not only do teachers know who their best readers are, but students are keenly aware of who reads well in their classes; teachers need not do a thing to promote or enhance their positions. Teachers often elevate status built on reading ability. Placement in top reading groups provides different learning experience for young people. Good readers are often selected for positions of honor and power that do not necessarily correlate with good reading. Children in top reading groups play on the schoolyard together. Their social bonds are perpetuated from an early age. Self-knowledge and self-esteem are techniques for building power in classrooms that seek to be inclusive. Teachers can learn style identification, acceptance, and expansion (Leaver, 1997).

STATUS

Differences between and among people are seldom just differences. Ranking and hierarchies soon follow. Children are quick to compete on physical lines: "My feet are bigger than yours." Adults compete too, sometimes with different categories or comparisons, as in "My feet are smaller than yours," with other body parts entering into the competition in covert, and even overt, ways. That is only the beginning. From kitchen hegemony ("I can cook better than you—this is my kitchen") to corporate takeovers ("We are bigger, therefore better"), the world promotes competition in many ways. In perceptions and practice, traits of race, gender, religion, and socioeconomic level are just some of the sources of enhanced or diminished status.

What is a schoolchild to do? Classroom contexts allow status to emerge as a negative force unless the members of its groups make conscious efforts to recognize its attributes, examine its effects, and change its course when necessary. It helps to have a teacher who is interested in studying status to build a cooperative climate.

Kindness, patience, and friendliness go a long way. By the *halo effect* of their words, teachers can enhance a child's status in a group by carefully worded, specific, and authentic compliments such as "I think that we need Shoshanna to help us all when we go to tutor. She really understands how to work with young children."

One of the ways teachers use to discuss status is to share interesting insights about someone or something with their students. The use of multicultural literature is one way to acquaint students with events, day-to-day characters, and heroes and influential figures from all walks of life, from all racial and ethnic groups. Whereas some individuals may believe that introducing literature about "otherness" is divisive, many others, myself included, see that emphasizing learning about multiple contexts and individuals can help see that we are all different, yet we are all the same. We are all cultural beings. Klassen (1993) refers to the "mirrors and windows" in multicultural literature, seeing our reflections, allowing us to see into the lives and perspectives of others. In her analysis of the use of multicultural literature, Schwartz (1995) incorporates thoughts from Anzaldua (1987) in urging readers to be a crossroads, to build bridges rather than walls. In all of our dealings, we have at times experienced being the stranger, crossing the border. To live in the borderlands means to put *chile* in the *borscht*, eat whole-wheat *tortillas*, speak Tex-Mex with a Brooklyn accent, be stopped by *la migra* at the border. Border pedagogy, also referred to as *critical postmodernism*, would have us read freely and widely. We can learn about inequality of all sorts; learn about people of all backgrounds who fight injustice; learn to protect the environment from the damages of humans all over the Earth; learn to respect all people of color, white being a color like any other.

VOICE

When students have voice in their classroom they are being listened to, by one another and by their teachers. To promote opportunities for voice, teachers take risks in diminishing some of their power. They must also condone their students' taking risks as they speak out through talking and writing.

In their work with students as coresearchers, Oldfather and Thomas (1991) came to use the term *honored voice*. It can occur when students not only find their voices, but their voices are "heard, taken seriously, acted upon, and honored" (p. 109). As the coauthors explain, self-expression becomes part of an interactive circle in which students shape their perceptions of their own self-competence and self-determination. That, in turn, promotes continuing engagement in learning that inspires further self-expression, self-competence, self-determination, and so on.

During Oldfather and Thomas's early work with their co-researcher students, the young people were fifth and sixth graders in a combination class. In one student's reflections a year later, she identified class discussions as the way she was able to learn that her opinion counts. Although arguing occurred, there was always the feeling of others accepting what she had to say, even if disagreement arose. The student, Nicki, explains, "This way, we can grow up believing in ourselves and we will want to participate in many other things, for example."

Talk

Clearly, the talk that teachers use with students can set the tone and make the difference for students (Garmston & Wellman, 1998; Ginott, 1972). Talk can be used in the classroom in many ways. From studies done over the years (Flanders, 1970; Marshall, Smagorinsky, & Smith, 1995), we know that teacher talk plays an overly dominant part of the amount of talk in any classroom. Unfortunately, true discussion and dialogue simply are not what go on in whole-class settings.

Teachers need to escape the dominance of their constant talk. The percentage of teacher talk as compared to all classroom talking has been estimated by some at close to 80% of all classroom talk. Many are also eager to escape the "bondage" of the initiation-response-evaluation pattern (IRE). A study conducted at bilingual classroom sites in California, Florida, New Jersey, New York, and Texas revealed that over 75% of student-initiated utterances are made in response to teacher initiations (questions, requests for information).

As mentioned earlier in this chapter, leaders of groups are sometimes selected from within for no better reason than they talk a great deal. Students of all ages are often unable to express themselves in speech before their peers when they do not feel confident. Therefore, one important role that teachers must play in building voice is to design groups in which a student can feel accepted, which can be done in several ways. One source of confidence is, of course, knowing something. Another way to promote voice for students is to distinguish between types of classroom talk. Although perhaps some consider it as old-fashioned, one type of difference is between a discussion and a dialogue.

Students learn to make decisions in life by making decisions and having opportunities to reflect on them. When they are individuals in a democracy, they are expected to make many decisions that affect their conditions in life. The factory model of educating children can result in adults who perform worker tasks. Through well-designed group activities, teachers can provide many opportunities for students to make choices and impact many real decisions of the classroom.

An important lesson for students is to learn to take many calculated risks. Good teachers however, remind them about social and political contexts in admonitions such as "You may say that when you are alone with your friends, but it is not language for the classroom."

Interpretation

Although teaching children to be independent is part of the common rhetoric in North American education, the opposite tends to happen. Typical practice teaches children to be dependent on external sources for directions, correct meanings, and truth (Delpit, 1995). Teachers of literacy classrooms have the potential to make a difference, and many of them do. Respect for student voice in response to literature has been a mission of those who promote *aesthetic response* (Rosenblatt, 1938, 1994). When speaking and writing express personal response, the interpretation goes beyond providing efferent information about such things as who the main characters are, the elements of the setting, or identifying the climax. Aesthetic response to literature promotes connection building for each student.

As previously mentioned in discussions of knowledge, small groups enhance the amount and type of student talk. *Reciprocal teaching* and *grand conversations* are two such formats that bring students and teachers together in small groups that can share power (Palincsar & Brown, 1984). When the teacher does not participate, groups still carry on in on-task ways that can bring about even greater production of ideas. As a variety of studies have shown (e.g., Short & Klassen 1993), student-directed response groups, such as literature circles, can allow for further gains. Students express themselves more, make more personal connections, take turns more fluidly and frequently, interact more, refer to their own lives, and explore the ethics of situations.

Possessing the power to discuss and interpret literature is important for students. Although students tend to talk more in small groups led by a teacher than in whole-class settings with the teacher, the quality of the talk is different. Students are often more free to speak their minds. As Lewis (1998) reveals, however, the power of the people doing the talking makes a difference on the amount and quality of talk that really does go on. Recordings of peer-led group sessions have shown that some conversations are good, but others are not so good for various participants. Social conditions outside the group will also influence what happens within the group.

Two students, Jason and Nikki, express themselves in very different voices. Jason's view of reading accepts the notion that he reads for "right" answers, and the group discussion serves to accept or reject his answers. Nikki, on the other hand, dominates the conversation. Along with the careful words of their teachers, a tool for changing the talk and the relationship is a recording of the students' book conversation. The power of the words themselves indicated that turn taking and less talk on Nikki's part would make a big difference in the overall quality of the exchange.

Writing

Powerful people throughout history have used words to help them gain power. Words have also effected the loss of power for many individuals—hence, the saying "The pen is mightier than the sword." Writing is powerful in adult society. Newspapers, magazines, books, and e-mail join white papers and documents of all sorts to influence and guide the population. Children, on the other hand, have traditionally written for extremely limited audiences. Teachers have tended to be their main readers except for parents. The advent of the writing process, assisted by the National Writing Projects more than two decades ago, encouraged teachers and their students to consider varied, authentic audiences for writing. Many classes do just that, engaging in various types of letter writing, newsletter writing, pen pals, journaling, and scriptwriting in addition to poems, stories, and essays.

Writing is no longer a lonely enterprise for many students. Dictation and language experience in the early grades enable students to work closely with adults and other students. Writing workshops encourage students to discuss their work with others. Writing partners and peer response groups are used in many situations, and students also collaborate on projects such as newspapers and anthologies of poetry and short stories. However, the voice that students adopt in kindergarten through sixth grade tends to be quite "soft." Students often have strong feelings, but the writing they do tends not to express emotion beyond platitudes.

Not only does writing empower individuals, but, as many adults and students know, liberation can come with the advent of word processing. The physical frustrations of writing with pencils and pens are alleviated. The spell checker brings a semblance of ability to almost anyone's composition. The power to move words and paragraphs makes editing relatively simple. The pleasure of seeing one's work in polished print lends authority to the words.

Children can experience the same empowerment. As Edinger (1994) points out, students can produce professional articles letters, stories, news articles, and poems with relative ease on word processors.

CHOICE

If power means the opportunity to make decisions and have influence, then students must have real choices in their classrooms to have power. Many writers have studied constructivist approaches to education (e.g., Kohn, 1996) and advocated approaches that give students authentic opportunities for decision making. Kohn mentions the success of teachers in Japan, for example, who even shy away from making authoritative statements that might short-circuit children's own problem solving.

In some settings, the possibility does become reality. Marilyn and Elizabeth, for example, have a multilevel class that serves first, second, and third graders. They call it a "1-2-3 progressive primary." It is one of several alternative education classes in their school district. Here is how the two teachers describe their situation in a letter to parents:

> *Our class uses a thematic approach to learning, with flexible grouping according to the needs of the students. Children are not limited by grade level barriers and instruction is appropriate to each child. Students are guided to become independent, self-directed learners. Children learn to accept responsibility for themselves.* Choice *is a key word in this environment.*

Although this type of multiage, multigrade classroom is rare in some states, it is prominent in many others. The belief system of the teachers has promoted many practices that empower their students over time. Ideally students do not just choose from a list of possibilities but generate the possibilities themselves.

The dichotomous needs of a democratic classroom require teachers to serve the common good as well as serve individual needs and preferences. Sometimes, when children have free choices, they repeat selections of friends to work with or topics to explore over and over. Such repetition may help a child deepen relationships or explore topics thoroughly. However, sometimes such power becomes a burden instead of a benefit to children. The child who always works with one friend may not know how to get out of choosing that person each time. The student who always chooses to write about a certain topic is limited in his or her scope of thought. Therefore, in addition to permitting free choice, teachers need to frame some choices for their students. Teachers have the responsibility to lead children into new relationships and topics for study. It is also important to recognize that some offers of choice are meaningful—"You may choose which type of bear to draw and color it appropriately"—whereas others are not—"You may color your bear with a brown crayon, a brown pencil, or a brown marker." Certainly, one individual should never make all of the decisions, and that includes the teacher.

Power and Social Justice

Studies of power can take students into many areas of inquiry. Because teachers want to empower students, they will listen to their questions and guide them to find answers. Reading the news can promote any number of questions about ethnic groups, social groups in schools, and family life. The status of children is a topic to which students are quick to relate. Investigations of all types of literature show that power struggles make stories. Whose stories get read in classrooms? What history is presented in the books? When students have engaged in their own searches, they are ready to explore the Bill of Rights to better understand and apply its guarantees and think about its interpretations. Telling students how to study power is probably not very empowering. As students from Sycamore school share, "Teachers are always asking their students' opinions because they believe that you can't teach an opinion. It would be too much like stealing the kids' own beliefs. We all have learned a great deal from one another" (Oldfather & Thomas, 1991, p. 119).

Teachers, in general, find it hard to open their agendas to student influence. Finding it hard does not make it inappropriate. It just means that it takes work to make things move.

POWER MINIVIGNETTES

The following groups, described in general terms, provide opportunities for children to experience power (P). Students are able to make their own decisions about significant parts of their assignments.

- The children plan and conduct research on their favorite books. They have the responsibility to work with a partner to design interviews and surveys. Then, after they talk to their classmates and record their data, they make a bar graph of their results. (Third-grade class)
- A 7-year-old girl explains, "This is our writing center. Our writing folders are all in special boxes, and you get to use the paper and these pencils. Although you may want to write at one of these desks, you are allowed to write anywhere you want to."
- Each student may drop one low grade before averaging his or her own final grade. (Fifth-grade class)

- The teacher explains, "You may choose any kind of animal you like to illustrate your poem. Refer to the books from our room library, if you like." (Second-grade class)
- One teacher explains, "Use the pocket chart to guide your choices. You should try to complete four of the six activities during the morning." (Grades 1–3 multiage classroom)
- The class meeting serves as a forum for clearing up the problem of mudballs at recess. Students suggest possible appropriate consequences and agree on the best one. (Sixth-grade class)
- Once a month, each student may sign up to spend a morning in the blockhouse. Three students may sign up together to build with the 1-foot to 3-feet-long wooden blocks, designing situations, playing them out, and then inviting visitors to tour the premises. Talking, planning, imagining together, the children create and re-create new environments. When the whole class gathers later in the day, they tell about their experiences that morning. (K–3 multiage class)
- The Listening Center has a tape player and five listening posts. Some of the recent tapes with matching books include *Strega Nona, Pinocchio,* and *The Gingerbread Man.* Children sign up to visit the center once a week and elect one person who takes over as the tape recorder's button pusher. Further communication among the group members is handled through eye contact. By the end of the school year, children have heard hundreds of stories read aloud because the Listening Center adds to their regular, "live" teacher read-alouds. (First grade)

On the other hand, these groups do not appear to have P:

- In Room 5, the teacher expects all of her children to work through their contracts in the exact order that appears on the ditto she prepared for them. (Fourth grade)
- After asking whether students have any questions about the designated writing topic, the teacher in Room 27 warns her students, "Do not leave your desk, and make sure that you work alone." (Sixth grade)
- When their cooperative group has an assignment, Paul complains to his teacher, "Sally has done all the writing the last four times. Why does she always get to do it?" (Third grade)
- Each morning the whole class reads in unison. The teacher leads with her voice and snaps her fingers to keep the children together. At first, the children say the right words, and the majority of the children point to the appropriate word. But, as they read onward, all but two children are on the right page, several children play with pencils and crayons, others lose their places, and, yawning, two children begin coloring. (First grade)

- The students in the eighth-grade literature class miss having their seventh-grade teacher. He had them sit in groups for discussions and assigned new literature circles every 4 to 6 weeks. They also wrote picture books to share at the local elementary school. This year they listen (part of the time) and take notes (as well as pass notes). (Middle school)

Children can experience power in groups that vary in size and activities that relate to all aspects of literacy instruction. With thoughtful teacher planning and standards setting, virtually any classroom learning opportunity can offer meaningful choice to students. As readers will discover in Chapter 12, "Building Power," teachers can design many opportunities to encourage student responsibility for their own growth in literacy.

> *[G]overnment of the people, by the people, for the people shall not perish from the earth.—ABRAHAM LINCOLN*

▶ 5

Circumstances That Promote Affection

I celebrate myself and sing myself,
For what I assume you shall assume,
For every atom belonging to me as good belongs to you.
—WALT WHITMAN

What is *affection*? It is belonging. It is care and understanding. It is listening to someone else. It is an attitude of respect and high expectations for self and others. It means trust.

Teachers must complete complex tasks as they organize their classrooms and schedules, develop lessons, and group students to meet the needs of individuals—often in environments of political change, poverty, and/or racism. When author Mike Rose traveled across the United States, looking at classrooms where positive teaching was going on for his book *Possible Lives*, he came to see that the good schools always had the following attributes: They were safe places, both physically and emotionally. The atmosphere was respectful, students and teachers toward each other and toward learning. They were vibrant—something good was going on, intellectually and socially, regardless of the structures that were used (Scherer, 1997). As he points out, the good news is that many classrooms demonstrate these qualities. Unfortunately, in the other half of that vision are schools that do not provide such supportive social settings. One of the key issues for both students and teachers, as well as staff and parents, is the lack of positive relations in schools.

A major qualitative study, completed by the Institute for Education in Transformation at what is now the Claremont Graduate University, revealed that within K–12 schools, all groups asked for individuals who care, listen, understand, respect others, and take the time to talk with one another (Poplin & Weeres, 1992). Regardless of their status or roles, students, staff, faculty, and parents saw the need for improved treatment of one another. When students, regardless of class and ethnicity, lose motivation and self-involvement at school, the consequences of their disengagement are difficult for all students. For those students who are considered to be at risk, the results are often dropping out of school and enduring the ensuing problematic consequences. Studies of at-risk students indicate that their engagement and retention in school can be enhanced by a caring individual. When schools change the learning environments for marginal students, the so-called risk factors can be reduced (Nieto, 1996).

In one model of school engagement (Finn, 1989), two central components describe student involvement. The first, *participation*, includes student behaviors such as coming to school, attending to rules, paying attention, and complying with teachers' requests. The other component is *identification*, which includes students' feelings of belonging and finding positive value in attending school. Although this chapter will focus mostly strongly on identification, it does not lose sight of the multiple interactions that occur with participation. Good classrooms are places where all students participate and identify. One teacher shared what his students taught him: A really good class is a "fence jumper"; it is one that students would jump over the schoolyard fence to get to. Something is always going on. You want to be there.

This chapter will deal with these indicators in terms of classroom climate and the motivation of individuals. People in the workplace, whether it be a business or a school, are more and more aware of the need for individuals to possess emotional intelligence (Cherniss, 1998; Goleman, 1995). The five dimensions in which individuals establish this intelligence, or "EQ," are self-awareness, self-control, motivation, empathy, and social skills. Those five dimensions help form the framework for the information presented here. They describe desirable attributes for all members of the classroom community, including teachers and students, parents and staff. The first focus here will be, however, on teachers.

TEACHERS WHO CARE

Teachers show that they care in many ways. They are patient and kind, and they respect others. But, as revealed in the work of Weinstein and Valenti (1995), traits of affection also include motivating classroom management and pedagogy right along with interpersonal relations. Promoting order and engaging students in challenging and motivating learning opportunities are aspects of care, in addition to being important ways to support growth in knowledge. Organized teaching based on learners' needs means care. Both teachers and learners demonstrate caring by expecting themselves and others to do their best and help maintain an orderly and productive environment for learning. Students who care are engaged in appropriate activities during learning time. In other words, it takes more than traditional notions of caring to grow community. As veteran teachers are fond of saying, "You don't just love 'em into learning."

Teachers are powerful models of affection in their interactions with students. Before good feelings can build between and among classmates, each teacher must establish the tone. This chapter will discuss the principles followed and the general ways in which teachers promote affection (A) for individuals in classrooms. Information and directions for selected, explicit practices will appear in Chapter 13, "Building Affection."

Several studies have used children's explanations to define a teacher who cares. Rather than collapse and summarize their findings, I report on them separately. I believe that readers will enjoy seeing their similarities and variances for themselves. In one (Rogers, 1991), fourth graders mentioned these teacher qualities: listening, trying to see things from a student's perspective, giving second chances, as well as "helping you with your work" and "keeping people from doing things they shouldn't." They saw teachers as being both nice and proactive.

In a study of what Latino children need for school success, Darder (1991a) found that children were clear about their expectations for teachers. The qualities that they mentioned over and over include someone who does not yell; is humorous, friendly, patient, creative, and flexible; is loyal, generous, kind, and trustworthy; and encourages the children to work in groups but permits them the choice to work alone and take on classroom responsibilities.

Students in a new alternative school at the edge of Harlem wrote essays about their first year (Jervis, 1998) that helped tell their story:

> 1. On trips teachers aren't always watching what you do. 2. There's a lot of gossip going on. 3. The teachers are very, very friendly. 4. If you have a problem they will talk to you about it. 5. Teachers trust us. 6. I like science because we get to experiment with things, not just read a science book and then write a paragraph about what you read. 7. They take us to a lot of trips.

Thomas and Montgomery (1998) studied children's explanations of the best and worst things teachers can do. Four rules emerged from the children's explanations and stories:

1. Don't yell at us; be gentle and ask others to be kind to me.
2. Please punish the right person; be fair.
3. Allow students to choose for ourselves.
4. Have a good sense of humor; have an attitude of fun.

The things that teachers do to promote active involvement and discussion are, indeed, appreciated by learners. Students treasure being treated in friendly ways that include listening and being trusted. Regardless of their socioeconomic levels or racial/ethnic backgrounds, students appreciate fair, fun, flexible, friendly individuals. As teachers work to relate positively with their students, they must identify the types of interactions and pedagogical strategies that build students' perceptions that they really do care.

When a group of practicing teachers describe attributes of good students, on the other hand, they do not necessarily include fun, in fact, neither funniness nor humor enter into the top 10 traits. They are interested in attributes that indicate motivation and will, ultimately, make resilient individuals.

1. Is persistent; puts forth positive effort
2. Is interested in learning, curious
3. Participates actively
4. Is creative; takes risks
5. Is a good listener
6. Has good attendance
7. Asks questions
8. Follows directions
9. Tries to do best work possible
10. Has good manners

Teacher–Student Relationships

One of the most influential analyses of teacher–student relations has been the work of Good & Brophy (e.g., 1973). Using the book *Life in Classrooms* (Jackson, 1968) as a springboard to classroom research, they reflect that not only are classrooms different, but life within the same classroom may be very different for the various students who "live" there. They conclude that there should never be identical expectations or treatment for all students; it is the identification of appropriate differences in teacher behaviors that is critical. Their summary includes suggestions for teachers if they expect to develop situations that can help low achievers as well as high. Kindergarten and first-grade teachers must place great emphasis on helping students develop school-related coping behaviors and reduce the emphasis that is so often placed on mastery of short-term achievement in content areas.

Suggestions include that teachers gain awareness of their own behaviors and biases. They must learn to possess and communicate positive expectations, such as enthusiasm for learning. They need to take time to know students as individuals and organize classroom activities so that they are able to interact with individuals and/or small groups of students. The progress of children should be monitored regularly so that the classroom activities can be adjusted, and teachers should learn how to help low achievers overcome institutionalized resistance strategies. They must also establish an instructional climate that can recognize specific, authentic accomplishments of students.

Teachers are cautioned against the regular instruction of the class as a whole, stressing that individuals' unique interests are not satisfied, the pace can never be appropriate for all, and the instruction can never be appropriate for certain students. Small groups increase the opportunities for children to be called on and experience involvement with the teacher. Teachers must take care in providing appropriate expectations and enough time for the small-group relationships to be of value. Praise needs to be given in specific terms for genuine reasons, criticism needs to be eliminated, and teachers need to exercise patience in waiting for all children to provide answers.

Although various types of leaders have been identified over time (Bonner, 1959; Hare, 1976), three categories consistently arise from the writings in group dynamics: (a) authoritarian, (b) democratic, and (c) laissez-faire. Because teachers are seldom, if ever, in positions to assume laissez-faire roles, really two leadership themes emerge for educators. There are leaders who share leadership functions (participatory) and those who do not (supervisory), and in classrooms there are situations that are predominantly teacher centered or learner centered.

Hare (1976) concluded that teacher-centered situations, in which task completion and demanding teacher behavior prevail, trigger reactions of student hostility, apathy, and other signs of withdrawal. Environments that are accepting and student-supportive, in contrast, lead to decreased anxiety, greater interaction, and positive feeling both in class and outside the classroom. Still, when there is ambiguity in permissive environments, particularly where group norms and goals are not clear, some students can have problems. Some students may do better with more directed instruction, and Hare describes them as those who are "dull, anxious, or dependent."

Bonner (1959) described effective leaders in problem-solving situations as those who ask good questions and create an opportunity for minority views to be expressed and held in the group memory. Because original ideas are disturbing, there can be a problem with settling for mediocrity in groups. Good leaders also not only provide substantive support for task completion but also give affective personal/emotional support as well. They promote the thought that every person is a potential resource person for the group as a whole.

Self-Awareness, and Intrapersonal Strength

An admonition that comes to us from ancient philosophy, one that has been repeated in a variety of ways through literary works to the present, is "Know thyself" (Nagel, 1994). Howard Gardner (1983), in his work with the multiple intelligences, explains the importance of intrapersonal intelligence. Not everyone is automatically strong in this attribute. This intelligence allows individuals to know themselves and their own personalities well to form and sustain plans. Each person with this quality has a strong sense of purpose, sensitivity to his or her personal motivations and goals, as well as a clear sense of self and reactions to others. Characteristics may include spiritual desire, access to feelings, sensitivity to experiences, and the ability to use contact with others in order to continue to know oneself. Although introspection is an individual process, it is regularly informed by social contexts. In education, the answers to "How did it go?" involve statements about other people.

Some individuals possess intrapersonal intelligence early in life. However, anyone may engage in activities that promote growth in this area. Although the impact of self-knowledge on group work is strong, the processes that develop introspection are not often social in nature. Also, many of the techniques could apply to both teachers and students, but they take on special characteristics as they relate to their different roles and levels of maturity. Teachers add to their effectiveness when they come to know their own stories and explore their own beliefs and values (e.g., Au, 1993). Educators who have not developed their own philosophies of education or who have never probed the impacts of their own culture on their personal values and decision making are in danger of making inflexible and intolerant classroom decisions.

Helpful in this regard is maintaining a reflective journal, a practice advocated not only by educators but also by psychologists and counselors. The process of self-reflection not only serves to highlight those values and concerns that arise in daily life but promotes metacognition. It is not unusual for individuals to say that they did not know how they thought about certain issues until they had to write about them.

Self-knowledge also helps build self-confidence. Through reflection on their own ups and downs, individuals can come to know that if they fail at something, they have the capacity to recover (Cherniss, 1998). They can see that recovery does truly happen over time. They can also see that if the worst possible thing does happen, it is not the end of the world.

Teachers work in stressful situations, making great numbers of important decisions that affect others each day. "Perfection" would seldom describe a typical lesson, for teachers must always adjust procedures to the context, both physical and social. Despite school efforts to limit interruptions, they are the rule, not the exception, during much of classroom life. Teachers must adapt constantly to such things as a student or a fellow teacher being absent, a new assembly schedule that interferes with library time, or the infamous messages from the office that arrive at key points in lessons.

To solve problems effectively, many teachers engage in action research. They write about conditions in their class, attempting to identify a problem that plagues their classroom work. By telling the ongoing story of changes they make in their own practice, teachers can record the things that they try in what is known as *move-testing* (Schon, 1987). When one idea does not seem to work, individuals move on to test a new procedure. Teachers soon realize that they have not yet "tried everything." On the other hand, their close observations may show that small victories are, indeed, occurring.

For teachers, self-confidence and positive self-esteem often come with experience. Raising skillfulness and lowering anxiety go hand in hand to promote positive esteem. Several approaches must work together to make it happen. Hard work is certainly one tactic. Working with colleagues is another way to succeed. Teachers who work together to plan and talk can serve as a support group for one another. Peer coaching is a technique that is supported in many school situations. Models of collegiality within the faculty make a difference for students. They enjoy the friendships of their fellow teachers. Teachers can build a more positive school climate when they are well acquainted with one another's classes.

Self-esteem for children is likewise critical. Many educators are familiar with programs that have been devised to foster positive esteem in students. Through activities, sometimes led by volunteer parents, classroom times have been devoted to examining values, telling their stories, and affirming their individuality and strengths. The long-term effects of such work are, however, varied. Although positive esteem can help students perform, it must be authentic and relate to the task at hand.

Reports of data gathered in multinational standardized tests and associated questions that students complete have revealed interesting cultural contrasts. Students from Japan who performed quite well responded in ways that indicated low personal self-esteem. Many U.S. students, on the other hand, responded in ways that indicated very positive esteem, despite low performance.

Esteem is best when students can take a look at their activities as complex; understanding "I am good at some things, but I need to work at others" would be a useful view. Students who learn about the multiple intelligences (Gardner, 1983) right along with their teachers can identify where they possess strengths and weaknesses.

Self-Control and Role Modeling

A set of rules similar to these may appear familiar to most teachers: (a) Come to school every day. (b) Be on time and come prepared. (c) Keep promises and plan ahead. (d) Be nice to others. (e) Request that your students do the same.

Until readers reach the fifth direction, their typical reactions are that the preceding rules are for students. Only upon reading the fifth item does it become clear that these directions are for teachers. Teachers do need to examine the ways in which their behaviors serve as models for students. This section will pursue further understanding of teachers as models.

Teachers Setting the Tone
Children can be expected to follow the modeling of their teachers, and teachers are wise to reflect frequently on the behaviors that they promote. The idea of "Don't do as I do, do as I say" simply does not work. The positive climate of any classroom allows knowledge to be gained and power to be utilized.

A teacher who begins with solid standards, using language that is understandable and techniques that are memorable, enhances classroom respect. Visuals such as posters, pictures, or overhead transparencies can help clarify the elements of positive citizenship. In addition, for groups to develop trust and respect, norms must be clarified and group members must attend to those norms. They know that a caring teacher will provide for their safety and well-being. Quite often, group members do not live up to one another's expectations because they operate from different perspectives about what is "proper" behavior. Conversations about how to get along are part of the important social cognition that needs to be developed.

Teachers also need to examine the words they use. Many classroom "veterans" with years of experience frequently say that they have never videotaped any of their lessons, and they do not want to. Still, what they say and how they say it make a big difference to others. The variables of voice tone, eye contact, body language, and silence lend to the impact of words that are used in daily discourse. Put-downs of any sort, through either verbal means or body language, must not be tolerated.

Although common practice does not always indicate it, the basic standards for teachers do not have to be different from standards for students. As a matter of fact, part of the distrust that can develop toward teachers occurs when they assume a different set of ideals and norms. Teachers sometimes engage in the very behaviors that are forbidden behaviors for students, such as talking during a performance, interrupting others, eating and drinking in class, and name calling. Rights and responsibilities, if they are to be different, must be clarified, and some are certainly justified in portraying the role(s) of the effective teacher—for example speaking to a visitor during a class session or correcting a student during a performance.

Norms for Students
Students who see their school as a caring and supportive environment in which they actively participate and have opportunities to exercise influence will feel attached to their school community and will, therefore, come to accept its norms and values. Mutual concern and respect, valuing individual members' contributions, attend to the need of the community. A caring

community conveys a set of goals and values while establishing the motivation within the group to abide by them (Battistich, Solomon, Kim, Watson, & Schaps, 1995).

Norms can be *rules* (guidelines for procedures) or *standards* (models of expectations, written or somehow demonstrated). Both are important for groups. Before student work begins, the norms must be clarified. It is not enough to set the ground rules once and expect success right away. Students often need to be reminded of norms after time elapses. Teachers do well to do the reminding by thanking the students for meeting the norms rather than waiting for things to fall apart and reestablish order. Reviving group memory when a group starts their activities on another occasion is also valuable. The process of "getting it" can be time-consuming, but it is extremely important for group success.

In working with a group of teachers one day, I gathered their following suggestions:

- Establish the rules.
- Model.
- Role-play.
- Have a group demonstrate.
- Establish time frames.
- Decide on acceptable talking levels and conversational habits.
- Set the expectations with clarity with reminders on the chalkboard or overhead or on posters for recurring activities.

Teachers are often unaware of how imprecise their directions can be. When children are not familiar with indirect ways of talk, for example, they may not respond in ways the teacher anticipates. "Would you like to sit down?" carries a different message from "Sit down, please" for many children. Many white teachers attempt to reduce an exhibition of power and be nice by expressing themselves in indirect terms. Their language may remove the very explicitness that a child from a different culture needs to understand the rules of their new classroom culture (Delpit, 1995).

For that and other reasons of motivation, teachers will find it much more successful, first, to involve the students in discussion of rules and procedures and role-play situations so that various language uses are made clear. Teachers may want to continue to use indirect ways of speaking but should do so only if the students have a fair chance to "translate." As mentioned in the chapters about knowledge, students are great explainers. They can make social information and skills clear as well as explain academic knowledge and skills to their peers. Teachers are powerful people, representing power because of their roles. But as Delpit explains, because so many teachers are white, they also come from a "culture of power" in the greater society. Without putting down other ways, teachers can share how certain ways of speaking, writing, dressing, and interacting are expected to participate smoothly in many arenas of successful daily life. Telling the stories behind the rules can make sense. Examining how television announcers speak, for example, could bring insights as to ways of talking for different purposes and audiences.

Students
The relationships between and among students are just as important as those between teachers and students. When students depict the sort of classmate they need to work with in groups, they are not concerned about IQ. Students surveyed about the types of groups that they preferred are much more concerned about the social behaviors of their fellow group members. Someone who is willing to do their part, follows through, and treats everyone with respect is what matters to them.

Affection within a classroom setting cannot be the same as that for a family setting. It is demonstrated in ways that are less physical, perhaps less emotional, but that can be just as unwavering and enduring. The stability that a class offers may be a safe harbor for students who must deal with difficult situations at home. A caring teacher certainly works hard, but the students must understand that hard work is a sign of affection for them, too. Kindness, patience, and friendliness go a long way, and the street is two-way.

Follow-through on guidelines tends to be most effective when the students have had a voice in setting notions of what is positive or negative. Just as groups come in different sizes and purposes, norms may also have a great deal of variance because of the nature of the roles and tasks that are involved. Context and purpose may vary factors from the type of clothing students worn to the quality of the language used.

Students can be expected to follow classroom rules. They need not be complex, and they need not be litanies of forbidden behaviors. Instead, they are best devised in a collaborative and thoughtful way. One simple framework might entail a devotion to courteous talk, compliments for one another, and commitment for self-assessment.

Using charts and other visual reminders can assist children in their performance. Teachers sometimes depend on their words alone, only to find out that what they have said was either not understood or not remembered, or both. Children are famous for "tuning out" and "forgetting." The need for cues extends to all ages of students. Many schools expect standards to be posted in classrooms for good reason. Some schools run off posters that denote expected behaviors, and they serve a useful function as long as they promote positive functions in clear and simple language. The best schoolwide standards have been constructed with the input of staff, students, and parents and are published with the public's gratitude for their contributions.

An important focus for teachers is to develop self-control among students, as well as with other participants in the classroom community, such as aides and parents. Consistency requires that everyone be on the same wavelength. Working with the principal and fellow faculty members is important to see that expectations are well known and that classroom norms are not in conflict. Jealousies and conflict can arise when one class does not seem to participate in the same way. From schoolwide silent reading times to library use and participation in assemblies, teachers can maintain many literacy-related relationships.

Motivation

Beyond possessing self-awareness and self-control, emotionally intelligent individuals are motivated. Motivation is what the KPA model is all about; resolving or avoiding student feelings of incompetence, powerlessness, and rejection—the three barricades to motivation. Teachers can promote high levels of intellectual accomplishment from all students when they help them mediate power and develop trusting relationships. Previous chapters have already discussed attributes of motivation, for it permeates every aspect of KPA.

As Borich and Tombari (1995) propose, effective learning can be enhanced or stifled depending on whether a student feels comfortable in the presence of others. Social guidance and cooperation are fundamental to motivation, and motivation plays a key role in promoting and energizing strategic activity. Positive relationships in classroom groups can create intellectual opportunities and prime each student's intrinsic motivation. Difficult relationships present barricades to learning and can promote emotional problems.

Cummins (1986) recommends an interactive, experiential model for working with students. It promotes positive reciprocal interactions and includes elements that represent KPA well: (a) genuine teacher–student dialogue, (b) "coaching" through guidance and facilitation, (c) encouragement for student-to-student talk, (d) encouragement of meaningful language rather than an emphasis on correctness, (e) conscious efforts to integrate language use with the curriculum, (f) a focus on high-level cognitive skills beyond factual recall, and (g) presentation of tasks that generate intrinsic motivation and do not depend on extrinsic motivation.

Although people do give one another tokens of affection outside of school contexts, they are not mandates for positive relationships, and they can create problems in school settings. Extrinsic "motivators" such as tickets, points, awards, and gifts can come to consume great amounts of time, energy, and money in classroom situations. In literacy classrooms, the wisest tokens are probably those that are free and use spoken or written discourse. In other words, a compliment or a note of affirmation can serve well. Good teachers avoid bribes but do not hesitate to say thank you for jobs well done. When affection is at its very best, it involves interest and empathy.

Empathy and Respect

In the words of British sociologist Basil Bernstein (1972), "If the culture of the teacher is to become part of the consciousness of the child, then the culture of the child must first be in the consciousness of the teacher" (p. 149). Familiarity with the attributes of the child extend beyond academic knowledge in a multigoal classroom. Teachers arrive at many schools from their own homes that are miles away. They do not know the surrounding community very well. They do not know the families. They do not understand the local characters, places, and events. They are wise to engage in activities that help to inform them, for otherwise they are simply drive-by teachers.

Benefit from Listening to the Children

Listening to students begins with listening to their names. Teachers encounter many types of names in schools with diverse student populations. With unusual letter–sound applications and multiple syllables, names are often mispronounced by the very people who serve as models of language use in a school setting. The diligence to get the spellings and pronunciations of children's names correct is a very basic sign of caring. The student and/or the parent are the best authorities, whether the last name is Csikszentmihalyi, Groening, Nguyen, or Waugh. Although many individuals shorten or Americanize their first names, the choice should definitely rest with them.

Good teachers also develop eyes in the back of their heads. They help the classroom climate by knowing who is responsible for what. Accusing the wrong person for misdeeds is sure to dampen the spirits of all the children. Instead, effective teachers do not miss a step; they can keep focused on a lesson and correct a misbehaving child with subtle signals at the same time. Until a teacher develops such a sense, she or he is wise to curtail accusations and use indirect methods, such as confidential written messages, to get to the bottom of puzzling problems. Teaching as social work always seems to involve a bit of detective work.

By taking an active interest in their students, teachers also can come to appreciate them as individuals, not stereotypes. When educators lump categories of students together (e.g., second graders, seventh graders, Latinas, bus riders, students with disabilities, athletes) they miss many opportunities for connections between their students and themselves. Listening to incidental conversation, both in and out of the classroom, can shed light on how specific students are responding to the classroom as well as to specific lessons. Additional insights are shared later, in Chapter 13, "Building Affection."

Try to Understand the Other Person's Perspective

Walking in someone else's moccasins can be difficult. Not only may they be a poor fit, but we often do not know how to walk in other types of footwear.

Different shoes take different approaches for handling rocks in the road. Physically trying on another person's shoes (or hat, or wheelchair, or skin color) can make a big difference in how we perceive the world and how the world approaches us. Imagining what others' perspectives are like is enhanced when literature is there to help. Rich resources in multicultural literature are now available through most libraries as well as a wide variety of catalogues, bookstores, and on-line sources. Teachers need not offer selections that only match the racial or cultural backgrounds of their children. If the student population is monocultural, the call for diverse literary experiences is even greater than if cross-cultural encounters are frequent in the classroom context.

Generational culture gaps can also be bridged by conscientious teachers. When teachers use humor, they may miss the mark because their students do not have the developmental capacity or vocabulary-based appreciation for their plays on words or narrative twists. Sometimes, it is best to change course. Sometimes, providing enough information through backgrounding can make a difference for lessons, both formal and casual.

Eliminate Thoughtless Criticism

In a review of psychological literature, Thompson (1998) concludes that perspectives of caring are different for individuals in nonwhite and/or poor cultures as compared to concepts held by those who are white and privileged. Recognizing that manners are multicultural and that civility can come in varied formats, teachers play a very important role in promoting caring for the classroom culture. For example, children in one classroom were discussing healthy things to eat for breakfast. Although the teacher was using materials that stressed cereal and milk, one child mentioned pizza, another mentioned a rice bowl, and another mentioned a burrito. When the teacher exclaimed, "Don't be silly! Pizza for breakfast isn't very good for you," she not only missed an opportunity to honor a child's knowledge but revealed her own lack of knowledge about foods and nutrition. Teachers need to be very cautious about casting their student's behaviors and answers in a negative light. Instead of promoting participation, such comments diminish it, if not shut it down entirely.

By the halo effect of their words, teachers can enhance a child's status in a group by carefully worded, specific, and authentic compliments such as "I think that the information that Joe brought in will help us all. He spent an hour at the library finding three great articles on George Washington."

Children, likewise, must monitor their comments and eliminate all put-downs. Taking on others' perspectives can help. Many people can, perhaps, remember their own parents or teachers asking, "How would you feel if that happened to you?"

In their study of first- and second-grade classrooms, Grant and Rothenberg (1986) noted the different emotional climates established by teachers in their classrooms. By the use of praise, teachers enhance climate; by their use of criticism, they diminish it. Friendly chats with students set up an open feeling and a warm atmosphere, permitting students to ask questions and talk about their personal interests. Allowing students to set the agenda by their questions and comments during group time permits them to have a greater sense of power than for those students who are cut short.

Educators must avoid the kinds of "teacher talk" that occur, typically, in low groups such as criticisms, low-level questions, and an acceptance of interruptions to the group's activities (Allington, 1983; Grant & Rothenberg, 1986; Hiebert, 1983). They must avoid making ongoing negative comments that do not hold up in polite adult society such as "You never have your book," "All you do is argue," and "Sit still." Instead, teachers can emphasize their own high-group behaviors, such as chatting with the children, speaking kindly, and paying devoted attention to the group's work: "I saw your mom outside the office after school yesterday. She loved the amusement park you designed." "This group is doing a good job of listening to one another."

Social Skills

A prominent finding of researchers Battistich, Solomon, and Delucchi (1993) is that the effects of cooperative group learning on academic achievement and social development will vary with the quality of the group interactions. Students who receive clear preparation prior to their experiences do better than others. Students can be engaged in discussing group goals as well as the interpersonal values that are important to group activity. During the setup time, participants can share insights and establish standards about fairness, respect, and responsibility. The effective teacher monitors unobtrusively during group work and then brings concepts and values up for discussion again in the activity wrap-up. Teachers make a difference.

In her explanations of the role that teachers can play, Cohen (1986) describes the differences between *direct* and *supportive* supervision. In the first, the teacher behaviors are explicit and they resemble behaviorist instruction. In the latter, the teacher gives feedback, encouraging the group to solve its own problems by asking questions and encouraging thinking. Facilitation and suggestions seem to serve students better than lectures and mandates.

Parent Relationships

The level of affect between parents and teachers is also influential in each student's ongoing sense of affection. Reaching out to parents and gaining their informed support will add to feelings of affection between and among students and teachers.

Contacting parents is a task that may seem threatening to many teachers, and when there are differences in culture and language, the difficulties can seem overwhelming. However, within teachers' attitudes and behaviors toward parents lie the catalysts for positive relations (Tinajero, Nagel, Flood, & Lapp, 1995). Analyzing the KPA triad of sociopsychological needs from the *parents'* perspective can help. Their relationships can be effective when they feel that they are cared for, that they have some talent or knowledge to offer, and that their opinions will be respected.

Teachers who do understand why some parents will not come to school can compensate with their own communicative behaviors and create a winning situation for their students in the long run. Leaving the door open and the coffeepot on and setting up specific ways for parents to feel wanted can start the process. Parents can be invited to gatherings that are designed strictly for social purposes, perhaps sharing performances of the children and providing chances to eat, talk, and laugh. They must not be invited to the classroom to be "fixed" or merely to be used.

Basic values treasured by parents turn out to be very similar to those of teachers. When groups gather to compare values, they come up with lists of very compatible qualities, such as honesty, fairness, learning, hard work, and respect for elders. Nevertheless, the ways in which those values are expressed may be very different from one cultural group to another, from one socioeconomic group to another, and from one age group to another. Students struggle when peers in their community offer friendship and respect for attributes that exclude school learning as being "white" (Ogbu, 1987). As explained further in Chapter 7, "Group Dynamics," values held by an individual's reference group are the ones that lend status and serve to cause conflict in values.

Parent involvement in public schools has been considered important for generations. The national Congress of Parents and Teachers (PTA) has been an influential voice for parents at school, district, state, and national levels. One of its main purposes is bringing "into closer relation the home and the school, that parents and teachers may cooperate intelligently in the education of children and youth" (Staff, 1990). Schools across the United States not only have PTA-type parent groups but also parent participation councils that discuss and respond to school programs. Other school–community committees and task forces take on continuing or ad hoc roles, with varying amounts of authority depending on policy as well as local procedures.

Although the explicit message for parent participation is often the same, the implicit realities are different throughout schools and districts. Parent groups work with varying amounts of power. Parents have little or no voice in school after school, and classroom after classroom, and it isn't merely a matter of administrative domination or of people "not caring." Opportunities—even those advisory groups required by law—are not always well publicized. Parents who need baby-sitting find the thought of leaving their children difficult and disruptive to daily living, which, for many, is stressful. Simply getting food on the table, children to finish homework, everyone's personal needs met, and everyone to sleep is a major chore.

Mehan (1989) depicts how varied the quality of family–school partnerships is when class differences exist among parents. In a comparison of schools in which one represented a white-working class community and the other an upper-middle-class area, factors were noted that constantly created inequality. The limited disposable time and income of the working-class people, coupled with inadequate skills in education, lack of child care and transportation, and perceptions that parents have no right to criticize teachers, meant a totally different level of involvement. Children in upper-middle-class homes come with the "cultural capital" of the dominant culture: knowledge, skills, norms, dress, manners, books, museums, concerts, theater, and style of interaction. When ethnic groups and economic levels are even further apart, so, too, are parent levels of participation.

Faltis (1997) concludes that schools need to find ways to serve as resources for the community, as opposed to thinking only that the community is a resource for the school. Such thinking is not unusual to North Americans who have heard, many times, "Ask not what your country can do for you . . ." His four-level approach to home–school relationships represents a reasonable way for schools to consider the gradual involvement of parents and families. This is a type of acculturation—the culture of each school is unique. The educator is the initiator.

Level 1: **Teacher–parent contact.** Get-togethers, perhaps home visits to learn about parents' or adult caregivers' daily experiences and the community where they live, permit insights as to how the parents may monitor schoolwork. More and more schools have home–school liaisons who can help orchestrate teachers' home visits. This phase is concentrated on gaining understandings and promoting trust.

Level 2: **Information sharing.** Through phone calls, letters, newsletters, and informal conferences, teachers may share information about important school dates and events, information about special phone numbers and community resources, information about the school board and its work, and information about help that parents can provide at home.

Level 3: **Participation in school activities and classroom life.** Times can range from a few minutes spent at the time of student arrivals or departures, to sharing the room and encouraging parents' "funds of knowledge."

Level 4: **Asking parents to help with school decision making.** This role is not for every parent, but it can be a boon. Most schools have parent advisory committees that would welcome more members. Creating and distributing a parent handbook is a valuable project. Other parent events can be devised in the spirit of "joinfostering," a term devised by Faltis (1997) to address the ways in which learning must address the social and cultural environments of the child.

> *They are not enemies; they are partners-in-conflict.*
> —SUSAN RICE

AFFECTION MINIVIGNETTES

These groups have A:

- Children have signed up for the Friday storytelling group. One girl's mother has come to share her short story of what it was like to be a girl growing up in Japan. She talks about her favorite games that she played. Then she and all of the group members listen carefully as, one by one, the children tell about games they played when they were very little boys and girls. (K–3 class)
- The children clap for their teacher who worked for 2 weeks to write and illustrate a book, just as they have been doing. (First grade)
- The fifth graders visit the kindergarten every Friday to share stories and journals with their kindergarten buddies. They have gotten to know each other well, and they have even created a friendship quilt together. Attendance on Fridays has been close to perfect in both classes. (5–K classes)
- A parent explains "Our participation is important to the success of this classroom. Many of us work in the room for 2 or 3 hours each week. Other parents agree to do tasks at home. We all listen to our kids read and guide them in at-home journal writing." (K–3 class)
- Five members of a group agree to work on a movie for their language arts class. They plan to work at one boy's house at two in the afternoon. They all show up. They all help. They all stay until the filming is done. They all do a part of the presentation at home. (Eighth grade)

These groups do not appear to have A:

- One student is told by other group members, "You have to do the drawing! You don't know how to write." (Third-grade class)
- Five girls scramble to get together when the teacher announces, "Get

in groups of four." Four girls whine at one, "Get out of here. You don't belong in this group." (K–3)

- Several students tell their teacher, "Nobody wants to work with Sara. She always tells everyone what to do." (First-grade class)
- The teacher has told her students that they will have an early recess if everyone finishes their assignments. Two boys play with an electronic game instead of completing their work, and the whole class thus stays in until the bell. (Fifth grade)
- A cross-age tutor writes back and forth in a journal with her second-grade "buddy." The day to write in journals is each Wednesday, and after being sick two Wednesdays in a row, her young buddy writes, "You didn't write! I don't know why you can't write to me!!!" ("Grade 17"—grade 2)

When students gain social insights, they not only get along well in the classroom but are preparing for life in the workplace. Every relational street goes two ways. An experienced teacher, chatting with fellow graduates from his teaching credential program, provided an insight that seems to lend well to ending this chapter. Something that he knows helped him to be successful in his work with inner-city upper graders was a set of sessions that had nothing to do with teaching—so he thought. It was marriage counseling. His teaching—and his private life—are both going strong.

> *Men [sic] being driven as we have seen, more by emotions than by reason, it follows that if they really want to agree and have some kind of common soul, it is not by virtue of a perception of reason but rather a common emotion such as hope, fear, or the desire to wreak vengeance.—B. SPINOZA*

▶ 6

KPA in Action

The good we secure for ourselves is precarious and uncertain . . . until it is secured for all of us and incorporated into our common life.—JANE ADDAMS

In any classroom, some groups may offer a KPA experience, and others may not. In the best of times, as indicated in Chapter 2, the classroom may become a community, exemplifying the intersection of knowledge, power, and affection. In building to that opportunity, an effective teacher sees that a variety of learning contexts occur for each child within the classroom. Just as students show academic greatest progress when teachers use a broad variety of strategies (Allington, 1998), classrooms that provide a great variety of well-designed groups promote growth for all learners (Raphael, Brock, & Wallace, 1997). The following narratives reflect groups that not only exemplify KPA for each member but also have the capacity to build knowledge, power, and affection for the class as a whole. Grade levels are not explicit in all of these vignettes, for some activities can cross several grade levels. In newsletters to parents and teachers, one principal has stressed messages such as, "Our school is preparing our children for the 21st century. We want them to enjoy adulthood as problem solvers, cooperative workers, self-starters, information managers, flexible thinkers, and effective questioners with positive self-esteem. Whether your child is in kindergarten or sixth grade, it starts right here" (Nagel, 1989, p. 1)."

DRAMATIZATION

For one small-group literacy activity, Grace gathers heterogeneous clusters of five children to act out their stories on the floor at the front of the room. After asking the children to tell what the story is about, she invites them to choose which parts they would like to play. To enhance each part as attractive, she adds comments: "Oh! The pig. That takes someone special. Who wants to be the pig?" After parts are handed out, students work on their own parts for the invented dialogue. Then Grace quizzes them, "Where does he come in? Is he going into the water? Why?" "Who wants to be Mother?" "Who is going to be in the water?" "Now what's going to happen?" "What's Mommy going to say?" "And now what? What are you going to say?"

Jaquaya, who has been grumpy about a lost barrette most of the morning, is happy to be the dog. She finally smiles a one-tooth-missing smile. Performance time comes soon, and all of the children say their made-up parts with enthusiasm. Their purposes are met as they fulfill their dramatic roles. They review and understand the story. They express their paraphrased interpretations of the characters. And when it is all over, Grace smiles and exclaims, "All ri-i-i-ght!" and claps for them all with sincere enthusiasm.

"DEAR" TIME

Liz and Marilyn are in a school that promotes silent reading time for all of its students, faculty, and staff. Every day after lunch the school has a Sustained Silent Reading (SSR) time for 15 minutes. Marilyn would prefer to call it "DEAR" for Drop Everything and Read because it is not always a silent time in their multiage classroom. As a matter of fact, the youngest children like to look at a book with a partner and share their perceptions as they go along. The children mix and spend time in various spots across their double classroom, preferring the couches and beanbags but not arguing when the softest spots are taken. The books that children choose are often from "their" colored plastic tubs, but several children explain that any book is fine. Children may also read other children's published pieces as the year goes on.

Marco and Charles find a spot on a beanbag and enjoy a book together. They are both first graders, and neither is an early reader. While they enjoy the book, they chat about the pictures and spend the time thinking about how much they like the animals. Each boy tells something that he knows about the animal and they also decide that they do not know some things. They both make up adventure stories as they go, inserting soft growls and howls where appropriate. For 15 minutes, Marco and Charles do not discuss other topics— their attention is totally on their book.

SINGING

Group singing, a daily thing to do, is fun for the children in Room 3-4, but they are also expected to learn the words correctly. They read from the sentence strips in the classroom pocket charts. Learning skills like beat, rhythm, melody, and echo rounds also becomes part of the experience. When the morning song is "This Land Is Your Land," the class sings all three verses, getting visual clues if they can read the chart, but also learning it through hearing it many times. One tune that is sung many times during one of my visitation weeks is "Pop Goes the Weasel," complete with gestures and sound effects.

COOPERATIVE GROUPS: RESPONSE TO LITERATURE

Each week, the children have one or two opportunities to work together in cooperative groups for language arts. Their projects almost always combine writing and drawing to express the ideas of one of the stories being studied that week. In one instance, the children are assigned to heterogeneous teams of four. Each group is given a large sheet of manila paper and five small sheets of colored construction paper. Their task is to create torn-paper pictures of a scene that includes appropriate representations of five important words they examined in the big book story that they just read. Although the activity involved in completing the work of art is serial in nature, the decision making is reciprocal. Each group needs to talk about what the words are, what the pictures will be, and where the pictures will go. Then individual children have responsibility for creating the shapes, gluing them on, and gluing the identifying words nearby. This particular project, although simple in design, is complex in its cooperative requirements. The children need to come to agreements about role responsibilities and correctness.

PARENTS AS PARTNERS

Bette has devised an at-home reading program called "Parents as Partners: Making Reading a Habit." Every week each child takes home a special reading packet, a laminated brown envelope that contains an interesting book for a parent to read to the child and a reading record sheet that lasts the whole month. To provide interesting books, the teachers have spent a great amount of personal money to get materials, mostly from a commercial book club. Children enjoy paperbacks such as *Lyle, Lyle, Crocodile, Cars and Trucks and Things That Go,* and *The Cat in the Hat.* The Friday mother-volunteer logs in minutes for each child on the permanent record sheet, and the Monday mother gets packets ready to go out again that day.

According to the Friday mom and the teachers, the program is very well liked. Everyone agrees that it makes a difference. The children are enthusiastic about the books that they get to take home. Perhaps because the books are the personal belongings of the teachers, they are treated with care. Reports of amounts of time spent reading are high, and there is universal participation.

TUTORIAL WITH A TEACHER

Marie is one of Grace's five students who go to Reading Recovery. Jane, the specialist teacher, greets first-grade Marie like an old pal when she walks in the door. The room is cozy and colorful, and so is the teacher, in her long printed cotton dress and dangly earrings. At 8:38, off they go for an action-packed session of 30 minutes that includes reading and rereading different books, phonetic word analysis in texts, alphabet letter writing, journal writing, word identification using plastic manipulative magnetic letters placed in a cake pan, and sentence building with cards cut from a sentence strip of Marie's own journal words. Jane keeps a detailed log of each event of the lesson.

The pace is fast, the talk is focused on reading and writing, and activities are pleasurable to Marie, who leans forward and allows frequent, small smiles to wash across her face. Jane encourages Marie the entire time. "I like the way you went back and you checked on yourself." "I like the way you did that." "Good, that's exactly what you're supposed to do." "Good, you remembered to point." "Wonderful." "Very nice." "Good!" "Do you want to read that last part again?" "How did you know that this word was *rain*?" "This is the word *to*." "Do *you* fly an airplane to school?" "That's exactly right." "Would you read that to me again?" "Good memory." "Good for you." "That was very nice." "Find *am*." "Excellent." "Do you want to put them in the envelope so you can take it home?" "I picked this out just for you. It's called *run*."

LITERATURE CIRCLES

After the first few months of school, students in Nora's fourth-grade class choose to work in groups according to their choices of novels. Nora introduces six core books, giving a book talk about each one to let all of the students see the book, hear a few passages, and get the gist of the story without all the details that would give away any secrets. After the introductions, each fourth grader fills out a preference sheet, listing their first three choices in order and telling why they would like to study each book. Everyone passes the books around for a few days to get a sense of how long or difficult each choice happens to be. When the groups are announced, most students get to read their first- or second-choice book. Nora makes sure that any student who is not in a first choice knows why, usually from a private conference or sometimes by her remarks on their choice papers that she returns.

The students select their own roles to play in the literature circle. Nora has a set of papers for all members of each group to understand the group process. She also prepares a small set of papers that explain each role, so that students know their tasks to perform.

DESIGNING A RUBRIC

After the second period class gets settled, Lou shares a few reminders about the anthology that they will be publishing and teases his eighth graders: "Remember, as king of this classroom, I have a right to have a bad mood." He is, however, in quite a good mood. He passes out a copy of a four-point rubric for their current writing but explains that he wrote it on the computer that morning and it is not very exciting. Instead, he needs them to help develop clear criteria. What distinguishes a one-point score from two, three, or four?

After establishing emphatically that "zero is nothing," Lou accepts suggestions from across the room. Students are in self-selected teams of four, and hands go up from someone in each of the nine groups during the exchange. Starting with a "one," Lou records on the overhead while students suggest, "Off-topic," "Didn't try," "No details," "Not worth reading," and "No connections." When someone offers, "Bad grammar," Lou smiles and declares, "Sounds like a rock band!" When another student calls out, "Might as well be a rough draft," the entire class nods in agreement, some saying yes and Lou declaring "I *like* that!" When the group moves on to describe a "two," suggestions include "Same old, same old," "Not really interesting," and then one student adds, "Might as well be a second draft." Everyone laughs, knowing that it is more funny than appropriate.

When the class gets to descriptions of a "four," the set begins with, "Might as well be your last draft." The kids say, "oo-ooh" and everyone smiles. Then the contributions continue: "Captivating," "Addictive," "Imaginative," "Stands out," "Memorable." The students are ready with criteria that they understand for the partner peer scoring that comes next. They are in good spirits. They have done a good job. Lou declares, "Outstanding!" to his class, and he means it.

SPECIAL BUDDIES

For one semester, Lisa's fourth graders wrote back and forth to students in a teacher preparation class. They wrote once a week and the college students wrote back. The college buddies visited the classroom in small groups over the semester, and everyone participated in an end-of-semester pizza party with buddy presentations to the gathered crowd. Their comments speak for them.

What We Think About Buddy Journals

Ray—I think buddy journals are fun because it's another person we can communicate with inside the classroom.

Rebecca—I think buddy journals are fun to write because you could learn about each other. You could learn to be a teacher so that you could be a teacher when you grow up.

Tracie—My buddy journal means a lot to me because it is the only time I am able to communicate with an adult, who can teach me many things.

Mary—I think buddy journaling is nice because we get to speak to grownups how its like being a college student.

Dan—I think buddy journals are really good because we can communicate with other people except our friends, parents, and teachers. I am looking forward to meeting our Big Buddies.

Jared—My buddy journal makes me feel that someone is actually listening to my thoughts and is giving me suggestions about school.

One middle-schooler in Chicago said about his school, "This is not a place that makes fun of you if you mess up." That's powerful.—MIKE ROSE

► 7

Group Dynamics

The social practices within which reading and writing are embedded largely determine the cognitive and social outcomes for individuals.—S. SCRIBNER AND M. COLE

As a subdiscipline of social psychology, group dynamics studies the changing, affective interactions between and among group members as they adjust to one another in the process of reaching goals (Bonner, 1959). Although this entire volume is certainly about the dynamics of groups, this chapter will highlight explicit descriptions of some of the basic concepts that have come from the traditional science of group behavior. I hope it will help readers as a resource for their personal research and problem solving. It joins with the next chapters on ability and size to provide ideas that can inform and support understandings of KPA. According to Bonner, "Human relations are holistic, not additive" (p. 64). Although we can separate various attributes of groups to study them, we must remember that groups are more than the sum of their attributes. In education, as elsewhere, groups are not predictable, and human learning is affected by other human beings. This chapter will cover aspects of group dynamics such as (a) its background; (b) group roles and tasks; (c) cohesiveness, motivation and socioemotional needs; (d) status expectations related to socioeconomic status, culture, and gender; and (e) diagnosis of group problems. Impacts of student abilities and group sizes will be handled as separate topics in Chapters 8 and 9.

BACKGROUND

Although educators began to pay a great amount of attention to group dynamics in the 1940s and 1950s, many of their perspectives sprang out of principles developed earlier by two social psychologists, Kurt Lewin and Jacob Moreno, whose research in the 1920s and 1930s supported the philosophies of John Dewey. Lewin and Moreno worked in independent realms, conducting studies in group dynamics as a science, but used their work to promote social reconstruction. Lewin set the tone for applied action research and is also known as the originator of the "T-group," the training group that brought many individuals to heightened self-perception in the 1960s. Moreno was responsible for the development of sociometry and role playing. Their work formed a base for subsequent generations of group dynamics scholars.

Studies of group dynamics and group work have been conducted with varying intensity over the years. Lewin established the first Research Center for Group Dynamics at the Massachusetts Institute of Technology. The National Training Laboratory in Group Development began in 1947 at Temple University, involving Leland Bradford and other spokespersons. The number of books and papers on small group processes was 584 works in 1955 and grew to about 2,700 in 1966, then to over 6,035 in 1977, but the growth of research was curtailed with diminished federal funding in the 1970s.

Other projects involving group work have been conducted at the various regional laboratories over the years, as well as becoming focus work for independent researchers at colleges and universities across the United States. For example, contemporary group research efforts have taken place at Stanford University's Center for Complex Instruction in conjunction with the scholarly leadership of Elizabeth Cohen. In addition, perspectives in social psychology have influenced the work of many literacy researchers, particularly during the last two decades. Examinations of the ways in which student and teacher–student interactions affect outcomes have been frequent bases for research reports in, for example, the annual meetings of the National Reading Conference and the American Educational Research Association and their publications.

The concepts presented here have had staying power. Many of the original insights come from the "heyday" of group dynamics research. Readers will recall chapters on knowledge, power, and affection, where more recent investigations have demonstrated these concepts.

GROUP ROLES

Group processes help students learn interpersonal skills, and they play important roles in the development of individuals' self-concepts (Schmuck & Schmuck, 1979). Each child brings unique characteristics to a classroom, but they are changed and shaped by what happens in the room. The roles that students take in a group have been described in various sets. Getzels and Thelen (1960) proposed two role patterns: *nomothetic* roles—formalized, institutionalized duties—and *idiographic* aspects—the variable attributes that come with their personal characteristics. Benne and Sheats (1948) also outlined two rather similar categories: (a) the group-task roles that focus on the job to be done and (b) the group-building and maintenance roles that help the group to function. These two patterns have accrued many other labels over time, one pair being *task* and *social-emotional* (Bradford, 1978)—terms that I will call on for further explanation; task roles get the job done and social-emotional roles keep the group going. These words are also the ones used to describe good leaders, for they see that jobs get done and people get along.

Task Roles

These roles are not to be confused with the jobs to be accomplished through groupwork. These are the roles that get the job done. Teachers, in their oral and written directions, set the course for their students to analyze a passage, write an essay, and complete a project. However, these include roles that are not usually assigned, and are not necessarily overt, but nevertheless occur in the context of problem solving. The roles may be played by different people at different moments because of the dynamics that always occur. Many publications, including tips for teachers, name a variety of tasks that might be performed by individuals. The following set of roles comes from the work of Benne and Sheats (1948). Recent, popular frameworks seem to have traits that stem from these 11 roles, although different terms are used in various adaptations. Simply knowing these task roles will not help readers. Instead, it would be wise to analyze the type of literacy situation, the goals for the group, and the size and maturity of the student group. Most groups start with a coordinator and a recorder, but the quality of the inquiry can improve with the enactment of these roles.

One person may serve in several roles, but some individuals may, informally, play most of the roles in a given group session:

- the *initiator-contributor*, who suggests new ideas or different ways;
- the *information-seeker* who seeks facts;
- the *information-giver*;
- the *opinion-seeker*, who looks for clarification relative to values;
- the *opinion-giver*;
- the *elaborator*, who projects how something would work out;
- a *coordinator*, who tries to gather separate ideas or activities into a group effort;
- an *orienter*, who summarizes ideas or activities that help accomplish the group goal(s); and
- the *evaluator-critic*, who examines the group's achievement in view of the task.

In addition, there is usually a *procedural technician* of some sort—a person who does routine tasks and gathers materials—and a *recorder* who keeps an account for the group memory. The recorder is, in most settings, also a reporter of some sort. Successful groups will have most of the task roles fulfilled at some point. Fulfillment of task roles, on the other hand, does not assure that a group will be successful. The roles must be enacted well and must function in concert with social-emotional roles.

In classrooms of young children, formalizing the roles can serve a useful function, despite the fact that the flow of discourse is, typically, not particularly smooth or "normal." One format might be to have these task roles: (a) coordinator, (b) recorder, (b) creative idea provider, (c) fact finder, (d) information giver, (e) summarizer, and (f) evaluator.

Social-Emotional Roles

Seven *social-emotional* roles support group work by helping members to get along.

- the *encourager*, who provides warmth and approval for contributions to the group;
- a *harmonizer*, who mediates disagreements and practices conciliation;
- the *compromiser*, who modifies his or her own ideas for the sake of group harmony;
- the *gatekeeper*, who keeps the channels of communication open and the process rolling;
- the *standard-setter*, who establishes a criterion to evaluate the quality of group achievements;
- a *group observer*, who reflects back to the group evaluations of processes that occur, and
- the *follower*, who goes along, passively accepting the ideas of others.

When teachers introduce these roles, students can find much to discuss. Their amplifications of what each person's words and actions might be would be very useful in setting the tone for group work and in clarifying how students should proceed.

In accomplishing tasks and fulfilling roles, the interdependence of group members varies. As presented in Chapter 3, Thompson (1967) described three formats for understanding the ways in which social interactions impact work. The diagram shown in Appendix F illustrates the ways in which I envision the Thompson descriptions. In *pooled* interdependence, all group members can contribute to the whole, but like so many swimmers in a pool, their individual contributions are important but do not necessarily interact. In *sequential* interdependence, one group member must perform his or her task before the next person can. Since members may interact during the process, their roles are more like those of relay teams in track and field events. In *reciprocal interdependence*, all members interact and their work affects the work of one another.

I find that an understanding of these formats has proven very useful for teachers in understanding how to promote conversation and true interaction within classroom groups. Although Western societies are noted to have many competitive attributes, examples of reciprocal interdependence are more and more abundant in everyday life. Many occupations require teamwork with accompanying reciprocal problem solving. More and more, think tanks in which people brainstorm and yield collaborative messages are for everyone. Whether they be staff of school faculties at all levels, builders of cars, employees of bioscientific firms, or developers of technology, people need to work together well. Individuals who claim that our students need to be competitive to get along in this competitive world have not kept up with the requirements of turn-of-the century workplaces.

COHESION, MORALE, AND SELF-INVOLVEMENT

Different researchers have also enumerated the sociopsychological needs of individuals in a variety of ways. They relate to their motivation for joining and staying in group relationships. As indicated throughout this volume, these three needs may be expressed as *knowledge*, *power*, and *affection* (see Chapter 2).

Esprit de corps, morale, and self-involvement play overlapping roles in the minds of group members, and it is not possible to say that they align in any precise way with the three sociopsychological needs of individuals. Instead, they develop as a result of KPA and serve with KPA as indicators of group health.

When teachers work with groups, they do not want anyone to be left out. The attentiveness of children, their on-task behaviors, are important to the cohesion of the group. The ways in which groups gain cohesion are also ways in which they motivate individuals.

Three interrelated aspects to motivation apply directly to the dynamics that occur in groups (Bonner, 1959). These factors "keep groups going." The term *esprit de corps* refers to the "team spirit" that can apply to feelings of group identification, regardless of the group size. The force of esprit de corps builds morale by enhancing the attractiveness of members to one another and fosters uniformity of behavior and persistence of group membership. Continued interaction and participation increase the degree of interpersonal attraction.

Another factor, *positive morale*, allows group members to keep members going strong in their relationships, in spite of adversities faced by the group. Morale characterizes any group with a sense of solidarity, regardless of its democratic or authoritarian structure. Members of a group with high morale and a group with low morale can look at an identical set of circumstances and see it differently. A high-morale group can see it as positive, while the low group sees it as negative. Morale makes the difference between satisfaction and dissatisfaction; it is the force behind seeing the glass as half-full instead of as half-empty. It is also a way of perceiving happiness, for individuals may be happy in even the worst of social conditions.

A sense of *self-involvement* occurs when the norms of the group become internalized as the norms of the individual member. They are not felt as external pressure, for they are values that each group member cherishes as a person. Another term that is frequently used for this attribute is *identification*. The individual's thinking becomes inseparable from the group's, and a sense of personal pride comes from talking about, or working on, the group's goals.

Esprit de corps, morale, and self-involvement relate to the socioemotional effects on individuals as they function in groups. They help keep groups going.

STATUS

The relative positions that individuals hold within groups come with the territory. Groups, as readers will recall, are networks of psychological relationships, and status is a product of the mind. Unequal status interferes with the attractiveness of group members to one another. It can disrupt cohesiveness and make groups unfulfilling for individuals, not because it interferes with feelings of friendliness but because it creates general expectations for competence or incompetence (Sharan & Sharan, 1976). Indeed, students can become more friendly in the process of confirming stereotypes of one another. Intricate forces operate to reinforce status relationships and negatively impact the needs for knowledge and power, but not affection. In other words, an individual might very well accept low status to achieve a sense of belonging. Many explanations of gang membership, for example, would support this notion.

Status also relates to the "invisible" groups to which individuals belong. Teachers will want to remember the difference between associations with overt and hidden groups. When a person is recognized by others as belonging to a group, it is a *membership* group for that person. Membership groups are quite visible. Parents join PTAs. Teachers join faculties. Students become members of specific classes. When a person identifies strongly with a group and relates to its values, it is a *reference* group (Hyman, 1942); members feel loyal and related. All social attitudes are acquired within a context that shapes perceptions of various objects, people, and events: "You've got to be carefully taught." Although a membership group can also be a reference group, people who share the same frame of reference are not necessarily in the same membership group. They can be in reference relationships that are invisible yet rigid and enduring.

Status is an issue of reference groups, not membership groups. When people show bias toward others, it is a result of identifying with a certain reference group. Also, because social attitudes are a group phenomenon, change is not solely a matter of an individual changing his or her mind. The implications of status for groups mean that, as students enter membership groups, they carry with them the perceptions of their other, reference, groups. Two of the most common reference groups for all individuals are culture and gender. The ways in which they play on group actions and decisions have been explored and documented enough to tell of their immense impact.

In school settings, gender and racial and ethnic differences have been shown to influence teacher expectations through stereotyping. Teachers' prophecies about children have been demonstrated to be fulfilled (Schmuck & Schmuck, 1979). Expectations for self are also involved. The ways in which children take on roles through the process of self-fulfilling prophecy have also permeated classroom research. Of course, the interpersonal reactions of teachers and students promote a circular pattern of expectations and fulfillment that can continue unbroken unless steps of intervention are taken. Status that emerges from racial and ethnic differences permits white students to be more influential than black (Berger, Rosenholtz, & Zelditch, 1983) and white students to be more dominant than Mexican Americans (Rosenholtz & Cohen, 1983). High-status students can be more active and influential than low-status students (Cohen, 1982).

When Peterson (1963) looked at girls and boys in the context of studying maladaptive behavior in groups, 80% of the passives were girls and 80% of the aggressives were boys. Low self-confidence seems to be a problem for girls in mixed situations as they go through school (Lenney, 1977). Whereas males approach relationships with self-identity in mind, females tend to see relationships as ways to create identity. The conclusion that girls are withdrawn, initiating less, and boys are aggressive has carried into modern literature, exploding on 1992 newspaper pages with the results of an Association of American University Women (AAUW) study of girls' lack of equal opportunities in the classroom. However, the ways in which gender differences are presented in the contexts of first-grade classrooms is less clear. Much of the gender research has involved children in adolescence and older (Gilligan, 1982).

Status based on academic standing is yet one other force that operates in classrooms. Those children who are seen as having more ability, particularly reading ability, can exert more influence than those who are seen as having less. When Slavin (1983) found that in mixed cooperative learning situations, black students make even greater achievements than do white students, some further thoughts emerged. Students were engaged who were often disengaged and inattentive in other settings. Nevertheless, their overall status was not necessarily changed because of the continuing influence of high-status classmates.

Unanswered questions about circumstances that affect young children persist because of the relative absence of dynamics research that has directly involved them. "Traditional" status issues may not hold the same force. Still, Grant and Rothenberg (1986) suggest from their findings that first-grade reading groups perpetuate status distinctions among students and create barriers to mobility. They also note that students in low reading groups are prepared for the possibility of downward social mobility and students in the highest groups within blue-collar schools are trained for upward mobility.

When Hatch (1987) studied status and social power in kindergarten groups, three sorts of behavior emerged in the child-to-child interactions: (a) *self-promotion*, which appears in statements of "I am . . . ," "I can . . . ," "I did . . . ," and are usually countered by responses of one-upsmanship; (b) *put-downs*, which include statements such as "You're acting silly," and get responses of offense or refute; and (c) *dominance* through giving orders, which are countered by statements such as, "You do it yourself." Young children use overt language. Their comments are indicative of problems that can spring up in groups, regardless of the members' ages.

As people take on different roles in life, their reference groups can change. Cognitive adaptations can provide new ways of seeing things because reference is psychologically determined, which, in turn, leads to a change in attitude that leads on to a change in actions (Lieberman, 1956). Membership groups that do not change in composition do not promote changes in thinking and action. Changes in reference groups are what make a difference. When individuals realize that they belong to the same reference group as someone else, they may form bonds with that individual. Promoting changes in status thinking, therefore, would certainly involve assisting individuals to identify with reference groups in new ways. One example of how that could come about is seen in "big blue marble" thinking: we are all travelers on Spaceship Earth.

DIAGNOSIS OF GROUP PROBLEMS

Bonner (1959) describes group problems as dominance, irrelevant behavior or horseplay, and laziness. Groups have problems when there are interpersonal aggressions, temporary escape or withdrawal from the situation, or general disorganization in which someone will not cooperate and blames others.

Benne and Sheats (1948) describe group problems as the *aggressor*, who deflates the status of others; the *playboy*, who displays a lack of involvement with

out of field behavior; and the *blocker*, who tends to be stubbornly resistant beyond reason. When a group brings pressure on an individual to conform and
there is a demand for that person to surrender selfhood, the reaction will also
be one of these three. In a mentally healthy individual, the choice to conform
must be his or her own.

I have renamed these problem types as the following: (a) Bullies,
(b) Bozos, and (c) Babies. They all create antagonism and slow the progress
of a group toward reaching its goals. Teachers are bound to recognize them.
Students are bound to know them. They can disrupt the dynamics of any
group relationship, no matter the size, no matter the age.

Bullies may not be particularly bossy, nor do they have to be mean in the
sense of a schoolyard bully. Instead, they are self-centered, using the time or
hogging the conversation for themselves. Bozos engage in behaviors that do
not lead toward the group goals. They may be very likable, they may be
funny, but they do not assume the roles or tasks that fit the situation. They
simply do not "produce." The Babies are the whiners. They stop progress,
and, like the Bozos, they take the group on side trips of their own making.
Even though they may have no argument with a particular goal, they always
find something wrong with the suggested means to the goal and provide no
suggested substitute.

Certainly other descriptions of "difficult" group members can be brought
forward. Issues of loss of civility and manners, for example, are present in current discussions of getting along. Nevertheless, the behaviors that actually
halt progress and dissolve groups can probably be tied back to the "Three Bs."

IMPLICATIONS

A negative classroom climate is characterized by competitiveness, hostility,
and alienation, with little chance for the development of positive self-esteem;
individuals develop feelings of anxiety. When the classroom climate is positive, students expect the intellectual best of one another, they share influence,
and they enjoy high levels of personal attractiveness to one another. In cohesive classroom groups, there are many clusters of interpersonal friendships,
and no obvious "stars" or "outcasts." Individual differences are accommodated, work groups can be changed easily, and if the group's norms relate to
academic involvement, there may be greater opportunity for productive
learning (Schmuck & Schmuck, 1979).

When educators understand the roles that make a difference in classroom groups, they can begin to convey those ideas to their students in age-
appropriate ways. When group health is of concern, specific elements can be
identified as needing enhancement. Knowledge of the various components of
dynamics can assist the search for improvement.

Therefore, classmates and teachers have the socioemotional tasks of working through communication, collaboration, and cooperation to establish that all class members do, indeed, have knowledge, that they all exert power in some way, and that they care about one another. Individuals who believe that they make a difference will stick with groups.

Group problems will, of course, vary with the individuals who make up the group. Students may play positive task and social-emotional roles in some settings and turn to negative behaviors in other group contexts. Readers are familiar with the difficult student who does well with a certain teacher or in a certain group. As mentioned at the start of this chapter, information from the chapters on size and ability add greatly to the understandings of group dynamics. Problems may exist simply because the size of the group does not provide for appropriate interactions for certain types of activities. Problems may also arise because ability considerations have not been made in keeping with the task(s) to be performed. If the membership does not include an individual who can serve as an appropriate model or mentor, the opportunity for goals to be met is diminished greatly. Also, in addition to supportive ideas in Chapters 8 and 9, the Questions and Answers in Chapter 10 may shed further insight on ideas presented here.

> *If I do not love the word—if I do not love life—*
> *if I do not love people—I cannot enter into dialogue.*
> *—PAULO FREIRE*

▶ 8

Research About Ability Grouping

*If children completed drill sheets and workbook pages,
and sat in their ability groups to discuss the story, the
spiral curriculum built into the basal series would
ensure that students could comprehend complex text.*
—E. O. KEENE AND S. ZIMMERMAN

The practice of ability grouping is grounded in widespread beliefs related to human capacity in that some students are more competent than others. It has been a common procedure, used in many districts, schools, and classrooms to accommodate individual differences in learning rates (Good & Stipek, 1983). Teachers have obeyed manuals from basal readers and have operated three reading groups a day with time designated to do skills exercises as seatwork (Keene & Zimmerman, 1997). Levels of reading ability, more than any other literacy behaviors, have tended to serve as determiners for grouping. As explained in Chapter 1, a common perception about ability groups in the early part of the 20th century was that they were good for the low students because they would receive more assistance in that context. Teachers have found in-class and across-class organizations to be "sensible" and convenient in dealing with the complex levels of expertise within their classrooms. Sometimes learners' differences are revealed by grades and test scores gathered in cumulative files; sometimes differences are delineated by inventories and assessments done at the start of the school year.

Research across the last 4 decades, however, would have us question the ways grouping decisions incorporate such criteria as IQ, standardized test scores in reading, or closer assessments of reading such as informal reading inventories (IRIs), miscue analyses, and benchmark tests. We are wise to question how groupings based on ability impact children's performance and their ongoing participation in school life. As Keene and Zimmerman (1997) remind us, children "certainly weren't becoming proficient, independent, confident, critical readers" while they sat in their ability groups (p. 61).

Students are, at any grade level, sure to demonstrate varying incoming levels of performance (Kierstead, 1999). Homogeneous grouping, however, does not produce higher overall achievement than heterogeneous grouping, according to Slavin's "best evidence synthesis" from 1987. Positive effects for homogeneous high groups are offset by negative effects in middle and low groups. Inequality increases over time because high-group students typically grow more than low-ability students. The only positive effects that have been achieved for reading have been from short-term cross-grade groupings in which students gather from several grades to use materials at their common level.

Convenient as ability groups may be for managing materials and work within classrooms, the larger picture across schools, districts, and states presents a dilemma. Low-group experiences are different from high-group experiences. Students in low groups experience differences in the quality of instruction and the level of learning (e.g., Barr & Dreeben, 1983). Unfortunately, ability grouping is a policy-based procedure that results in ethnic and class-related discrimination. Not only has it demonstrated harmful long-term effects on children in low groups, but it also raises many moral, psychological, and sociological issues. Because grouping tends to isolate groups by race and/or ethnicity, the practice has been associated with institutional racism. Methods for determining ability are questionable, and "homogeneous" groups are really quite heterogeneous in ability. These factors have been supported by a wide variety of research data and arguments from court cases, as presented by Welner and Oakes (1996). Their article is only one of many that have made a cumulative, convincing case against tracking and ability grouping.

The scheduling dictates of a typical public school day have made "three reading groups" a common practice for reading instruction over the years— sometimes by teacher choice, sometimes by administrative mandate (Slavin, 1997). Many parents also support the practice in seeking the prestige of high-group placements for their children. A change to flexible and heterogeneous grouping patterns has been slow to occur. Many teachers decide that ability is still the best way to group students for reading, as concluded in a study of 100 teachers in four districts of California (Nagel, Flood, & Lapp, 1990).

Today ability groups have not disappeared, even in areas that have generally accepted inclusive philosophies for student assessment and placement. For example, ability still drives the homogeneous placement of gifted students, often into classes segregated with the intention of meeting their special needs. Somewhere near 25% of our nation's academically gifted students are educated in public school classrooms—or schools—identified as for the gifted (Association for Supervision and Cirriculum Development [ASCD], 1990).

Picking up where Chapter 1 left off, this chapter will focus on conclusions of studies over the years. The paragraphs that follow will describe some of the key research that can help educators understand the ways in which ability grouping relates to the following: (a) procedures in group formation, (b) curriculum and instruction in high and low groups, and (c) social impacts of group membership.

GROUP FORMATION

At best, ability grouping procedures have been faulty. Often, they have been harmful to children through prejudicial placements. The distribution of students to high, middle, and low groups appears to be associated with parents' incomes and occupations. In their influential work, Cicourel and Kitsuse (1963) determined that students with low grades and low test scores are always placed in the low group if they are from low income families, but middle-class children with identical grades and scores are put in middle groups—or end up there due to parental intervention. Many teachers can attest to the power of PTA parents, for example. Rist (1970) suggested that teachers tend to set up "ideal" students in their minds—well-behaved, clean, with good work habits. In turn, they group children according to these preconceived notions that include perceptions of lower-socioeconomic children as belonging in low groups. Placement by "teacher observation" and "teacher judgment" has presented opportunities for teacher bias to play a role in group formations that affect children for the rest of their lives (Sorensen & Hallinan, 1984), although Haller and Waterman (1985), in confirming that the low groups had disproportionate numbers of poor and black children, assert that there is no evidence to support that the situation can be blamed on the racial bias of their teachers. They suggest that it is critical for educators to deal with the differences in children's preparedness to succeed at school reading tasks. Nevertheless, they confirm that children's work habits, behavior, personalities, as well as situations of home environment are considered by teachers along with ability as they place children in reading groups. Parents can affect the group placements of their children by influencing the teachers' perceptions of their children's ability and/or motivation (Goldenberg, 1989). Such assessments are typically made by teachers at the end of the school year, thereby making it convenient for the next year's teachers to form groups with ease. Such procedures recognize correctly that children do have multiple attributes that impact, success, but, clearly, some of those have the potential to change as the context and the teacher change.

The inadequacies and invalidities of standardized tests and independent reading inventories (IRIs) have been revealed in the work of Wesson, Vierthaler, and Haubrich (1989). How children respond to specific questions does not translate into how they interact with a variety of texts through inquiry, study, and retellings. Students present different profiles, varying with the measures being used. Decisions that influence group placements for years can stem from a "bad test" day. Opportunities to change groups during the school year are infrequent, if not completely absent. Moving down is more frequent than moving up, based on students' not completing their work rather than on reassessments of capability.

Weinstein (1976) conducted a study of the first 5 months of first grade in three classes where children were ability grouped. She examined student mobility, finding that the children most likely to be reassigned are those in the middle groups and that their movement takes place only during the first few weeks of school. Thereafter, reading group assignments are virtually unchanged and no bottom group student reaches the highest group.

CURRICULUM AND INSTRUCTION IN HIGH AND LOW GROUPS

Some of the negative effects of ability grouping for students in low groups include the difference in the amounts of time spent reading. Allotted time is not the variable, for the actual time engaged with a teacher in instruction and responding in a group tends to be similar across all group levels (Graden, Thurlow, Ysseldyke, & Algozzine, 1982). Instead, the amount of actual reading in the context of the "reading" period is less for low groups. More specifically, it is the amount of *silent* reading time that is very different, according to Allington (1982). In his study of groups in grades 1, 3, and 5, the low readers read more words out loud and did far less silent reading. Hiebert's 1983 review of studies of first grade reading found that higher-ability groups are more involved in literacy activities that involve meaning and low groups focus on decoding instruction.

The types and qualities of questions asked by teachers also differ from one type of group to the next (Hiebert, 1983; Shake & Allington, 1985), with students in low groups being asked recall questions that do not expect higher, analytic levels of thinking and problem solving that are more likely to occur for students in high groups. Cognitive outcomes for high group members are also enhanced by the greater amount of silent reading they do, as opposed to the oral reading that can dominate in low groups (Wilkinson & Anderson, 1995).

Cook-Gumperz, et al., (1981) studied classroom learning environments in an ethnography that revealed that the access to learning opportunities is quite different among levels of groups. The types of learning materials are also different, with low groups being expected to do more drill work in skill materials and having less exposure to works of literature. In elementary classes, the relationship of phonics instruction to the total amount of instructional time is greater for students in low groups, allowing far less time for discussion and comprehension activities. The types and qualities of questions asked by teachers also differ from one type of group to the next (Shake & Allington, 1985), with students in low groups being asked recall questions that did not expect higher levels of thinking. Eder and Felmlee (1984) found that discussions are more likely to take place in high groups; low groups have structured activities that do not allow low children to engage in communication.

One large study, accomplished across 21 classes of eighth graders, looked at the quality of discussion and achievement in learning new material. All students worked individually, then in collaborative groups, and again alone. Above-average students worked in groups with below-average students as well as in homogeneous groups with other high-ability students. Below-average students worked in both heterogeneous and homogeneous groups as well. Group compositions were above-below, above-above, or below-below. In all configurations that included above-average students, the quality of the discussion and of the assessment outcomes for other group participants was enriched, including when the other participants were of high ability. In the final analysis, the benefits of heterogeneous groups enhanced the performance of the lower students, with benefits that outweighed the advantages to high students when they worked with other highs (Webb, Nemer, Chizhik, & Sugrue, 1998). Such benefits are measured by tests of reading proficiency, but the positive modeling of other students can go beyond reading accomplishments. Students can benefit greatly from learning about others' life experiences through their broadened perspectives and deeper understandings. If, indeed, the highest level of thinking is empathy, it can best develop in well-designed heterogeneous groups.

In a study of 36 classrooms—11 with homogeneous ability groups, 11 with whole-class group instruction at grade level, and 14 with whole-class group instruction above grade level—Kamil and Rauscher (1990) discovered that there were no essential differences between groups after a year, according to standardized tests of vocabulary and comprehension.

SOCIAL IMPACTS OF GROUP PLACEMENT

Years ago, Hickerson (1966) wrote about the ways in which ability grouping condoned the labeling of children in slow groups. His writings seem quite current in that they reveal how ability groups bring about inappropriate expectancies related to racial groups and socioeconomic levels, which he labeled as "castes." Positive modeling by other students is not as evident in low groups, and not only do situations within low groups shape behavior in negative ways, but the amount of teachers' controlling talk is much higher and their expectations of behavior lower (Schell & Rouch, 1988). In addition, student attentiveness in lower groups is found to be far less than in higher groups in studies conducted by Felmlee and Eder (1983). Also, as Bristow (1985) notes, poor readers end up being passive, rather than active, readers because of the interrelated factors that make their group experiences frustrating.

Children end up being sorted by class, with children from lower socioeconomic levels placed in the low groups. As students continue into upper grades, tracking polarizes the students into "proschool" and "antischool" groups (e.g., Abraham, 1989). Statistics for low groups change in later years simply because their populations change as students leave school.

Other researchers have concluded that ability grouping involves difficulties in teacher morale. Teachers frequently do not wish to teach the lower groups because of the social implications that set in for them as well—they come to be seen as "low" teachers. Teachers of high students tend to be seen as high teachers, earning praise and rewards that they do not necessarily merit by their teaching excellence (Bachofer, 1990).

In addition, interactions between students and teachers in high groups tend to be more task oriented, providing greater, appropriate assistance to those students who probably need it less (Peterson, Wilkinson, Spinelli, & Swing, 1984). In first grade, teachers allowed children in low groups to "tell" the words to one another (Hiebert, 1983) instead of promoting wait time or providing other instructional clues.

In her study of the effects of reading group assignments in first and second grade, Juel (1990) explains:

> *Reading group placement in first grade did not in itself seem to have a negative (or positive) effect on growth in reading development. On the other hand, being placed in a reading group where performance in learning basal words was carefully monitored and remained high—whether this was a low or high group—did make a difference on final reading achievement. Reading group assignment in first grade, however, largely determined reading group assignment in second grade.* (p. 234)

Results of grouping for low groups may be dismal, but if the benefits of high grouping for high-ability students were clearly established, policymakers might be correct in continuing to promote ability groups for the benefit of those students. However, that notion has not been borne out, except for some data at the secondary level that suggest that high-ability students were able to make slight test gains when they were in homogeneous classes and, at the same time, received an enriched curriculum (Good & Marshall, 1984).

In their study of eight first- and second-grade classrooms, Grant and

Rothenberg (1986) concluded that children in high groups have more opportunities to engage in self-directed modes of learning as compared to lockstep work completion in low groups. Students in high groups also enjoy a warmer socioemotional atmosphere (through more teacher–student chatting) than children in low groups. The two researchers also found that student attentiveness in lower groups is far less than in higher groups, as did Eder and Felmlee (1983, 1984) in their studies of first grades and Hiebert (1983). In the Grant and Rothenberg (1986) study, events took on different meanings in blue-collar compared to white-collar classroom settings. Teachers in blue-collar classrooms use more praise and more criticism, regardless of groups. Still, interruptions to low groups appear to be tolerated across the board, regardless of socioeconomic level.

In their 1985 study, Hallinan and Sorensen examined the relationship of student friendships and assignment to reading groups to determine that group assignments encourage stratified friendship patterns, resulting in divisions by race, social class, and ethnicity. Weinstein (1991) also clarified how teachers' comments make children aware of the status that is based on reading group placement within their rooms. She determined that static group placement has a significant impact on children's self-esteem and their levels of test anxiety, with the gap between high-group and low-group children widening as the school year progresses. Incidentally, she noted that low reading group students receive more praise, but in the face of other factors, it seemed not to help students' self-perceptions.

Eder, in her 1981 study of one first-grade classroom, found that the learning contexts for high-ability and low-ability groups are different. Although she did not measure the extent of the group influence on academic progress, she found that the teacher permits more interruptions to lower group meetings, the low students are more inattentive during lessons, and the teacher spends more time managing the low children's behavior. Eder concluded that, by placing children with beginning learning problems in the same group, their difficulties are compounded. Contextual differences were also noted by Haskins, Walden, and Ramey (1983), who determined that low students in 20 kindergarten and first-grade classes have smaller groups and that teachers spend more time with those groups, a finding different from the shorter time noted by Weinstein.

Hiebert (1983) concluded that low-group children, after only a few months in first grade, report more negative feelings toward reading and their reading groups and that classmates rate children in high reading groups as having higher social status.

Beyond their impact on the learning experience, ability groups have also had implications for students' social status. High-grouped and high-tracked students are awarded higher social status than their classmates in lower groups (Good & Marshall, 1984). The stigma of being in a lower group becomes a problem for students, even inviting labels of "slow" and "dumb" to get attached to group members.

The conclusion that must be drawn from the large number of studies conducted in elementary schools is that ability grouping is detrimental for students in low groups. Regardless, ability grouping was a common procedure into the 1980s, used increasingly over the years in many districts, schools, and classrooms to accommodate individual differences in learning rates (Good & Stipek, 1983; Kamil & Rauscher, 1990). Dissemination of research information to practitioners is always a scattered and slow process. When vested interests are at stake, the process is further impeded. Parents of children in high groups are usually the most vocal in dealing with school administrators. Parents of the children who are most hurt by ability groups are, politically, the least influential (Thelen, 1967).

ALTERNATIVES TO ABILITY GROUPING

The ways in which students may be grouped are many. Not only are many formats possible, but many purposes and vehicles may be used. For example, groups can be developed around skills, interests, social growth, lesson content, or task completion. Groups can change with varied leadership from teacher to students to others, such as guests. Sizes can be designated from tutorial pairs to whole-class groups. Memberships can vary with matches to purposes, for social reasons, and with choices by chance.

First-grade teachers who were committed not to use ability grouping participated in a year-long study of alternative patterns in their classrooms (Nagel, 1992). The study showed that each of the six studied contexts had a very distinctive pattern of groupings, determined largely by the teachers' personalities and beliefs. As individuals' views of literacy goals broadened, their uses of many different sizes and types of groups expanded, as did their acknowledgment of students' existing knowledge and their need for power.

Explorations of ways to group students cooperatively permeate the work of such writers as Slavin (1980), who suggests that the key to all forms of cooperative learning is to arrange students into teams in which the members can help one another. Other studies have focused on peer work groups, including the work of Stodolsky (1984). She outlines a system for distinguishing various within-class groups that, along with the work of Manarino-Leggett and Salomon (1989), influences the categories presented in Appendix A.

CHANGING PRACTICE

Although conclusions of research and academic writing had discouraged ability grouping for years, the beginnings of change within schools were promoted by prominent, popular publications. In the late 1980s, several re-ports advocated that schools end their grouping and tracking procedures. A well-publicized, widely distributed volume was *Becoming a Nation of Readers: The Report of the Commission on Reading* (Anderson, Hiebert, Scott, & Wilkin-son, 1985), whose impact was truly felt in schools and school districts. Among its many assertions was the following:

> *Whatever cute name may be given to a reading group, the children know their place. They evaluate their own abilities on the basis of the status of their group. The low-group students in one school may be at the same reading level as the students in the average group in another school. Yet, the low-group students in the one school may view themselves as poor readers, and teachers may have lower expectations for their progress.* (p. 89)

The authors go on to say, "It is a sad fact, but frequently true that, 'Once a bluebird, always a bluebird' " (p. 90). They assert that schools "must chal-lenge all students to meet high standards yet ability grouping in the elemen-tary grades, and tracking in the secondary grades, prevent this, especially for students placed in the lower groups." (p. 17)

At the end of the 20th century, documents from various organizations re-flected concern about, if not outright condemnation of, the sorting of children by perceptions of innate ability. Noted experts in reading, depicting their similarities and differences about reading practices, all agreed that teachers should not use ability groups (1999). The National Governors Association (1993), for example, advocates the formation of groups by methods other than ability determination. Policies and frameworks advocate flexible group-ing in states such as Texas, Massachusetts, and California that serve diverse populations in their large, urban centers (California Department of Educa-tion, 1998).

As Barr (1995) concludes, after years of intense study of elementary school grouping, a model that has merit—one that I agree with—would en-courage flexible use of diverse groups and diminish the use of traditional ability groups.

Excellent resources in journals and books can provide further specific in-formation and guidelines for classroom implementation of flexible grouping. Books (e.g., Radencich & McKay, 1995) and articles about flexible grouping (e.g., Flood, et al., 1992; Cunningham, Hall, & Defee, 1998) join dozens of ar-ticles and books about specific small-group strategies (e.g., Short & Klassen, 1993). Such resources are valuable extensions of this volume.

Nevertheless, whether widespread change will really take place resides in the ways teachers design their own classroom groups. School policies and procedures, particularly in times and places where faculty and parent decision making are active, will depend on the interpretations of the people at the table and the individuals behind the doors of our nation's classrooms.

> *Good teaching cannot be reduced to technique: good teach-*
> *ing comes from the identity and integrity of the teacher.*
> —*PARKER PALMER*

▶ 9

Group Size

Two heads are better than one.
Two's company, three's a crowd.
—*OLD SAYINGS*

When educators and their students plan instructional groupings, the selected size can make a difference in terms of who does what and how for how long (Weinstein, 1991). To begin with, the sizes of classes themselves are impacted by legislation and policy at state and district or zone levels that impact budgeting for teachers' salaries and classroom space. Budgets are controlled by legislators and administrators at various levels who select and interpret studies or recall personal experiences as they influence school funding. The sizes of within-class groups are usually determined by teachers. To assure attention to curriculum and to their students, they evaluate needs and schedules, counting the number of hours in the day and days in the week. They, too, are concerned with budgets—budgets of time and materials. As teachers well know, they frequently spend their own money to enhance instruction for their students when the school does not provide the appropriate materials. How materials—books, manipulatives, equipment, technology—are to be used by students impacts the teacher's determinations of group size and management.

However, considerations beyond time and money always enter in. Group sizes are determined by influential individuals who work from varied backgrounds of knowledge and belief. Their decisions must examine the benefits to students and teachers. Unfortunately, details from decades of research about dynamics related to size are not particularly well known. This chapter will provide a sketch of some the findings that could assist educators in their planning. It will portray well-established notions from classic group dynamics literature as well as summarize developments from recent projects.

SIZES OF WITHIN-CLASS GROUPS

Old sayings often hold truth, and those at the start of the chapter have been verified over time. Two heads probably *are* better than one for critical literacy. Early studies of academic work show the advantages of group study over single tutorials and of writing to a group audience instead of to the teacher only (Bonner, 1959). Working with another person does have cognitive advantages, and partnerships are, perhaps, the most workable of groups in terms of ease of formation and smoothness of dynamics. The work of Schwartz, Black, and Strange (1991) has confirmed that dyads perform better than individuals working alone. The size of the group can make a difference in the level of interpersonal communication that occurs, but groups of any size have certain advantages over individual learners. The opportunities for interaction, discussion, dialogue, and communication, as well as for praise and criticism, lead to understanding as well as to cohesion.

Not that working alone is not a good idea at times. For sure, independent writing and thinking have a proper place in the K–8 school day. We know that one person does not make a group, but whether a student is ever truly alone in a classroom context is actually a point of discussion, according to some theoretical perspectives. The teacher is in constant relationship, even though not in constant close proximity. The ways in which teachers place themselves in classrooms put most students in face-to-face contact with them for most of the day, albeit across a crowded room. When teachers partner with students, they can provide excellent scaffolding as long as the relationship is comfortable. Sitting at the same side of a desk or table may make a difference in how the talk proceeds. Women make up the vast majority of the teaching population, and they tend to be quite comfortable with face-to-face encounters, for they have practiced them all their lives. Men and boys are more into parallel play and conversation; side-by-side communication while focused upon another thing is common. Teachers could very well give students a choice of placement for conferences or consultations with students.

The impact of being with teachers in small groups is more positive than being in large-group or one-to-one settings. An individual in a group is in a very different psychological position as compared to a solitary individual with a more powerful teacher. Modern examples can be been seen in the success stories of Asian American students as they prepare for lessons and tests in study groups. In small groups, members have opportunities to maintain eye contact with one another. Individuals who would not speak in a whole-class setting talk freely in the small context. Students with soft voices may be heard more easily, and their fear of making mistakes in front of others is minimized with fewer people watching and listening. In small collaborative groups, students are able to assess the membership and exert power more comfortably when other members do not stand in the way. Educators who participate in tutoring programs would be wise to reflect on the impact of group dynamics on their effectiveness with children. The perfectly personalized attention given in a one-to-one tutoring situation may not be more effective, in the long run, than a teacher with two students because of the quality of the discourse.

As in the second saying quoted earlier, three people *can* seem like a crowd, compared to two. Groups of three are likely to have special problems, just because of their size. One person may be "the odd man out." Allowing expressions of an additional person simply takes more time. Because of the strong tendency for pairs to form dyad coalitions, third persons are often left out (Cohen, 1986). A more recent study (Jaich-Yokley, 1990) found that first graders exhibited more exploratory behaviors in dyads than triads. Not that threesomes cannot work. They can, but part of setting standards for their group work might involve cautionary explanations about inclusive, and other size-attentive, behaviors. If the third individual happens to be the teacher, status creates a difference going into the relationship, and students still enjoy dyad conditions.

Advantages of groups of at least four seem to be well founded. Student investigations accomplished in groups scored higher than individuals alone (Jaich-Yokley, 1990). The impact of being with teachers in small groups is more positive than being in large group or one-to-one settings, according to Morrow (1989) in studying young children's responses to questions. In his early work, Bonner (1959) determined that consensus decreases as the group size goes from 5 to 12. Leaders have a more positive effect on discipline and problem solving in small groups. A group of five may hold a discussion in 15 minutes, but the time is not long enough for 12.

Teachers do not want any student "left out" of the learning process. According to Cohen (1986), if group discussion and interaction are the goal, groups should be no larger than four or five. As the group grows beyond that, the chance is high that one person will remain left out of interaction. The satisfaction and agreement of individual members decrease when the group size increases (Bonner, 1959). The work of Hare (1962) concluded that, as groups grow in size from 5 to 12, the potential for consensus decreases as the size increases. Members of larger groups do not feel that they have had time to make important contributions. Also, in small groups, leaders have a more positive effect on discussion and problem solving.

Gordon (1966) promoted the idea that young children learn little when they are taught as a large audience. She pointed out that many children do not have the visual or auditory acuity, the behavior, the problem-solving ability, or the perception to function well in large groups. Also, the children least able to change are the ones unlikely to allow themselves to learn in that situation. Face-to-face groups support student learning better because of the teacher's ability to get clear feedback from each child.

It would be foolish to say that *all* groups are superior to individual learning, but cohesive groups can speed and deepen both cognitive and social learnings. The Deutsch (1949) studies were pivotal in determining that individuals in cooperation learn more than individuals in competition. Since that time, increasing interest and research about cooperative groups have allowed for great volumes of theoretical and practical work to be published.

In larger groups, members participate less and teachers control more. If a group is too large, dominant members tend to emerge and monopolize the talk. The only time when large groups function well is if they are also composed of smaller subgroups or task forces with functions within the group. The whole-class group is a frequent instructional unit, and its size has been the focus of a great deal of interest over time. The class size reduction efforts in North America at the end of the 20th century received a great deal of public attention.

CLASS SIZE

Times do change. Class size in California went from 80 during the early years of the 20th century to 40 back to 70 after World War II and now to 20 (California Teachers Association [CTA], 1998).

A well-known report conducted in 1978 by the Educational Research Service concluded that "the relationship between pupil achievement and class size is highly complex" and that findings are "contradictory and inconclusive" and "do not support the contention that smaller classes will of themselves result in greater academic achievement gains" (Educational Research Service, 1980, pp. 68–69). The report went on to warn that "policy decisions pertaining to class size and pupil–teacher ration involve factors that are complex, varied, and often emotionally charged. These require the weighing of the possible pupil benefits, the possible teacher benefits, the facilities utilized, the financial costs, and the possible political consequences" (p. 70).

Teachers, however, have expressed intuitive concerns about group size. Entwined with their concerns about meeting all their groups and holding conferences with all their students' parents are their longings for fewer students. The sizes of within-class groups, the nature of their activities, and the time that each teacher may spend with the groups are all directly influenced by the size of the classroom group. Because of the prevailing notion that managing three groups is wise time management when the typical day's events are considered (Slavin, 1997), there are significant differences between what goes on in a class of 30 compared to a class of 20. Three groups of 10 each would mean that all the small groups are simply not small enough for effective dynamics. Groups of six or seven in a small class begin to reach more optimal size for appropriate interactions, as alluded to earlier.

Because lowering class size and lowering costs can be at odds, the realities of large classes continue. Quantity of students may not always directly relate to quality of education, but group size does carry great impact. Teachers have desired smaller classes for a long time. Although the words quoted here (McKenna, 1982) are those of a Georgia teacher, they could well be those of a teacher from many states:

> *My colleagues and I are told that class size doesn't affect student achieve-ment. All teachers, on the other hand, who live with the problem of large classes on a day-to-day basis realize that class size is, actually, the main problem. This inability to prove what all experience shows has to be the great failure of educational research. (p. 93)*

Class Size Reduction Efforts

In the Beginning Teacher Evaluation Study (BTES, 1978), the frequency of contact with the instructor was found to be strongly related to student attention. When there are fewer students, each student gets a greater portion of the teacher's time and has an opportunity to participate more. Teachers, in turn, have greater opportunities to monitor behaviors and progress with fewer students. In one field study, when teachers did have class size lowered, they did not automatically change their methods. Nevertheless, they did increase the amount of individual contact with children, giving more explanations, checking on papers, and providing encouragement. Teachers reported feeling more confident about planning the next day's lessons (Cahen et al., 1981). The reciprocal influence of teacher on student and student on teacher is enhanced when there are fewer students and a limited quantity of time.

In seeking out and sorting through the class size research, Glass, Cahen, Smith, and Filby (1982) ended up analyzing the results of 77 studies on class size and achievement. They concluded that smaller classes, regardless of the subject, outperform large classes in academic achievement three out of five times. In their meta-analysis of *affective* outcomes in 59 studies, the odds jump to a nine-to-one ratio in favor of smaller classes, with positive effects on student attitudes, interest, and motivation and teachers' morale, satisfaction, and attitude toward students.

More recently, Project STAR in Tennessee conducted a 4-year study under the guidance of three education laboratories. The research methods included controlled random selection for class memberships in one of three class types. Students could be placed in a class of either 13 to 17 or 22 to 26 students. The larger classes had two formats, one without a classroom aide and one with. The STAR results support the "small class advantage." With diverse student samples that were large (6,300 students in 79 schools), the project shows students' average scores going up in every subject within small classes. There were significant differences on all measures for both girls and boys. The advantage on standardized test scores averaged about 0.2 of a grade level at each grade. However, for white students, scores went up only about 0.16. For minority students, the scores went up an average of 0.35. The benefit to minority students was two times as great (Finn, 1989). The statistical information from this project was widely reported, and, despite efforts to deflate its findings, it remains as a respected research document.

Smallness also makes a big difference in student behaviors. In Project STAR, students' engagement with their teachers increased as the number of contacts increased and more questions were answered in the small class setting. Children were on task more of the time, not being able to "hide" in the crowd, and not spending time waiting to have needs met. Teachers took on more roles and could not ignore children. The study revealed that class size reduction brought fewer grade retentions and less need for special education placement. The findings also indicated that students going on to larger classes in fourth grade still had positive effects from their small class size in the primary grades. They continued to outperform their counterparts in academic and social measures.

In 1990, information from Project STAR was used as a rationale for Project Challenge to reduce class size to 18 in Tennessee's poorest school districts. As a result, grade retentions were reduced, and the districts improved their rankings by an average of 20 (out of 138 schools) in reading and almost 30 in mathematics. The Tennessee studies, it should be noted, involved certificated teachers in all instances, as did class size reduction in Indiana (Prime Time), North Carolina (Burke County), and Wisconsin (SAGE). In addition, class size reduction was enacted in 20 other states. All projects reported positive effects.

Documented by researchers at Stanford University, the large downsizing movement in California began with legislation during the summer of 1996. In a first look at teachers and students, noticeable changes occurred in business as usual. Observers noted differences in learning environments and teachers' practices. Days in smaller classrooms were less chaotic. Parent involvement was enhanced, and students were treated in more equitable ways (Kirst, 1998). The fact that vast numbers of reduced classes were taught by novice, "emergency permit" teachers differentiated the California move from other states' efforts. The size and complexity of the changes to be made, particularly in large, urban school districts, meant that acquisitions of resources and space were not always timely. The quality of the individuals covering classrooms varied, denoting wide variance in the experiences of students.

When teachers work with twenty or fewer students, they can address individual children with greater ease. However, the news about class size would not be so gratifying if it did not also mean that it gives teachers greater opportunities to work with small, within-class groups. A teacher might possibly interact meaningfully with four groups during a literacy period of 90 minutes. Therefore, in a class of 20, the groups would have 5 students in each. If the class size were 30, the group size would have to increase to 7 or 8 students, and instructional efficacy would diminish, as indicated by size factors described in Chapter 9.

Philosophies about where to cut class size have differed in various contexts over time. In the United States the prevailing belief has been to give children a solid start. On the other hand, downsizing efforts in Great Britain were focused on secondary levels, not infant (primary) schools. While reduction of class size in the United States has emphasized downsizing in its primary classrooms, efforts have now also included English classes in high school. But there, as with many contexts in the elementary schools, teachers in the larger, unreduced classes came to resent the negative impacts on scheduling and facilities in their schools (Korostoff, 1998). They, too, want the enhancement of their physical, academic, and social conditions that having fewer students can bring.

As dynamics literature has supported for some time, group size makes a difference, including the whole class group. In reading, teachers were able to achieve higher average levels of performance in less time. Students remained on task, and teachers were aware of each student's individual progress. Students get to speak more often, they get to be listened to, they get more attention of their teacher, and their classes are, indeed, friendlier places, bringing about greater engagement in learning. Clearly, small classes are making KPA more humanly possible.

Far from the madding crowd's ignoble strife
Their sober wishes never learn'd to stray . . .
—THOMAS GRAY

► 10

Common Concerns About Groups

Can't we all get along?—RODNEY KING

The gathered explanations, research reports, and vignettes in the preceding chapters have, I hope, helped to create a vision of KPA, but educators may still wish to address their specific needs. The following suggestions have arisen from my work with various groups of inservice teachers. The narratives here will, I hope, help readers to see how various teachers work with challenges. Additional insights may be gained from Chapters 11, 12, and 13, which will discuss specific classroom activities and practices that teachers might select to build knowledge, power, and affection.

PREPARING FOR GROUP WORK

Promoting good group interactions takes careful planning with the guidance of the principles of KPA. Group work requires flexibility if democracy is to be honored; you must be willing to forego perfection. As we know from our adult contexts, democracy is "noisy," for differences in opinion are omnipresent. Students will—perhaps, should—have disagreements from time to time. Therefore, you will want to teach them how to handle different points of view with civility. Role-play a case situation using your best dramatic gestures and voices to emphasize pointers about what to do and what not to do. Students will want to act out civil conversations (see "Agree to Disagree" in Chapter 13).

See that decisions are made in four arenas:

1. Group goals are clear; everyone knows what the group is supposed to understand or accomplish.
2. The tasks to be completed are understood and roles are delineated.
3. The group membership is appropriate to the goals and tasks.
4. Norms for work habits and social habits are clear, with evaluation systems that include rubrics for cooperation.

Keep Group Interaction Notes

Learn to forecast your students' interactions by keeping notes on group dynamics over time. Create a casual class sociogram (Appendix G), being sensitive to the need for the extreme confidentiality of your note taking. Who likes to work with whom? Who are "difficult" group members to work with, and for whom? Who are the members of groups that work with success? Use your informed knowledge about each child and his or her ways along with your gentle authority to help pave the way to social success. Some students may have to work into small-group work slowly. Independent work is necessary, at times, for some. Do not, however, make the mistake that some students should never engage in group work. Opportunities for cooperation are not a privilege; they are an educational necessity.

Use Dual Grading Systems

Teachers who give one grade for the entire group make a mistake. You will want to let individuals earn good grades for carrying out their roles and contributing to the group effort. You will sacrifice group esprit de corps, however, if a group grade is not arranged. A dual grade system is usually best (Slavin, 1983). Many handy grading rubrics may be bought through commercial outlets, but it may be wiser for you to discuss grading with students as you prepare them for their upcoming group experience. They will not only benefit from their empowerment, but you will all benefit from designing a system for grading that is more in line with the context and the activity. Grading through self-reporting and peer reporting can be appropriate as long as the students discuss a clear vision of being fair to one another. Individual grades can focus on both academic and social contributions.

Deal with the Three *B*s

Admonitions of "Be nice" or "Get along," are not enough for most groups. The bottom line, although you will find ways to express the following ideas in more positive language, is that the group must have no Bullies, Babies, or Bozos (see Chapter 7). They are the individuals who spoil the group process for everyone. Bullies are those individuals who want to boss everyone else around. Babies are the ones who will not go along with the group's plans or carry out their individual tasks; they whine and claim, "I don't want to do that." The third group of spoilers, the Bozos, are the ones who seem to be the most difficult. They are the ones who clown around or simply do not do their part. They appear to be happy to let the worker bees carry out group tasks. A more positive way to promote important values might be to encourage students to collaborate, cooperate, and participate. Students can create specific guidelines for group behavior. Peer reports for individual grading can help extinguish Three B types of behavior.

Cooperative groups are a regular phenomenon in Liz and Marilyn's multiage classroom. On Friday mornings, cooperative groups are formed to work on projects that integrate the curriculum, usually activities that are based on learnings that relate to science or social studies. Some weeks the students choose their own groups, in which case the children usually like to select friends at the same grade level. During other weeks, the teachers announce that they are doing the choosing, and they set up groups of three and four in which all three grades are represented. They always place writers with non-writers. Sometimes the groups turn out to be all girls or all boys, but most groups have variety in terms of all four attributes—age, gender, ability, and work habits.

Before the children set to work, however, the teachers go over the game plan, explaining the directions that are written on a photocopy for each group, as well as giving pointers about how the specific roles in each group are to be done. For example, one day's groups each had three or four members who were asked to think of all the ways water is important for people. Then they had to decide on the five most important ways and develop a mobile on a hanger that represented their thinking.

The "Co-op Group Jobs" are the same ones that have been in force all year. The reader reads all directions, the recorder writes down the group responses, and the reporter reports back to the class when the large group gathers to share what happened The monitor distributes and collects all supplies. This preplanning session takes about 15 minutes, and the teachers elicit from the children how things should be. Setting standards each time, even though they are familiar, helps them be present in the students' minds as they proceed to work.

Whole-Class Group Preparation

Working together is important to the development of classroom community. Small groups or independent work is not appropriate all of the time. Everyone can usually benefit from planned presentations, plays, class meetings, broadcasts, and guest speakers. Whole-class relationships can flourish with choral readings, antiphonal poems, or read-alouds that are comprehensible to the group. The shared culture that occurs when all class members know a particular story well is gratifying. Honoring a special "Word of the Week" can bring word study to everyone's attention and expand opportunities for it to be heard and used.

Whole-class opportunities that do *not* work are usually skills lessons that aim at one level of expertise. Introductions to certain new skills are reasonably done within a whole-class context, but skills practice is best done in other settings. You know that your children will always have differences in ability; children are still children, with vast ranges of prior knowledge and talents. Repetitious phonics drills, for example, have no place in the whole-class group. Meeting needs for phonological growth can be done best in small group settings or tutorial work.

Build Community Through Reading Aloud

Ed reads aloud to his sixth-graders every day after lunch. Although his students participate in several other types of reading groups, he finds that the half hour spent enjoying a book together as a whole class is well worth the time in providing common ideas, common language, common in jokes, and common characters with which to identify. He tries to choose books that are interesting and kid oriented, but he will not read from a book that will "jump off the shelf" on its own anyway. For example, he has never read a Judy Blume book aloud.

He tried *Shadow of a Bull*, a Newbery award winner from the 1960s, and was pleasantly surprised. As usual, thanks to a small literature grant, each student had a copy of the book to follow along. The sounds of the words, coupled with the looks of the words and the occasional pictures, helped everyone tune in to the meaning of the story. Visual learners and auditory learners all felt comfortable. In the book, Manolo, the main character, deals with growing up in a community in Spain where bullfighting is highly respected. Ed's girls were willing to listen, once again, to a "boy's story" because the boys had earlier agreed to listen to *Summer of the Swans*. The *Shadow* book was full of terms in Spanish, which pleased the Spanish-speaking students. The complex terms in the book were, this time, mostly words that they felt quite comfortable with. Although Ed pointed out the glossary of terms in the back of the book, not everyone needed to use it. The English-only students were busy flipping back and forth during activity times to practice the new terms.

The book about growing up and struggling with family affected everyone. The students' conversations about the book were very touching. The "Dear Abby" letters that evolved as a project related to the book were outstanding. The students worked with partners to write lengthy letters and then compose thoughtful responses to one another.

Determining Group Size

The size of within-class groupings should vary according to function. Some activities have many possible "right" sizes. Choral readings can be of chorus size or of quartet, trio, or duet size. Thinking about the ways in which "real" literacy activities occur in the adult world can give some clues as to options that might be reasonable. Groups for Readers Theater and plays can vary greatly. Casts of thousands may be inappropriate for most plays, but the number of actors can—and does—vary. Best practice would suggest that all students play significant roles. Rewriting some plays to engage students is a reasonable thing to do.

On the other hand, teachers often attempt to hold discussions with classes of 30 and more and should not be surprised when many students speak little and others benefit little from a too-large context. Class discussion can seldom be effective with groups of over 20, and even then requires careful questioning and monitoring. Good teachers can pose questions with certain students in mind. They allow all students the opportunity to think about possible answers through the use of purposeful wait time. Then they call on students who are likely to answer with success. Success for all occurs through well-managed group process.

When face-to-face discussion and group cohesion are desired in student-led groups, memberships over five lose their power. Many studies over time have supported the need for small classes. As some of our schools engage in class size reduction movements, we must recognize that political initiatives are based on teachers' "intuitive" voices only in part. The size of the group definitely does make a difference. (See Chapter 9 for further details).

Teaching to Half the Class

Katherine and Kim divide their multiage class in half for a short time each afternoon. The older students go with Katherine to listen to the next installment of a book chapter or a series of short stories that are appropriate for their elder status in this classroom. The young children go with Kim to listen as she reads picture books that are more in line with their ages and interests.

These times are beneficial for the children. The physical grouping is relatively compact, and the time is very interactive. Children who would never have much to say in the larger whole-class group come alive in the half-class setting. The time is used mostly for reading, but the sessions never end until the students think about their reactions to the story and what it has to do with them and their lives.

TEACHING SKILLS IN GROUPS

The first step for skill-based instruction is to identify exactly what you are teaching and have a sense of who does or does not know particular skills. Then, opportunities are plentiful. A teacher may work directly with individuals or with small groups of students who all need the skill. Tutors, either adults or other students, work well with children in most settings. Students who have mastered a skill can benefit from the challenge of teaching it to someone else. Teachers must, however, make sure that students of high ability are not always helping others. Their roles as tutors can be personally gratifying, but only up to a point. Daily tutoring would be inappropriate, and frequent weeks without tutoring would be suitable, in order for students to have extended times for their own learning activities.

Computers, tape recorders and players, and VCRs belong in all flexibly grouped classrooms. The varied technology can provide consistent presentations of information and skills and can serve as accepting "listeners." What *is* important is to remember that KPA can remain intact in a balanced program that promotes skill development in a context of motivating experiences that bring students together for many authentic purposes.

Preparing for Skills Instruction

At the start of the school year, getting the children to work as a whole is Sophia's primary goal. She begins with the desks arranged in paired rows, creating a climate and expectations for all of the children. When the groups work at their desks, she assigns seatwork that they can all reasonably do. However, the students come from very different backgrounds and have incoming levels of performance that go from very little exposure to words and numbers to facility with second-grade material. To deal with the children's varied needs, Sophia institutes skills "clusters" after the first few weeks of school. When they meet with Sophia or her instructional aide, who comes for 1 ½ hours after recess each morning, the instruction is then differentiated to meet their respective needs.

The skills clusters are led, almost daily, by Sophia and her aide. To Sophia, she is just the kind of aide to have. She was a teacher in Bolivia, and her presence is important to the program's success. She meets with the students who do not yet know the letters of the alphabet while Sophia pulls up two other collections of children to practice reading and engage in skills work that she has diagnosed to be appropriate and important for the members of the groups. The groups meet on the floor with Sophia in the southeast corner or with the aide at a table in the northwest corner. Except for the work that they do directly in contact with the teacher or the aide, the children all have identical seatwork projects. They may, however, interpret their assignment in various ways, for they all write in their journals.

DETERMINING GROUP MEMBERSHIP

Although teachers should be the ones to make sure that groups have appropriate memberships for various activities, one important decision they make is to see that the children do the choosing at times. Children enjoy the opportunity to work with individuals who are easy companions, and they can be astute about selecting appropriate individuals. When the camaraderie of friends will not interfere with task completion, honor children's power to choose specific individuals. Chance is also a satisfactory vehicle in some instances. Coming together for literacy activities can be dictated by shared interests, by drawing lots, by group sign-ups, and by numbering off or choosing a certain color. Ask the children to come up with new ways to establish groups. Drawing a popsicle stick with another child's name from a container is one way to determine partners. Diverse groups can be just as effective—or more so—as homogeneous groups for many purposes.

Nevertheless, an educator's thoughtful design must be a constant thread if knowledge-/skills-based lessons are to succeed. Sometimes grouping by teacher design allows for a range of abilities or similar skills needs. Including a high-ability student in most learning group memberships is a smart thing to do. Teachers are wise to establish situations in which positive academic and social models are present. (See Chapter 8 to review ability grouping.)

Fellow Students

David and Taylor are friends in the multi-age classroom. They are both six years old. When they write a story together, they make agreements to guide the process. Their main rule is that the person who draws the original picture is the boss. He dictates what the words of the story will be, even though the physical task of writing is shared evenly between the boys. One boy does one line, the other the next, and so on. Since Taylor did the picture this time, he begins: "Me and David are . . ." but then he looks around and gets distracted. David grumbles, "Taylor, tell me what's next!" When Taylor repeats exactly the same words, he reminds him, "Yeah, I already wrote that." Taylor then goes on to finish, ". . . are playing around on the vines." David finishes filling line one, and then announces, "Taylor, it's your turn." So the boys continue their reciprocal writing with Taylor's next idea: "Nat is on the hill."

This is, clearly, Taylor's story, David's stories are all about baseball teams and heroes or about television cartoon heroes. He explains, "When I help him, he's the boss. Then when he helps me write, I'm the boss."

Changing Group Memberships

Group memberships can change with the goals and the activities. Logical sequences in the curriculum and instruction can signal time to change group formations. Some groups serve ad hoc purposes and need only exist for a day or two. Others can last for 6 weeks or a quarter. Except for the whole-class group, no group needs to last all year. Change should definitely occur whenever any group is becoming a "caste."

Be sensitive to the labels assigned by others and the ongoing feelings of group members. Otherwise, do not feel compelled to change groups too frequently (more than every 3 or 4 weeks). Students need time to develop and appreciate a working relationship. Do make small changes when you have investigated and confirmed that discord stems from more than trivial difficulty. Do disband groups when you see that their purposes have been met. Take anecdotal notes to reflect on the need for change.

Retain your authority always, making sure that skills groups are designed by you, but there is no need to be authoritarian about all group memberships. Remember, though, that student choice presents its own set of dynamics problems because friends are, as students admit, too friendly when they get in school work groups. Have students fill out thoughtful evaluations of group work. Use a variety of systems, and tell students why a particular change is being made.

From One Team to the Next

During the spring semester, after the kids know each other quite well, Lynn has her sixth graders do "team jobs" (see Chapter 11) each week. The students work in teams of five, except since her class has 32 students, she has two teams with six members. Their jobs include a leader/reporter, poet, orator, artist, and inventor. The teams sit together as home-base work groups as well, which allows the members to discuss their projects during the course of the day, sharing materials and helping each other with ideas. The students fulfill their five (or six) designated roles for the week, and then they rotate jobs. After 5 weeks, Lynn changes all the teams, although when the kids begged to stay with their teams, she agreed to do so—once. Planning the group rosters takes time, but she knows it is worth it. She makes sure that she separates the four students who always seem to be complained about in terms of their work habits and follow-through. She has also discovered that her coaching efforts make a difference. She has a private conference with each of the four students, and when she makes sure the topics appeal to them and that they understand what to do, their performance is much more dependable.

Too Together

In the multiage room, students are free to choose their work partners for many activities. Joseph and John seem to be inseparable for many weeks, writing stories side by side, sitting on the couch for 30 to 40 minutes at a stretch, examining six or seven books, and discussing what they think they are all about. The two first graders also have the effect of drawing one another into and out of work completion. Finally, the teachers decide to separate the two first graders part of the time. As they realize, the boys' constant togetherness, perhaps not harmful in itself, does exclude other people from their lives. It is good to get to know other people.

MANAGING MULTIPLE GROUPS

Work. That is what students are in the classroom to do. Make that standard clear. Writing, drawing, planning, taping, problem solving, discussing, and listening are all just fine. Model well, and set standards well and high. Research (e.g., Short, Kaufman, Kaser, Kahn, & Crawford, 1999) indicates that students interact well and display a high level of expertise in groups when the teacher is not present. It seems that students in focused groups will accomplish more than students who are simply sent off to do seatwork. Recognize that traditional seatwork has a very low success rate for time-on-task behavior and the acquisition of new learnings. Small groups really are a good way to go.

Plan ways in which a variety of group leaders can help groups succeed. Teachers and aides are the most obvious status figures, but guests and parents can also serve well. Student leaders are usually marvelous. Computers, tapes, videos, and other motivating technology can serve as automatic "leaders" urging students on. If centers are to be used, talk/walk the class through each center, allowing for a mental run-through. Then, make sure that students have clear directions available to review and tangible reminders, such as task cards, to guide them.

Children learn responsibility through opportunities to be responsible, but they are still children—not adults—and they are certainly not angels. Think of how you and your colleagues would work together at various group projects. You may realize how reasonable your students' level of participation is. They usually do quite well.

Structured Centers

In addition to devoting time for other literacy activities, Ginny runs four centers in her second-grade class most days. The children come to two centers each day, so the content for the centers changes every 2 days. The format for the centers changes every few weeks, but Ginny enjoys the current configuration because it is productive and it sustains the students' interest well.

She establishes herself at the Teaching Center, varying the guided reading with the group that is before her. A second center includes three easels, where familiar big books are set out and students play teacher and student with a partner. The "teachers" get to use the wooden pointers, but both partners read simultaneously. The Listening Center has six posts, and Ginny makes sure that she rotates the tape/book sets every 2 days. The fourth center is the Songs and Poetry Center where some choices are available. Two or three people may use the overhead projector that has been placed on the floor in the front corner so it is not distracting to the rest of the class. They may select their favorite verses from the notebook of transparencies and whisper-read or whisper-sing. Other students may read from the collected poetry and song books that are in a special tub at the library center.

Literature Circles

Lou has found great success when his eighth-grade students work in literature circles. Several parents have told him that since he instituted circles, their kids always brag about what a good class they have. The groups currently running are self-selected according to the book. For each available book, Lou has filled a big plastic box with the set of books and the related materials. The students take on predesignated roles, and then Lou monitors the student groups as they go about sharing their literary response activities on their own. This is the third year that he is using circles, and the roles have changed somewhat over time. Right now, each group has a discussion director, a vocabulary enricher, an artful artist, a connector, a summarizer, and a passage master.

THE TEACHER'S ROLE

The part played by each teacher will vary with the type of group, but it will also vary with the calendar. At the start of the year, teachers exert authority far more often through lectures and modeling in direct leadership roles within all sorts of groups. Once the classroom norms and procedures are established, most teachers will want to promote opportunities for independence. By spring, children can lead class meetings, literature circles, study groups, and computer sessions. Teachers still lead classes, but their authority can be indirect. Students can have far more range of choice when they know how to handle it.

Transfer of Power

When Cindy transferred from a middle-class school to one that served a low-socioeconomic community, the types of discipline problems were different and the number of student conflicts exceeded what she had been used to. She felt fortunate to attend a workshop in conducting class meetings as a language arts activity. The format was based on the work of Rudolf Dreikurs, and the procedures allowed students to use their oral language skills in discussing problematic situations and their possible solutions. The meeting topics were always based on agenda sign-ups. Anyone, including Cindy, who had tried several ways to solve a problem with no success was allowed to have a presentation slot at the next meeting.

The opening procedure for each meeting was to go around the meeting circle and have each participant offer a genuine compliment to a classmate. This time for compliments was most valuable in establishing a sense of friendly caring. Every phase of the meeting was quite structured, and all talk was handled in order, allowed according to clockwise movement around the circle. Someone who did not choose to speak the first time around could pass and participate after having time to think. The rules for participation were quite clear. They allowed students time to think and precluded any individual from "hogging" the conversation, including Cindy. Meetings went from daily to three times a week to once a week.

By the middle of the year, Cindy knew that class meetings were a success. She decided that the class officers who were elected in November could increase their duties beyond planning parties and activities. She worked with the class president and turned over all the meeting leadership responsibilities. The class secretary recorded items for decisions on the overhead projector. The sergeant-at-arms recorded bonus points earned by polite participants. Although there were times when decision making became difficult and Cindy was asked to intervene, she came to play a role that was similar in most ways to that of her students.

WHEN TO FORM ABILITY GROUPS

Establishing some temporary groups by ability is reasonable, but it is *not* all right to keep them in same-membership formation over time. It would be foolish to discard a group of students who enjoy learning together at their level. When groups are composed of students of varying abilities, goals of skill attainment can promote discord. Rather, group work must develop the sharing of insights, work, and talents that can be mutually beneficial to all members. According to Cohen (1987), cognitive goals should be related to concept development, not to the acquisition of hierarchical skills.

There are appropriate times when gifted/talented students may be clustered. "Club" approaches to certain parts of the school week have shown to be successful (Renzulli, 1986). Some students may have interests that bear no resemblance to the inclinations of other students. Students who have low academic talents may be most comfortable working together at learning some things. When they are not harassed by the presence of students of higher ability/status, they may have opportunities to be tops, be leaders, and be the ones to garner praise.

After-School Clubs

Terry's school provides after-school clubs for the students each Wednesday. On that day, the official school day ends early, and clubs run for 90 minutes, attracting students of all sorts. High-achieving students are advised to participate in certain groups, but any student who is dedicated to joining a particular group is permitted to do just that. Each club runs for a semester, and students may rejoin for a second semester or move to a different club.

All of the clubs incorporate literacy projects. Students can select to write articles for the school newspaper. The Art History Club produces works of art in various styles as they study periods from history and create a display for the school, explaining their works through written explanations that go on the wall next to the various projects. Students hold an "opening" that requires them to give minispeeches as family, friends and fellow students come by.

You may discover that you have questions that are not answered by the suggestions in this chapter. If you continue reading and you discover that you do not find ideas in other chapters of this volume, you may want to ask your students or their parents. Their ideas can personalize solutions to needs in your context, and even though the answer may not be a "perfect" one, it will be right for you. In addition, the organizations and individuals listed in Chapter 14 can serve as rich resources.

▶ 11

Building Knowledge

The way we diagnose our students' condition will determine the kind of remedy we offer.—PARKER PALMER

What is *knowledge*? It is the demonstration of expertise that is respected by the group and useful to the group's purpose(s). It is the possession of information or access to resources. It is the ability to build knowledge.

Most educators know that medical models are not healthy to use in education if we approach students as if they have something "wrong" with them, if we see them as "ill." The term *diagnosis* has come to have many negative connotations, representing dissonance, and possible prejudice, of privileged teachers encountering ever more diverse students. Therefore, it seems out of place for Palmer, in the chapter-opening quote, to use the term *diagnose*, given his love for teachers and students and classroom worlds. However, he is battling the mindless stereotyping that some educators do, looking at students as being all the same and therefore needing the same teaching.

The dictionary (*Webster's*, 1959) explains that diagnosis is "scientific determination; critical scrutiny or its resulting judgment." It goes on to explain that diagnostics is the *art* of diagnosing. I like that, for teachers are constantly engaged in the art *and* science of knowing what to teach to who and when, not to mention how. Their prevailing quest, and that of their students, is to know why they do what they do, and to ask "So what?" about their daily endeavors.

When educators look at the work of other professionals, we can identify the sorts of things we all need to do, whether it be in business, law, medicine, or education. I do not agree with the comparison that teaching is more like preaching than it is like the other professions. Not that teachers do not preach sometimes, not that they do not work to save "souls," and not that they do not engage in counseling activities. But in an era when we focus on designing tasks and contexts to serve the traits of individuals, we apply the same sort of rigorous analysis and problem solving that the "learned professions" do.

Professional work is also detective work (Sagor, 1992), and analyzing what is *right* is as much part of the diagnosis as what is wrong. Furthermore, to remedy is to "make better." A remedy may be that which counteracts an evil. In times when so many lament the social ills that befall us all, I am convinced that diagnosis—ongoing diagnosis—is a very reasonable consideration for building knowledge.

In any day, most classroom schedules devote a great deal of time to reading and language arts. Some general ideals include the following: Class assignments cover a variety of topics that cross all children's experiences. Instruction incorporates rich field and classroom activities that build concepts for all children in multimodal ways. Individual assignments build on interests and prior knowledge. The physical environment has appropriate books and tools for learning. Students have opportunities for oral sharing at all grade levels. Students read silently for extended amounts of time in many types of materials. They are expected to think in complex ways, and they can use strategies to help them think and remember.

Canned lessons and static, impermeable groups will not do, but classrooms present a daily "Rubik's cube" of decision making for every teacher. Every student's individual schema plays a dynamic part in the complex processes of learning to read and write, speak and listen, and using the language arts to learn across the curriculum. In the meantime, teachers do not do it all. They should not, for when students do their part, they also learn. As Chapters 4 and 12 also indicate, empowered students can do great things. The ways in which they can share and teach one another are able to extend and reinforce their own learnings. Teaching is a powerful way to learn.

This chapter shares information about classroom activities that teachers can use to address the knowledge that students already possess and help lead to further knowledge. The suggestions are intended as examples of tasks that involve discourse and promote cognitive growth.

HONORING STUDENTS' PRIOR KNOWLEDGE

Teachers create a more level academic playing field for their students when they link lessons to children's prior knowledge. Effective group activities incorporate topics for reading, discussion, and writing with elements that are familiar to the student. Regardless of their levels of reading prowess, students can think at high levels as long as the subject is one with which they are comfortable. Many teachers come to know this phenomenon through their work with students in using questions and activities that relate to familiar topics.

Holding conversations or doing assignments at a comfortable level builds confidence for handling content at more difficult levels.

Topics That Cross All Children's Experiences

Some concepts transcend the differentiation in students' incoming knowledge levels and are common to most cultures and lifestyles, to many levels of academic ability and socioeconomic positions. People must eat and sleep; they live in neighborhoods with various businesses and stores with families in homes that are furnished and are characterized by many interrelationships, including pets. Yards and parks have trees and plants with animals of one sort or another. People enjoy music and games, they enjoy celebrations and artistic experiences, they travel from place to place, and they participate in viewing television shows and movies. What comes from such explorations is that children realize that they all have rich experiences and common types of experiences but unique experiences because of the panorama of their individual circumstances. To focus on similarities and rejoice in differences is a way to promote participation and communication.

Depending on the ages of the students, partners or small groups can create skits, essays, stories, or plays that represent the following topics:

animals	homes	sleeping
artistic experiences	movies	strange things
businesses and stores	music	television shows
celebrations	neighborhoods	travel
families	pets	trees
friends, young and old	plants	weather
games	silly things	work

Comparing and contrasting one person's version to another would be one way to work with the ideas. People always have similarities and things that make them special. Finding our culture in others brings us together; so does finding uniqueness in things that appear identical. Using synthesis, as in "If we put our families together . . . ," would have interesting results. Students of all ages can enjoy picture books such as *Everybody Cooks Rice* (Dooley, 1991b) or *Everybody Bakes Bread* (Dooley, 1991a).

Doing the "How To"

This language arts unit of study is based on students' individual interests—a hobby, a sport, or a collection. It is an intensive, thematic exploration of things students love to do. They may be cat lovers or bicyclists, rock hounds or golfers, stamp collectors or Barbie collectors, just to mention a few of the interesting things that they explore. Through the years, I have worked on the "How To" project with students in third through eighth grades. Over time, I also have learned that partners work better than individuals in completing the multiple tasks with greater depth of thought through the benefits of discussion.

During this long-term experience, usually lasting about 6 weeks, students write stories, essays, and interviews. They analyze and sentimentalize, and they give speeches and demonstrations. They also provide data in a variety of forms, including flowcharts and graphs of survey results. The activity builds multiple skills, and the motivation of bringing to school their dogs, motorcycles, fishing rods, or baseball cards (and much more) leads students through the rigorous academic work that is involved.

A state publication describes the How To (Nagel, 1996) in some detail, including the unit's original collaboration with Terry Kristiansen. The table of contents below provides some insight into the activities:

Written Report	*Oral Report*	*Special Format Pages*	*Creative Projects*
Outline	Catchy Opening	Foreword	Songs
Introduction	Background	Title Page	Magazine Ads
History	Equipment	Table of Contents	Surveys
Steps	Mini-Demo	Vocabulary List	Questionnaires
Famous Person	Closure	Flow Chart	Commercials
Powers/Pitfalls	Questions	Bibliography	Machines
Interesting Experience			Hobby News
Interview			
Closing			

BUILDING CONCEPTS FOR ALL STUDENTS IN MULTIMODAL WAYS

Connecting to remembrance is done through strategies that assist all students as part of effective teaching and are particularly wise to incorporate for second language learners:

- *Visuals*—Teachers use maps and charts, globes and models, graphs of all sorts, diagrams, photographs, cartoons, drawings, posters, paintings, books, overhead transparencies, films, filmstrips, computers, and videos to establish recognition and build new understandings. Materials may be purchased or, in many cases, created by the teacher and students.
- *Realia*—Teachers and students bring "stuff" to school. They bring it from home, the schoolyard, travels, biological supply houses, and museums. It starts with show and tell and goes from there. Clothing and animals, art objects and trinkets, toys and machines, food and plants, or tools and souvenirs are some of the things that cross the classroom threshold.
- *Compare/contrast*—Showing how new ideas are like or unlike known things is a way to think and remember. The use of Venn diagrams or T charts of likeness and differences help the thinking process.
- *Visualization*—Using familiar words, teachers can take students into their imaginations to create scenes and situations. Students can use the pictures in their minds to draw on as they speak and write. Although teachers may guide the imagery, students create scenes, characters, and situations through their own creative efforts.
- *Figures of speech*—The use of similes and metaphors is certainly not reserved for the literature classroom. Good teachers use them all the time, in both their language ("It smells like rotten eggs") and their demonstrations ("These fruits are the planets"). Using them and encouraging student use in their writing helps identify them in the work of others.

ASSESSING FAIRLY IN MULTIPLE WAYS

Self-Assessment for Teachers: A–Z

Good teaching means being attentive to learners and their needs. With classrooms ever increasing in diversity, educators must examine their practices in terms of what will make a difference for students of many cultures. One tool that might assist teachers in assessing their practice is the 26-element list provided in Appendix I, "Strategies for Multicultural Teaching, A–Z" (Au, 1993; Banks & Banks, 1993; Cummins, 1989; Darder, 1991a; Diamond & Moore, 1995; Moll, 1992; Scarcella, 1990; Sleeter & McLaren, 1996; Tinajero et al., 1995) The suggestions are not new, and to some teachers the need for them may seem quite obvious. Nevertheless, providing an education that fulfills all elements for each child is difficult to do in some classroom contexts, for a variety of reasons.

The A–Z opportunities are entwined with issues of knowledge and power. Urban schools may not be as equipped as suburban schools. As the socioeconomic level of the school lowers, the enactment of these important strategies may become more difficult because of lack of resources. The suggested activities in Chapters 11, 12, and 13 about building K, P, and A will address elements of multicultural teaching.

Assessing for the Positive

Make sure that the assessments you use are effective and valid. We have all seen how a group of children who cannot identify the main idea on a standardized exercise can turn around and do a fine job of telling a friend what a story is about. We must give our students credit for what they *can* do. The mode of assessment makes a difference in results and can be employed to build additional capabilities. Teachers who see their work as developmental for each child rather than "remedial" will begin to escape the clutches of thinking that something is wrong with the child who simply has not acquired certain learnings yet. Positive mind-set on the part of the teacher will help inspire the child. Teachers who, for example, look at the things that emergent readers know such as the front and back of a book, what an author is, and left-to-right directionality can build on progress rather than the child's lack of phonological ability.

I suggest that other types of *positive* analysis can help us look at children with different lenses. For example, a "traditional" end-of-the year student placement card typically lists negative elements and attributes that a child may or may not have. Teachers want to have as few "bad apples" as possible. I share some alternatives here that would help teachers sort children equitably and perhaps more reasonably:

Listens

Shares

Self-disciplined

Friendly

Funny

Resilient

A leader

Peacemaker

Flexible

Enthusiastic

Empathetic

Every group needs to have models. Every class needs to have students who are strong in reading and writing and social skills. Teachers would be the first to admit that they need the "good apples." The growth of community and of solid academic expertise in groups of all. If we are to engage in "glass-half-full" thinking, the behaviors we want to honor must be explicit.

Portfolio Assessment

Ongoing portfolio assessment is one tool by which teachers can see not only the quality of students' writing but also the ideas put forth and the quantity usually involved. Teachers need to gain expertise in how to judge student reading and writing, not just how to note errors or correct punctuation and capital letters. Miscue analysis, running records, and holistic assessments are useful, especially to examine over time. Commentaries from student observations provide rich anecdotal data. Informal reading inventories permit students to read orally and silently and to talk to the teacher on a one-to-one basis. Using such a tool can help a teacher's understanding of how the student solves problems to achieve word recognition and comprehension in reading. Story retelling can easily be part of the informal reading inventory, allowing assessment of the student's cognitive connections and sense of story structure.

Perhaps the most powerful technique is the day-to-day examination of "ordinary" classwork—not just grade sheets, but the content of written and oral responses. Teachers who listen and read with care, document their impressions, and reflect on their data are those who can gain insight into each child's learning. Teachers who mark answers wrong without probing further to find out why will gain little insight into the learners before them.

In her fourth-grade class, Polly keeps a notebook with a page for each of her students. When she is analyzing student writing or listening in to their various groups in action, she makes note of what seems to be needed. At least once a week or more for each child, she pulls together a "workshop" group. In some cases, the workshop is for a rather advanced skill that only a few kids are ready to develop—for example, "Let's try to understand how we use personification." In others, the skill may not be bound to paper and pencil but can be a refresher in interpersonal skills couched in terms of talents for group leadership. Polly also teaches a minilesson in a particular skill once or twice each week, highlighting technical aspects of reading or writing that she wants the students to apply that week. It may be the correct format for a friendly letter or a review of a strategy such as webbing.

In her kindergarten class, Lina invites small groups of children and their parents to come into the classroom before school starts each year. While moms and dads fill out papers at a parents' table, Lina works with the group of three or four children to note their responses to typical activities. She reads aloud, has the children paint, and listens to each child.

As an assessment of linguistic intelligence, a portfolio allows each student to collect and display works that represent competency:

Writings at various stages in process

Examples of best writing

Lists of readings and writings

Logs, journals, and final reports

Audiotapes of discussions, readings, and storytelling

Videotapes of performances

Peer assessments

Collected teacher assessments

Retelling, Recounting

Students provide insights when they talk about a story—giving a teacher information that far exceeds that of standardized assessments and explicit questioning. Students who may not perform on a multiple-choice test can show their understandings in other ways. Literacy occurs all day long, not just in language arts class, and this technique travels well. For example, listening to a child "talk through" a story problem can offer far more insights than a numerical score. Talking—even briefly—to students about science or social studies can reveal a great deal about their abilities to read and conceptualize in those content areas. Once a teacher has put a child at ease, the talk that occurs can offer a great amount of information to the trained adult who listens. Home cultures influence the narratives that young children experience and use (Heath, 1986).

Four types of narratives follow. The teller organizes his or her speaking or writing to center around a theme and proceed in order of time.

- *Recount*—a narrative guided by questions: "Tell us what happened when. . . ." "What happened after . . . ?" "Were you surprised to find out that . . . ?" "And then . . . ?"
- *Account*—a self-guided narrative, as exemplified by show and tell or journaling. A clarifying question may be asked at the end.
- *Eventcast*—an ongoing narrative of a current event (as in sportscast)

that uses the present tense or of a future event (predictions), telling how it will go in the future tense.

- *Story*—Usually a past-tense narrative that goes beyond a simple account of facts strung together. A story has a beginning, an ending, and a problem and usually contains the resolution to the problem.

Children will always benefit from having more than one way to recall what they have just read. Furthermore, they will benefit from listening to teachers vary the ways they use narrative.

Letter Writing

When students write to another person, they portray their likes and dislikes and ongoing interests and activities in their own words. Not only does the information provide points of common interest for a teacher to develop in relating to students, but the written page serves as a valuable document for analysis of writing skills. Some writing assessments may be satisfactory, but because a student can express more in this authentic format, writing about comfortable topics. The audience should be someone in a different place—another classroom, another school, another city, another part of the world. The use of e-mail will produce a different sense of tone and structure. Letters, in general, seem to generate longer and more thoughtful pieces.

Student and Parent Interviews; Interest Inventories

Children come to school with vast varieties of experiences and perspectives. Some kinds of prior knowledge are more school-applicable than others because of their overlap with the curriculum of the district, school, grade, and class. The sort of parent–child talk that goes on in the home may or may not pave the way to school talk. Some experiences come to be more transferable because of their similarities to the teachers' experiences and views (Heath, 1983).

Any professional teacher is a detective, looking for clues that will help unravel the mysteries of how a student can best learn. Finding out what students know is a process. It may start with an interest inventory. Assessing a child's interests and information of a personal nature, such as pets, favorite kinds of books or foods, favorite TV shows, and hobbies can also affect the relationship with the teacher and enhance the quality of instruction. Children have many interests and "favorites" in common, but they also have unique profiles of combinations of those traits, just as adults do. Interest inventories of many sorts are available, published in books as well as in formats that can be duplicated readily. However, the one you devise yourself and refine over time will be the most appropriate and meaningful.

The Multiple Intelligences

Howard Gardner's *Frames of Mind* was published in 1983. That book, and its sequels and takeoffs, reveal the importance of thinking beyond mere academic strength in children. Books by the dozens have done a good job of describing activities that are based on multiple intelligence theory, and Gardner himself continues to identify intelligences as he works with his theory. We know that high grades and IQ are no guarantee for success in life, if happiness, not money, becomes a measure. Discovering the ways in which students can have talents that are logical, spatial, bodily-kinesthetic, musical, linguistic, interpersonal, or intrapersonal not only can help know the child in whole ways but can help the teacher bolster self-esteem in the context of classroom life. Curriculum can be designed in which students with particular strengths can highlight their abilities while learning and achieving in other ways. Teachers must use caution, however, in designing programs with opportunities that are too focused, too narrow. Just as a class with members who are all "SPs" on the Myers-Briggs temperament scale is not a healthy mix for learning, activities that limit a student's application of talent to just a few strong areas would be a big mistake.

Linguistic Intelligence

Linguistic intelligence allows individuals to send and receive words, paying attention to their sounds, meanings, structures, and functions. This intelligence seems to reveal itself in two ways for individuals: sending and receiving. Senders (speakers and writers) encode sounds and arrange words into meaningful oral and/or written patterns. The vast variety of possible arrangements may highlight sounds, rhythms, and meanings to convey ideas. Linguistic elements such as cadence, tone quality, and volume become important when words are delivered aloud in oratory. Speakers may wish to convince others, recall information, explain ideas, or conduct inquiry. Writers may have purposes that are personal, imaginative, or informational.

Receivers (listeners and readers) decode the sounds and confer meaning through constant comparisons of their own prior knowledge to the words in context. Linguistic intelligence allows them to determine the intents and meanings of authors.

Is Linguistic Intelligence (Literacy) Your Strong Suit?
The best way to know whether you are strong in this area is to think about the things that you do in life. No standardized test can give you a better indication. You may reflect on your own behaviors or ask close relatives or friends. When you work with other students, ask them. Interview their family.

Some key questions follow. Few individuals could answer positively to all of them, but someone with linguistic intelligence would answer yes to most.

Do you enjoy speaking to others in many different settings?

Do you like to read?

Do you tell jokes, stories, or tall tales?

Do you have a well-developed vocabulary?

Do you tend to remember names, dates, places, or trivia?

Do you enjoy word games or crossword puzzles?

Do you enjoy writing?

Can you listen well as an active listener?

Do you enjoy spelling with accuracy?

Do you do well in school, in general?

The only way that teachers can begin to accomplish their challenging tasks well is to use multiple forms of assessment over time, to become capable diagnosticians, planners, and action researchers. Effective teachers use a great variety of groups that incorporate a wide variety of activities, use a broad spectrum of resources for reading and listening, and address many audiences for writing and speaking.

ADDRESSING COMPREHENSIBILITY

Kids must be able to understand what they hear and read. Group tasks must incorporate materials and input that are comprehensible. Some pointers that would help teachers to serve and advise students follow. Just as Goldilocks found the porridge, the chair, and the bed that were just right in the home of the Three Bears, students should be able to encounter content that is at a "just right" level of difficulty. Students who work within the zone of proximal development (Vygotsky, 1978) can advance with the assistance of a teacher or more knowledgeable peer.

- Provide reading materials for self-selection that are in the readability range for students.
- Gather reading materials in abundance. They should include a variety of books, magazines, and pamphlets that address students' current or possible interests.
- Demonstrate and model using overt actions and clear visuals. Allow students with varied language backgrounds to learn from more than just the words.

- Consider the duality of this criterion (K). In the arena of reading, knowledge represents content knowledge (How much does the student already know about dinosaurs if the book is about dinosaurs?) and skill-related approaches (What techniques does the student possess to recognize words in and out of context?).
- Ask, "Does the student understand the task?" How do you know?
- Are various modalities addressed? Will students have reinforced understanding from realia and auditory sources?
- Is there repetition? If students encounter multiple places where they know what to do, they can grow in confidence and competence.
- Are second-language learners accommodated? Have you used "sheltered" techniques?
- Do you know what out-of-school activities and engagement with print the students enjoy?
- Do you allow opportunities for oral sharing at all grade levels?
- *Note*: The work of Stephen Krashen has helped educators understand comprehensible input.

DESIGNING GROUPS

> *Place emphasis on learning rather than teaching. Construe learning as a process of participation.—E. WENGER*

To form groups with reasonable memberships, teachers will find several tools useful. Certainly the information gathered from assessments is important to think about. Group tasks and materials must be selected to meet students at their necessary levels of expertise. In addition, the sociogram can assist in seeing who may or may not have an opportunity to get along with ease. Another item is a quick questions chart that may remind teachers of important concepts.

Sociograms

The process of sociometry has been used for decades. As mentioned in Chapter 10, sociograms are *confidential* charts that help teachers see students' preferences for working partners. They can identify which students help enhance group work and which students will have a more difficult time and need assistance in negotiating the challenges of working with others. Although a sociogram is intended to assist with social analysis, indicating who will get along with whom in group settings, it is also a wise tool for establishing the academic possibilities for groups.

The sociogram shown in Appendix G consists of a grid that lists students down the side and across the top. The left-hand list represents "choosing;" the top list represents "chosen." The teacher asks each student, in confidence, to write or tell the names of students that she or he could work well with in a group. Then each student may also name one person with whom she or he might not get along very well. The top choices could be numbered to refine the process, but that is not necessary. Although the preparation of the grid is time-consuming, it can serve as an extremely useful tool for group formation (Miller, 1974).

Quick Questions for Small-Group Design

1. Does the group have five members or fewer?
2. Are boys and girls balanced?
3. Are leaders distributed?
4. Are shy or special students distributed?
5. Are students matched with at least one person identified in their sociograms?
6. If students are with "star"/difficult classmates, have you coached them about getting along? (adapted from Gibbs, 1987)

CREATING INSTRUCTIONAL OPPORTUNITIES

Instruction is a design for learning.
—G. SALOMON AND D. N. PERKINS

Team Jobs

As the title indicates, this format gives jobs to teams. They work in collaborative research and use creative expression to portray and convey their found knowledge. The goals of the team include (a) problem solving, (b) self-expression, and (c) socialization.

Purposes

1. Students will apply higher-level thinking skills through discussion, reading, writing, and listening.
2. Give students opportunities to explore topics that are not part of the daily curriculum.
3. Provide ways for students to express various talents, multiple intelligences.
4. Establish channels for creative expression.
5. Provide for community building.

Team Jobs Schedule

1. Once week before the presentation, select a topic with student input.
2. Assign students to a heterogeneous team of five or six students if they are not already in groups. Make sure, behind the scenes, that at least one very capable student is on each team.
3. Designate a half hour each day for team jobs discussions and research.
4. Allow 1 week for preparation. Expect homework time to be devoted, and allow for the minutes in scheduling other homework.
5. On the designated day (Friday seems to work for most classes), hold presentations. Set time limits for groups accordingly. Hold high expectations for active listening of the audience.

   - The leader calls his or her team forward. He or she introduces members and states their responsibilities.
   - All team members present their work, explaining visual pieces, reading written pieces, or performing songs.
   - The class offers verbal praise and fills out holistic evaluations, group and individual. Points on a six-point scale work well. Some individuals prefer 10 points per job. Student evaluations are reviewed by the teacher and turned over to team members.

6. Each team rotates jobs weekly.

Responsibilities

Depending on the size of the group, select from these jobs:

1. Leader/recorder
   - Serves as a model of being a cooperative and helpful team member.
   - Encourages team members and assists in any way possible. During Team Jobs Presentations, introduces each member and tells what he or she will be presenting.

2. Orator
   - Gives an informative speech on the topic, using note cards, if appropriate. One audiovisual aid should accompany the talk.

3. Poet
   - Creates a poem using a style designated by the teacher or self-selected.
   - Reads the poem aloud and offers background and/or interpretation.

4. Author

- Writes a fictional piece or essay that somehow relates to the week's topic. The author's piece is not a report per se. The piece must not merely duplicate information the orator shares.

5. Artist

- Creates and presents a two- or three-dimensional project that relates to the week's topic, explaining the media and methods employed, and perhaps offering interpretation.

6. Inventor

- Creates a three-dimensional product (or detailed plans) that can somehow enhance life in relation to the week's topic.

7. Songwriter

- Writes and presents a song (a recording is all right) that expresses information and feelings related to the topic.

Possible Topics (but choose what's best for your context.)

winter	cowboys	air pollution
snakes	the brain	The Forty-Niners
George Washington	prepositions	Mary McLeod Bethune
circulatory system	trees	teachers
flowers	etiquette	the best book
soccer	our hero	

Grading

1. Each leader turns in an overview sheet at the end of the week.
2. The teacher also assesses group and individual accomplishments.

TEAM JOBS

Team Name_____   Date_____

Topic_____

Group points for this week_____   Total points_____

Team Members	Job	Points Earned
1. _____	_____	_____
2. _____	_____	_____
3. _____	_____	_____

Skills

To build K, teachers must use direct instruction but do so judiciously. Wise practitioners avoid skills-based lessons in whole-class settings, once the initial teaching and analysis of needs have been done. They can find plenty of activities to do with whole-class groups that build community and esprit de corps. Singing, storytelling, read-alouds, shared readings, and student or guest speakers are all appropriate.

For skill development, teachers are wise to use small groups. Heterogeneous groups are fine for most teaching, but homogeneous groups are useful if children clearly have a shared need for direct instruction.

Ideas for skill activities abound in basal materials, and commercial sources of grouping ideas for word study serve teachers well. Open-ended questions and projects are more effective compared to identical skills completion lessons: "Everyone will use their own particular talents in this play. You may draw, paint, write, speak, or sing. You may also make up a dance if you remember to write the directions clearly." Standards are set high: "You have to have read the story if you want to talk in discussion group. Everyone will tell us about the contribution that he or she made. Prepare your writing for publication. Keep a log of the number of minutes and hours you spend preparing."

Four Stages for Helping Learners

1. Find out and analyze what the student can and cannot do on his or her own.
2. Identify the kind of support needed to bring about improvement.
3. Devise and institute a procedure that can offer the necessary support, understanding that it may involve materials, other people, or both.
4. Gradually withdraw the support to encourage independent activity by the learner using the new strategies. (Vygotsky, 1978)

PROVIDING MOTIVATION AND "INTERESTINGNESS"

Some of the questions to answer about a learner's motivation include these: Does the child expect to enjoy? Does she or he expect to be successful? Is the student on task in the classroom? Much has been written about motivation. As with many dualities in education, motivation has questions related to intrinsic and extrinsic motivation. Having addressed those issues in Chapter 3, I hope to provide further ideas here.

Oral Sharing and Presentations

Children of all ages are interested in each other. Their words appeal to one another, and they enjoy peer presentations (Dodge, 1989). When young children stand before their classmates and share items for show and tell or "share and stare" in older grades, when students share experiences through storytelling, when they present mock television shows or "evening news," when they do how-to demonstrations and explanations, or when teams of children share the results of their inquiry work, their communications are typically well received and understood. Many other ways to do oral sharing are popular, as represented in Appendix H, "Literacy Activities for a Democratic Classroom."

Build Excitement; Present Novelty

The anticipatory experience is a critical part of joining any type of lesson to the child's schema. Although many teachers are familiar with the "anticipatory set" of the seven-step lesson plan promoted by Madeline Hunter, the prelesson connecting is important regardless of the model of instruction that follows. This motivating experience is designed by the teacher to make the learning relevant as well as to "hook" students into the learning opportunity. Posing questions and pondering mysteries, presenting intriguing possibilities, and providing puzzles add to the interest of visuals, real objects, and tools such as parts of videos or tapes. Teachers can make lessons attractive. They are defeating their purposes when they begin a new task by saying, "Open your books to page 34."

Provide Encouraging Feedback

Although teacher's notes from observation are important, it is extremely important to discuss lessons directly with the student and engage in reflection together. The shared perspectives will provide clearer insights, the attention provided in the conference will provide a sense of care and purpose, and the communication will inform the child about next steps far more effectively than a mere score or grade or a hastily written note on an assignment. Students find poor grades and lack of specific feedback unmotivating. Teachers need to couch real assessments in situations of encouragement. Precluding final assessments with clear rubrics, peer assessment, and self-assessment opportunities allow for greater opportunity for success. Motivation will occur when students *know* what to expect and are given *power* to deal with circumstances in a context of *affection*.

Provide Appropriate Tools for Learning

Students who have access to necessary materials will learn more effectively. Locked cupboards and hands-off policies keep materials safe and clean. They do not motivate or support learning. Work to provide student-accessible shelves and drawers that hold paper, scissors, glue, and books. Work with students to assign appropriate monitors and establish necessary norms for the use of shared materials. Designate ways to use videos, journals, word processing, fieldwork, video discs, record players, tape players, or CD players.

Design Rich Field and Classroom Experiences

The kinds of projects and learning opportunities that are offered to children can bring them to common understandings. "Learning by doing" is a very important means for grounding knowledge that will be retained. Not only are a variety of experiences that go "beyond the book" useful, but they can promote other aspects of KPA beyond knowledge. The ways in which children pour, cut, measure, draw, sell, act, and write are important for their understandings and for memorability.

Taking children outside the classroom is an important factor in building a store of shared knowledge. Going to places within the schoolyard or the neighborhood can be just as important as traveling to museums and sights of some distance. Field trips are often handled in ways that are educationally erroneous. The field trip to the zoo at the end of the year when the calendar is crowded, the zoo is jam-packed with kids, and the weather is hot can sometimes do no more than leave memories of being hot and tired for young children. Choosing the time for learning can include the proper season.

Consider Time

In addition to the time considerations mentioned in Chapter 3, two tips seem practical here.

Eliminate common distractions. Teachers are quite familiar with the parent at the door, the announcement on the loudspeaker, the assembly in the morning, and the messenger from the office hovering somewhere near the right elbow. They all interrupt the flow for students in any group. Work with principals to protect classroom time as precious. In addition, do a self-analysis of time wasters. Forgetting (yes, *teachers'* forgetting) is a big time waster. Assigning students to be rememberers can help locate materials, set up centers, set the timer, turn in lists, and more.

Promote paying attention to one another. Assure one another that you will communicate clearly and care about what other people have to say—including teachers *and* classmates. Certainly teachers want to model involvement and point out that the appearance of attention is not enough. Students of all ages have many thoughts roaming through their minds at any given time. Providing motivating tasks and using effective eye contact and tone of voice make a difference. Gaining commitment on the parts of students is an ongoing process that begins with providing information. As Caine and Caine (1994) point out, students are not always "there" when they are there.

Foster Remembering

Helping memories last and providing enough time for things to sink in are also tasks of the responsible teacher. Teachers must provide cognitive experiences that will not allow knowledge to slip on by in all-too-familiar condition. Building "unforgettability" is a critical task. The following techniques make a difference.

Less Stress

Attributes of and rationales for a low-stress environment were mentioned in Chapter 3. What teachers will want to add to their classroom context are things that the children select as helpful. Many individuals are very satisfied with special techniques—music by Mozart, warm and natural lighting, modulated voices, comprehensible and varied tasks that relate to real life. Creating a KPA context in general will also lend to the lowering of anxiety and allow for "good" stress to proceed. High expectations are not stressful when they are reasonable.

Stress often surrounds standardized testing for students and their teachers. Realizing that such testing is not going to go away even though it does not yet fairly test some students means that it must not be allowed to consume excessive time and emotions within healthy classes. Short-term cram sessions not only raise anxiety but the promote further senses of "I can't do it" for some students. They are self-defeating. On the other hand, ongoing incremental preparation techniques that are embedded in regular instructional practice can—and do—occur in effective settings. Aligning tests with curriculum in interesting ways is the only way to promote KPA. Game formats seem to work for many classes. Activities that link new vocabulary to old ideas work. Seamless connections from grade to grade, teacher to teacher work in helping to teach new things, not teach the same things over and over.

Mnemonic Devices

Building "unforgettability" is a very important task. Good groups in and of themselves help memories last. In addition, students can use special techniques to attach new ideas to old. Most educators are well aware of using comfortable sayings that have words starting with letters that also represent more difficult terms. "Every good boy does fine" helps with the musical staff; "Many very eager men just sit until nearly pushed" helps with the order of the planets. Rhymes are also easy to recall. "When two vowels go walking, the first one does the talking" may not have full applicability, but it does tend to stick in people's minds, as does "*I* before *E* except after *C*" As some students explain, "When I try to remember the list, I create a picture in my mind." Teachers and their students can make up devices that fit their topics and their levels of creativity.

Cognition and Metacognition

Strategies that help students to think and remember are many. I will remind teachers of three in this section, not because I have anything new to add but because they may be overlooked in their importance or even seen as "old" ideas in some contexts.

SQ3R has been known for many decades. It works, but classroom teachers overlook its use (or do not know about it.) The initials have inspired slightly altered versions along the way, but I have found this to be an effective acronym for an effective process.

Taking a *survey* of reading material prior to doing any actual reading is the first step (S). Noting pictures, graphs and charts, and maps, as well as captions, titles, and subtitles, gives the reader a sense of what is about to be experienced. It helps establish connections with prior knowledge and may do some backgrounding. The *question* step (Q) goes hand in hand with surveying. It may involve reading over questions at the end of a chapter if the material is a textbook. With texts and other works, the questions are also those that the reader poses during a survey. What does the reader want to find out, clear up, solve? (This takes practice.) The 3 Rs are *read, recite,* and *review.* This means that the reader reads, then makes sure that he or she can tell what has been read (section by section), and, finally, takes the trouble to review to make sure that the recitation has been accurate and complete. Using SQ3R as a group endeavor helps ingrain its habits as an individual procedure.

KWL also has admiring derivatives. The original Ogle (1986) version serves well. When students are about to begin a lesson or a unit of study, eliciting what they *know* is part of tapping prior knowledge. Determining *what* they want to find out establishes goals for learning and corresponds to the Q (question) phase in SQ3R. Setting purpose is important to the effective acquisition of knowledge. Thinking about what has been *learned* is part of the closure process, and it can certainly lead into another set of questions in ongoing inquiry. Teachers use butcher paper, charts, and overhead transparencies effectively. It is important for students to be able to review what they have said and to note their progress as they continue to learn.

Several *graphic organizers* are possible, and good overviews of various types are available (e.g., Flood & Lapp, 1995). Clustering as a prewriting technique (Rico, 1986) is one that helps many students. As its originator hoped, students use it to hold their many ideas and begin the process of organizing them in visual relationships. The process activates both hemispheres of the brain and serves to lower anxiety toward writing because once the ideas are on paper, they can be drawn on as a resource. Mind-mapping charts used as a postreading activity help reinforce the ideas of what has been read and can serve as tools for recitation and review (SQ3R). Students with visual strengths attest to their success as study tools.

Three Types of Tutoring

When the Tutor Is a Coach
This type of tutoring is recommended when the tutor is a volunteer or a parent. The training is minimal. It is not intended to supplant teaching in any way. The Topping (1998) model is one example:

1. The tutor prompts the tutee to talk about likes, dislikes, and interests in various contexts.
2. As time and comfort develop, conversations and vocabularies between the two develop.
3. The tutor helps the tutee select reading materials, noting how to choose "good" books.
4. The tutor demonstrates and discusses parts and features of books, noting their usefulness.
5. The tutor reads aloud to the tutee.
6. They may read favorite (also self-made books) aloud in synchrony.
7. They select the "best" books for repeated readings.
8. The tutee may choose part of texts to read unaided, but the tutor and tutee select how help will be given from time to time.
9. When the tutee is reading whole sections of text with comfort, the two focus on discussion of ideas.

When the Tutor Is a Teacher
Teachers have worked with individual students to provide support and direct instruction in many contexts. Informal before- or after-school sessions can provide useful, temporary assistance. More formal, sustained programs have appeared in recent years. Classroom teachers come to the tutoring task with insights and developed skills. Since teachers have primary responsibility to their classroom programs, difficulties arise in finding appropriate times and designating the necessary funding. See Chapter 6 for a narrative that

looks at one Reading Recovery session in which the tutor is a highly qualified teacher working with a student from a public school first-grade class.

When the Tutor Is Another Student

Success stories of students working well with younger children abound in professional journals of the key literacy organizations. Fifth graders have been studied in their work with kindergarten students (Heath, 1995) and fourth graders' work with second graders. The results have been positive and reciprocal, for although new learnings benefit the younger child, the older student benefits from the experience of teaching. As presented in Chapter 3, the construction of meaning comes from complex interactions among cognition, metacognition, and motivation. Teachers are constantly involved with all three elements as they plan and interact and plan again. All "real" teachers know the pleasure of truly understanding many things because of having taught them. Students, even young students, are no different.

"K" MINIVIGNETTES

Current Events

Lou works hard to get his language arts students to think and contribute to discussions. Before school one morning, a bearded man drove slowly by the front of the Hall Middle School in an old gray van that was covered with pictures and slogans protesting abortion. On one side of the van were two gigantic baby pictures, one of a healthy baby, one of a contorted, aborted baby. The students were all attentive to the loud message blaring across their school grounds: "Abortion kills!" Students stood in small clusters of four and five students, chattering about the man and the pictures, as the first bell rang.

As soon as the students got settled in their seats, Lou began. Although he had been inside working on an assignment on the classroom computer, he started by mentioning he heard that something unusual had gone on outside. One student described the van and the man, and then Lou fired off several questions, all in a row: "What does that do to you?" "Does it make *you* think?" "Do *you* have an opinion?" "Two boys respond first, dealing with the idea of abortion. Their comments included, "Well, there's adoption." "I think it's okay for rape and incest, but young girls should put their babies up for adoption." Then Lou asked, "Girls, what do *you* think?" Their answers were full of their responses to the van: "It was *disgusting*!" "I don't think it's right." "He shouldn't do that." For every comment Lou probed further. Then he continued, "Why do you think he would come to a *middle* school?" On goes the conversation.

Lou knows that he needs to "go with the flow" when something of note happens outside the classroom time frame. He makes sure that he capitalizes on such "teachable moments." Students are glad for the opportunity to talk to defuse the emotions of the situation. Lou is glad to have the opportunity to ask hard questions about events that are real and shared in the students' lives. He also knows, after about 10 minutes, when it is time to move on to the day's agenda with "Well, we have lots of things to do today."

Sentence Strips

One activity that the children do with the whole group seated on the carpet is one that involves cooperation. Long, card stock strips containing sentences from a current big-book story are passed out to class members throughout the rows of seated children. The distribution seems to be random, but children who are the most capable are avoided. Card holders quietly discuss with nearby children what they think the sentences say. Then Sophia reads the story from the book again, pausing after each sentence to have that card brought up and inserted into the pocket chart hanging on the nearby wall. In most instances, children struggle together, sounding out the words on the card, matching what they find to what they remember from the teacher's reading. The children are all engaged, looking and talking.

In one situation, Maria is sure about what her sentence says because her friend Cynthia is sitting next to her and immediately tells her the words at the beginning of the activity. Maria's knowledge about her own card gives her the confidence to look around and then travel about the group, giving advice and searching for the sentence cards as they come up. The moving, chatting children begin to resemble an outdoor marketplace—busy but controlled. When her sentence comes up, she remembers it and proudly takes it up to the chart.

Cheating? In the sense of standard notions about this kind of helping, perhaps, but the collaboration gives Maria confidence, and she is very pleased to place her card swiftly and assuredly. In the meantime, Cynthia is involved because she is finding all of the sentences.

This chapter could go on for many, many more pages. Dozens of ideas and opportunities to purchase materials related to achieving knowledge cross most educators' desks each month. Teachers know that wonderful activities exist in the files of colleagues, as well as in libraries and stores. Textbooks have sections of suggested activities that are often overlooked yet high in quality. Teachers are adept at inventing opportunities for students when they engage in collegial discussions and dialogues.

Probably some of the best learning activities for each teacher's groups reside in the minds of students, to be withdrawn in the true spirit of *education* (from the Latin, meaning "leading out"). Classroom communication must be clear with instruction flowing in two ways: *with* the grain of children's knowledge as well as teaching *against* the grain, bringing the challenge of new ideas and material to what is already known or accepted. Teaching is effective in ways that are both *yin* and *yang* (Nagel, 1994).

> *Many people give up on learning after they leave school*
> *because thirteen or twenty years of extrinsically motivated*
> *education is still a source of unpleasant memories.*
> —*MIHALY CSIKSZENTMIHALYI*

▶ 12

Building Power

*The rich children were never smacked . . . It
was obvious that he feared their parents. The
poor had no such protection.*—HAIM GINOTT

What is *power*? It means the opportunity to make decisions and have influence.
It means having choice as well as a voice. It means having rights and responsibilities along with a vote. It means social justice. It means being listened to.

Teachers are very influential. They plan lessons and arrange classroom
environments. They control classroom discourse, designating who talks
when. They touch the lives of their students in long-lasting ways that can be
positive or negative. They can change children's destinies. They can also
share their powerfulness with their students in determining the course of
events in their classrooms, preparing them for life in a democracy.

The ways in which citizens share power are important to consider in a democratic context. Most educators could not support a full-blown Summerhill-
style approach to educating youth, permitting students to choose to do work
or not. Still, they support activities that promote choices for children. They
can promote literacy activities that allow students to use their voices through
speaking and writing for a variety of audiences. Finding frameworks within
which student decision making can proceed is an important task of the KPA
classroom teacher. Some tried-and-true measures that have been with us in
education for a long time, such as having students serve as teachers or perform classroom jobs, bear regular revisiting. Some more recent methods, such
as literature circles, book clubs, or leading parent–teacher conferences, are
finding their ways into common practice.

This chapter will share descriptions and narratives of practices, activities,
and tools that can enhance power for students in classrooms. Ideas that follow are organized by the same three concepts—voices, choices, and votes—

used in Chapter 4. The activity segments are not intended to be complete "recipes" but are presentations of ideas that can serve as springboards to readers' own creative applications.

VOICES

Students as Guides

Giving responsibility to children to lead a group comes comfortably to some teachers. One day Sophia has Cynthia direct one of the small groups for an around-the-world-type flashcard activity. The leadership role comes to her naturally. She sits on a chair and tells the children to join hands, stand up, and make a better circle when they sit down on the carpet around her. Then she tells who to hold the cards and when to pass, but she supports them in a kind, not bossy, way. When two boys get off task, she takes one by the shoulders and turns him to face the right way. Then she says to the group, "Don't tell the answers. Let them think." Her authority is accepted, partly because it was designated by the teacher but also because the activity is well handled by the 6-year-old girl.

Knowledge from Home

To enhance academic learning, teachers want to understand students' prior knowledge in order to attach new learnings. According to Delpit (1995), power issues often have to do with how well the things that children learn at home match what they learn at school. Students will be empowered by knowing, and the ways in which home literacy is enacted will affect the presence of each child in the classroom social setting. The sorts of information will be varied.

Chapter 3 provided a list of possible topics that seem to cross all children's experiences. Another way of finding children's expertise, however, is to listen to children's comments and read children's journals about what they did over the weekend. Here is a sample:

Marco—Went to the hockey game

David—Rode his bike all over

Linda—Played with her dog

Manuel—Drew pictures

Lisa—Played soccer

Insightful teachers help children use their experiences as springboards for literacy activities. Topics can be entered on students' lists of possible writers workshop subjects. Examples can be drawn from hockey, bicycles, dogs, drawing, or soccer during classroom lessons.

Portfolio Presentation

Students who maintain portfolios are eager to share them with others. One proper setting is, certainly, at school. The proper guests are many. Some schools engage in student-led conferences with parents (Countryman & Shroeder, 1996). Others invite community members to meet with portfolio-sharing circles of students (e.g., Kerns, 1999). The opportunity to share samples of work collected over time provides an opportunity for student and teacher reflection; it develops a picture of change and growth. The selection process alone is one that empowers students and informs their future goals for work, as students and teachers review the numbers and types of completed projects. To reflect on levels of success promotes critical thinking. To discuss the portfolio's content with interested adults and peers promotes self-esteem and an opportunity for social cognition. Teachers can find many interesting way to help their students frame their rationales for selecting work and reflections about their quality.

12 Steps for Learning

The framework that follows has been adapted from Woolfolk (1998, p. 509). It shares 12 functions that can be initiated by a teacher in a traditional setting but can also be *learner initiated* and therefore empowering. With just a shift in control from teacher to students, the activities can grow in meaningfulness and memorability. From dealing with a textbook assignment to solving a problem, students benefit from considering the following:

1. *Expect*—Set the purpose for doing a particular activity. Answer the questions: "Why? So what?"
2. *Motivate*—Look for ways to make it relevant to your life.
3. *Use prior knowledge*—Ask what is already known, what is needed to complete the assignment.
4. *Pay attention*—Identify key features and main ideas.
5. *Encode*—Generate images, mnemonics, or multiple examples to help memory.
6. *Compare*—Look for similarities; draw diagrams and charts to relate to known ideas.
7. *Generate hypotheses*—Come up with possible alternatives and solutions.
8. *Repeat*—Review and reflect on the material.
9. *Get feedback*—Seek answers to self-posed questions.
10. *Evaluate*—Ask, "What do I know now? What do I need to find out?"

11. *Monitor*—Check for own understanding.
12. *Synthesize*—Make charts; construct tables; seek higher-order relation-ships between and among new ideas and prior knowledge.

Readers will notice that many of the elements of KWL and SQ3R appear in the 12 steps.

Ways to Speak and Write

Langston Hughes (1962) wrote these lines: "I play it cool, I dig all jive; That's the reason I stay alive." He expressed what is well known to most people, usually intuitively: that we use different ways of speaking in different situa-tions, and we would be foolish not to. It can be dangerous to use some kinds of talk in the wrong context.

Educators are well aware of the various influences of dialects and lan-guage use that are home or culture based. Debates about "Valley talk" and ebonics emerge in newspaper reports. Although various individuals have different ways of referring to "power" language, and controversies abound, a prominent thought is that the use of English and flexible ways of using it can provide access to many advantages of mainstream culture.

Role playing can become a base for studies of the ways we choose vo-cabulary, intonate words, and connect words and sentences. Teachers may want to use Martha's idea (in Delpit, 1995, p. 40) to distinguish between "For-mal" (standard) English and "Heritage" (informal, at-home) English. She in-vites her children to a formal dinner at which they use knives, forks, and spoons from formal table settings, eat "formal" food (not finger foods), and use formal language. Lessons about other ways of speaking and writing may emerge from such an experience. Many educators refer to standard English usage as "TV talk"—the kind that television announcers use. Role playing can add to the interestingness and memorability of formal language use, but teachers will want to use caution. Depicting commercials and the news will usually work, but some types of talk that are now quite common on television shows are unacceptable in K–8 school settings.

Interaction Analysis

Talk can be used many ways in the classroom. From studies done decades ago (Flanders, 1970) as well as the present, we know that teacher talk plays an overly dominant part of the amount of talk in any classroom

Although many writers have developed systems of interaction analysis for classroom discourse, the process promoted by Flanders is one that has demonstrated lasting value in a variety of contexts over the years (Tway, 1991). It uses an observation technique of recording verbal events in 10 cate-gories, and it can serve as an instructional or a research tool for action research. The chart shown as Appendix J may be used for marking during a lesson, in which an observer makes a tally mark by the appropriate description of classroom interaction every 30 seconds. The process can be refined by making a grid that the observer marks every 30 seconds. The areas for observation include four ways to look at indirect teacher talk (accepts feeling, praises or encourages, accepts or uses student ideas, and asks questions), three ways to look at direct teacher talk (lecturing, giving directions, and criticizing or justifying authority), and two ways to look at student talk (response to teacher, student initiated). Anything else is seen as silence or confusion.

This set of categories ignores other, student-to-student conversations, but it explores a critical arena of talk in classrooms. Teacher–student talk determines a great deal about the relationships that occur. Because Flanders points out the tremendous amount of teacher talk that dominates classrooms, some have interpreted him as saying that student talk is good and teacher talk is bad. Instead, his message can better be interpreted to encourage an examination of the *sort* of teacher talk that occurs. A teacher who talks more in the first four categories and less in the second three is also creating a positive climate for learning. The Flanders categories also provide a simple framework to think about types of talk in increasing complexity for a beginning teacher.

Word of the Week

In many classrooms, and in some entire school communities as well, a special "word of the week" is selected by students and teachers because of its relevance to current studies, events, or holidays. Teachers and children *use* the word in as many situations as possible and enjoy using the word in daily discourse, giving it ever-deepening meaning and memorability.

Cooperative Groups: Response to Literature

In Sophia's room, the children have one or two opportunities to work together in cooperative groups for language arts each week. Their projects are almost always combinations of writing and drawing that express the ideas of one of the stories being studied that week. In one instance, Sophia designates children to be in heterogeneous teams of four. Each team is given a large sheet of manila paper and five small sheets of colored construction paper. Their task is to do torn-paper pictures of a scene that includes proper representations of five important words that have been examined in a big-book story the class just read. Although completing the work of art is serial in nature, with one person adding on the work of the other, the group decision making is reciprocal. Each cluster needs to talk about what the words are, what the pictures will be, and where the pictures will go. Then individual children have responsibility for creating the shapes, gluing them on, and gluing the identifying words nearby. This particular project, although simple in design, is complex in its cooperative requirements. The children come to agreements about roles, responsibilities, and correctness.

Students as Partners

Partner reading involves two students reading the same writing. The procedure has several adaptations. In all, one member of the partnership is a stronger reader. One technique we use successfully with fourth, fifth, and sixth graders is a version of a technique called neurological impress. The procedure was to have the partners read simultaneously, with the weaker individual of the two pointing to the words as they are read.

A related partner activity is echo reading. It involves two readers, but one reader becomes the trailing voice. Yet another technique is to alternate voices, by the sentence, by the paragraph, by the page.

Literature Discussion Groups

As indicated in previous chapters and portrayed in Chapter 6, teachers who learn to trust their students and understand the power of peer discussions to reach multiple literacy goals may be assured by the research. Focused discussions and dialogues in peer-led groups will successfully enhance comprehension, promote higher-level thinking, and increase motivation (Almasi, 1994). Many types of groups work very well.

Effective teachers guide students with clear norms, perhaps beginning with the most simple, presented in Appendix K, as a framework for constructing their own set. Teachers who remember that discussion is not an assessment tool will help students find success. Teachers who themselves belong to book discussion groups with peers can be the most effective at facilitating and believing in the opportunity. My best suggestion to teachers is to begin a discussion group for adults if you are not already in one. It will establish you as a model with plenty of insights. The empathy will provide a personal opportunity to promote KPA.

Making Movies

Students love to make videos as a group work assignment. In Paul's class, the finished product is expected to be 3 minutes long, and the theme is related to a current curricular topic. Many students have access to video cameras because of family equipment, but Paul also arranges for a school camcorder to be used during lunch and after school in the "studio" corner of his sixth-grade classroom. There, the walls have floor-to-ceiling bulletin boards that are easy to change. Students receive a handbook, indicating the anticipated procedures and expected process and product. Then they submit a storyboard with related dialogue written out on a separate sheet of paper. It is the responsibility of the students before they receive a "contract" to proceed to shoot. Movies can be evaluated according to many criteria, including how well they communicate an important message. Interpretations may, of course, be varied and plentiful, but the point is that viewers "get" something to take away.

Facilitative Frames

When students engage in inquiry, their teachers rethink their roles. Quite often, such teachers begin to refer to themselves as guides-at-the-sides or facilitators. Structuring inquiries is a very different task from teaching in explicit, direct ways. One type of plan is a *facilitative frame*, a means by which to intrigue learners and assist their pursuits. Each frame serves as a broad theme within which students pose questions; conduct research; engage in physical activity; get involved in complex, collaborative problem solving; create interesting products; and achieve long-lasting learning through individual and social construction of meaning (Nagel, 1998d).

One such theme is *The Student's Survival Kit* . The learners write a handbook and prepare an associated kit of "tools" that would help a student survive in their particular school context. One sixth-grade class wrote theirs for the fifth graders. Its table of contents included such things as "School Supplies," "How to Do Homework," "Spelling Tips," "How to Get Along," "Correct Letter Format," and "School Rules."

Book Club

Students who are enthusiastic about reading, or who want to be enthusiastic, will find a book club a logical opportunity. Clubs may or may not take place in the frame of the regular classroom day, depending on the social context of the room and the school. The formats for clubs vary, but everyone is obligated to read the book and meet at the designated time and place to discuss the book. Most conversations are "grand" conversations and are not directed by questions with right or wrong answers. The teacher, if present, takes on a membership role. Student leaders are fine, and they often succeed with questions they design using materials based on Bloom's taxonomy.

Poetry Is Power

In *Rose, Where Did You Get That Red?*, and *Wishes, Lies and Dreams*, Koch (1990, 2000) shares examples of his students' poetry that are modeled after the works of famous poets such as the 18th-century William Blake, someone who would not typically be considered as a "children's" poet. Teachers who have embraced Koch's books in their teaching of poetry to children will understand these words from a different context (Torres, 1998): "I speak here of poetry as a revelatory distillation of experience, not the sterile word play that, too often, the white fathers distorted word poetry to mean—in order to cover a desperate wish for imagination without insight." Poetry permits students to express their questions and emotions and deepest thoughts. They may represent their pursuits of justice and care. Children's poems need not be mere ditties for entertainment.

Writing haiku, specifically, helps students to express simple but deep observations. The short, three-line format is friendly to all ages, and the attention to numbers of syllables help writers find a sense of accomplishment.

CHOICES

Independent Book Selection

For students of all ages, the importance of self-selected reading has been verified by many individuals (e.g., Fader & McNeil, 1968; McCracken & McCracken, 1978). Each child has an opportunity, usually at the same time, to choose a favorite book from a shelf. Children sit alone or in pairs on the carpet, looking and chatting about books, reading the books that are familiar with accuracy and pleasure. Children also check out a library book once a week from the school library. Library time at one school is under the supervision of classroom teachers this year. The woman who served as the librarian/aide for many years lost her job in the process of severe funding cuts in this school district, so teachers take turns doing checkout duty.

Light Reading

Students, like their adult counterparts, do navigate to "light" reading materials. Building in responsible selections would not be to eliminate such popular materials as cartoon books and mysteries (Nagel, 1998d) but to increase the numbers so that each student could check out two books, one in the light category and one that meets interests but is of a more serious nature.

"Quaker" Reading

This idea has come down from a set of ideas by Gross (1989) and seems to work best with upper-grade students. Once a particular piece has been read through once silently, each student chooses a favorite part to read aloud. The part is, however, to be read aloud without raising hands for a turn, just when no one else is reading. Skipping randomly around the room is fine, and one part may be read by several people in the course of the reading. This technique asks students to concede to one another, with humorous results at times. It capitalizes on self-expression, while at the same time providing an interesting way to practice oral reading. The teacher is not in charge of saying who reads when.

Reading Task Boards

A favorite time for students is when they choose centers to visit during their language arts time. Centers can be constructed in a great variety of ways. One version is to establish activity (task) centers that may change with the curriculum, but the centers themselves and the norms for work at them do not vary much. Many teachers control the size of group at each center through a card system or a reading task board. The activities to be chosen differ with the classroom. Some suggested centers that apply across many grades include Classroom Library, Overhead Projector, Game Center, Shared Reading Center, Computer, Listening to Tapes, Tape Recorder, Writing Center, and Meet with the Teacher. Other choices, dependent on school opportunities, might include a visit to the school library, or interview with an interesting community member or fellow student, or storytelling in the room. Some possibilities would depend on the grade level. Young children love to "read the room" with a special "wand," examining the student work that is posted as well as the many charts and posters that accumulate in most classrooms. The VCR may have a section of a video to watch and respond to.

Ways to Report on Books

The more books that students read and enjoy, the better they can read. Reporting on books provides a vehicle for students to review and reflect on what they have read. Not all books require reporting, and reports may be varied across students' inclinations to serve their purposes. Some techniques that "work" and provide practice in various writing genres include the following:

1. *Create a newspaper.* Using the book as the theme, write front-page articles, editorial pages, advice columns, sports articles, and obituaries. Draw comic strips, illustrations, and political cartoons. Work with a partner or a small group to put it all together.
2. *Write a travel brochure.* Using a brochure from a travel agency as a model, entice other travelers to go to the place in your book. Highlight attractions, things to do, travel arrangements, and accommodations.
3. *Create and perform a song.* Based on the themes and plot, share the book with others through lyrics and melody.
4. *Act out a key scene.* Select a pivotal time in the book. Gather actors for the key characters. Write the script based on the narrative. Practice. Invite the audience. Perform.

5. *Create a timeline for the wall.* Use words and pictures to summarize key events, and arrange them on a visible, attractive time line to share your book. Avoid giving away secrets.

6. *Write a book review.* Read reviews from the city newspaper section. Then share the book with its highlights and low points. Evaluate its impact on you and its potential to reach other readers.

7. *Create Venn diagram collages.* Compare and contrast your book to another one that is familiar. Use cut or torn magazine pictures to represent events and concepts from the books. Fill the circles and overlapping area of a poster-size Venn diagram.

When Students Are Leaders

Many activities that are traditionally led by teachers do not have to have an adult at the helm. Children learn from one another in many ways and find other children to be quite interesting in their presentations of activities and information. Students are able to present skits and plays, reports and speeches, and share group work. They can also show flashcards, do pocket chart activities with words and poems, play hangman, lead a guess-the-word game, lead songs and chants with word cards, play baseball questions, and play guessing games about words or ideas. Teachers can analyze all the tasks that they do and discover not only that many of them are appropriate for students to do but that the activities will increase in motivation for other students and will deepen learnings for the "student teachers."

Students of all ages can achieve leadership in many ways. Writing for authentic audiences is certainly a way to empower individuals. Literary journals, newsletters, newspapers, and magazines provide many opportunities for publishing. As a matter of fact, the information in Appendix L has been provided for this book by students—university students. I had the good fortune to teach a literacy class recently. As one of their assignments, all of the students contributed their best tried-and-true ideas for vocabulary study from their years of working with students in K–9 classrooms. Two students served as the appendix editors. Not only did they appreciate one another's insights, but they enjoyed the process of reflecting on their practice.

VOTES

Class Meetings

A literacy activity that makes a difference is the class meeting. Not only does it allow for student voice, but it serves as reasonable tool for conflict resolution in a classroom setting. As long as the meeting is structured well and students know the ground rules, it allows students to have their say in doing authentic problem solving. One format that has met with repeated success in classrooms at most grade levels is one that probably originated with Rudolf Dreikurs. In the Nelsen (1996) format, the agenda is written by the members of the group (class). Any person, including the teacher, may enter a few words to indicate their concern, sign it, and date it. Everyone has a turn to talk for the opportunity comes around. Game playing order goes clockwise. The teacher may serve as leader until a student leader takes over after a month or two of practice. Here are the basic procedures:

1. *Sit in a circle.* I prefer the floor for all ages.
2. *Give compliments.* Before any focused conversation occurs, the tone is set by a round of compliments. The leader of the group begins, and each member shares a positive comment about a recent, positive contribution of another classmate. I tend to say, "No clothes compliments."
3. *Read the agenda item.* Ask the agenda author (student A) whether the problem is still a problem (it often is not.). Ask the other involved person (student B) to tell her or his side of the story.
4. *Offer comments and suggestions.* Pass an item around, such as a speaking stick, so that just that person may talk, one at a time. Other students' insights into the disagreement or suggested consequences are welcome. Make sure that lessons about logical consequences precede regular meetings.
5. *Write down suggestions.* A recorder could use an overhead transparency.
6. *Read and review the suggestions.*
7. *Ask student B to select a suggestion that seems helpful.*
8. *Vote to confirm.* We use hand signals. A positive vote is thumbs up. A negative vote is shown by waving hands, palms down, over laps. If the vote is negative, it opens up a new round of discussion.
9. Student B selects when he or she will do whatever the chosen activity/consequence is.

Most class meetings are timed and focused. All agenda items that remain undiscussed are tabled until the next scheduled meeting. Our class went gradually from meetings once a day to once a week.

Favorite Book Contests

Beth has her students participate in the selection of the California Young Reader Medal each year. She reads each one aloud and, when all have been shared, has students vote. Another teacher has students create their own book contest. Each student may nominate a favorite book in a category that everyone agrees on. Then they all prepare persuasive posters and present short book talks.

Elections

Many school have student councils, with representatives elected within each classroom (grades 4 and up) and officers elected on a schoolwide basis. The poster making and speech writing and delivery are often endeavors of just a few individuals. Elections can have influence within classrooms, but teachers and students will want to decide whether traditional offices (president, secretary, treasurer, sergeant-at-arms) have meaning for them. When the job descriptions are explicit and the implications of hard work are clear, officers can be helpful.

Directions to Take

Voting can be helpful for many of the management issues that confront teachers. The democratic process allows students to have a greater sense of buy-in for such things as designated homework nights, topics for bulletin boards, games for recesses, when to go to the school library, how to arrange the classroom library, and who to invite as a guest speaker. Students need and appreciate decision-making opportunities that affect their school life.

"P" MINIVIGNETTES

Choosing Partners

Sophia often designs lessons that require paired collaboration. Late in the semester, when the children know each other well, she wants them to learn to use the open-ended dictionaries that she has photocopied for them. After she provides detailed directions as to how the project is to be done while the children all sit in a large circle, she demonstrates exactly how their finished papers will look and gives directions to the children as to how the partner groups will be made. Then she has all the children stand on the carpet before her. They begin their process in which one boy and one girl from different groups find one another to become a pair. Through a procedure that consists mostly of eye contact and reaching out of hands with just a few verbal requests, the matching up process looks very much like awkward adolescents at their first dance. Very shortly, 10 children remain standing like statues within the masking-taped perimeter of the carpet. Sophia does not intervene except to nod her approval of the partnerships as they form and go off to get to work at tables, desks, or on the floor.

When only four children remain, two are girls—Rose and Maria—and two are boys. Maria, who refuses to look at anyone or make any overtures whatsoever, looks as though she believes that someone is going to come along and grab her, but it does not happen. According to Sophia, Rose has earned a reputation of being someone who does not like to do much when she works. Maria is probably standing because her stone face has kept other children away from her the whole time. At last, after almost 2 minutes go by, she looks up, grabs the hand of the boy who reaches out to her, and the two children march up to be recognized by their teacher. Then they settle on the rug, lying on their stomachs to study the dictionary together.

The boy who walks up near Rose does so without any negative expression on his face, and the two of them walk to a table that can be used for group meetings. However, Sophia intervenes in this last choice, placing this last boy and girl in separate groups to make three in each of two other teams. She has been noticing much progress occurring for the boy, a shy but capable child, and fears that this partnership would be too discouraging. Rose is put with the top girl and a boy who is of middle academic ability. In their new, respective threesomes, the two participate—even doing part-time jobs as writers, with lots of advice from the group members.

The boy–girl combinations around the room have various approaches to responsibilities that they work out for themselves. In four of the dozen groups there is a decision to alternate the writing responsibility, and in the other groups the responsibility is evenly split between girls and boys. Maria is very businesslike in her relationship with her partner. After talking for a long time, they finally write. Then they go for a brief conversation with Sophia who is stationed at a student desk in the center of the room. Maria leads her partner, holding his hand and acting quite assertively, even in her explanations to Sophia. The activity is a social success, and even though their sentences need many corrections, the two go back to work with enthusiasm. The children are all happy to correct their sentences according to Sophia's suggestions, for their pages will go into a class book, adding to the five currently hanging on the wall for students to read.

Name Cards

In Jeff's kindergarten class, the children serve as teachers on a regular basis. The day Emily volunteers, she sits on the big wooden teacher's chair in front of the group gathered on the rug. She hold the class' giant flashcards, each with a student's name carefully printed on it. Then, she holds the card steady and waits for the identified classmate to raise his or her hand. Later, Jeff explains, the children will read one another's names.

Cooperative Group Roles

In Liz and Marilyn's multiage class, the teachers frame some of the choice making in cooperative groups. One day Marilyn is in charge of the standards setting while Liz sits near her side, drawing up the group memberships for that day. Marilyn punctuates her points with admonitions: "We shouldn't hear anybody saying, 'I'm not doing that [job]. I'm not doing that one.' Remember, next week you will have a chance to have another job. You must be willing to help anyone. You are responsible for your own behavior. You are not to ask a teacher for help unless everyone in the group sees it as a problem."

When the 15 groups settle, they are spread out in spots throughout the two classrooms. All of the groups choose spots at tables except two—one group in which a third-grade member, a boy, sits in an armchair surrounded by the other three members on the floor at his feet; another group whose four members are nestled on a section of the floor behind a divider. As the roles become apparent in each group, the recorders tend to be almost all third graders, with only two second graders holding the pencil. Although the teachers provide no spoken grade-level expectations for various jobs, the children have come to expect writing ability in their recorders. On the other hand, the roles of reporter, monitor, and reader have first graders spread among them. In one case, in which first-grade Eddie wants to be the reader, he is not able to read the directions well. However, his teammates coach him through the process. At the end of the work session, each group member fills out a slip of paper to share what job they did and tell how the group work went for that day.

> *She made us learn. We had to get in the books. There was this tall guy and he tried to take her on, but she was in charge of that class and she didn't let anyone run her.*
> —*A YOUNG BLACK MAN QUOTED IN LISA DELPIT*

▶ 13

Building Affection

*If people who do not understand each other at least under-
stand that they do not understand each other, then they
understand each other better than when, not understanding
each other, they do not even understand that they do not
understand each other.—GUSTAV ICHHEISER*

What is *affection*? It is belonging. It is care and understanding. It is listening
to someone else. It is an attitude of respect and high expectations for self and
others. It means trust.

Many of the key ways in which teachers promote affection for their
students are also simply dynamic ways to teach. Some practices may not immediately strike onlookers as strategies for affection. Nevertheless, they are
activities that are *interpreted* as caring by their students.

Students, when asked to recall their lives at school, remember most the
active things that occurred. In one fifth-grade inquiry, students were able to
reminisce about the trip to the zoo, cooking stone soup, learning to dance, eating chocolate in class, painting a mural—more than any books, any teachers,
any worksheets, any topics (Nagel, 1998e). So often, activities such as those
indicated in this chapter are cut from educational programs as being "frills."
However, they are the very ways in which students may tie in to the big
ideas of the curriculum. For the important roles they play in motivation and
memorability, I see them as essentials.

Previous chapters discuss many important factors that relate to student
motivation. Certainly the literacy tasks that teachers assign, as well as the
classroom contents that they design, can make a difference for students to feel
involved and be engaged.

In addition, students want a safe place, one that can be exciting but must
be familiar and comfortable at the same time. Such thinking is in keeping with

analyses of intergroup relations (Gudykunst, 1991). Effective communication can take place only when the uncertainty and anxiety of working with others is reduced. In working successfully as a teacher and coach of gang members, Hasan (1998) explains the value of adapting Nel Noddings's (1992) concepts of care. Students from "dislocated, disordered, declining" neighborhoods need love and respect from their teachers and continuity in their lives. Playing fair, keeping standards high, building trust, and acting proud are all attributes that work with even the most difficult students who are seriously at risk. A sense of ownership plus a sense of family can provide a successful atmosphere.

This chapter will suggest ways to promote affection for students through participation and identification. Students respond when they are being listened to; they like to learn through active learning and appreciate teachers who help them, so ideas for active participation and help will begin the chapter. Because students want to have a safe environment free of negative anxiety, norms and expectations will be the focus for the next segment. Students grow in their feelings of belonging when they have opportunities to grow in self-awareness, self-control, motivation, empathy, and social skills. Those qualities will be explored next. Finally, ideas about parent involvement and rewards will conclude the chapter.

LISTENING TO THE CHILDREN

Care About Kids' Culture(s)

Based on advice gathered from children of all ages and insights that have been shared from ancient times, if I could only recommend one strategy it would be to *listen*. Only then will others have voice. Only then will they know you care. Get students to talk to you—in class, outside class, in the hall, on the yard. As you do, you will start to understand the things that your students really care about.

Certainly ethnic culture is one area for listening and learning. Students are your best sources of information, for your assumptions about a particular ethnic group may get in the way of what really happens in the context of your particular context. Native Americans, for example, share many points of pride, but the traditions and current ways will vary from state to state and from reservation life to urban life. Set up times for students to write and talk about the influences of culture in their lives. It is better for students (or their parents) to define themselves rather than be defined by others.

Another way to listen to children is to learn about the influences of popular culture in their lives. Here are just a few topics from pop culture that kids participate in every day: shows, music, stars, television characters, humor, and fashions. As Gordon (1997) indicates, "As painful as it may seem, watching MTV, listening to current music, and attending popular movies can help provide a connection to what is current in students' lives" (p. 57). Then demonstrate that you have listened by making reference to their world. Your references to their world definitely do not mean that you need to adopt their preferences. It does mean that your willingness to reach out to them can enhance their willingness to reach out to you.

Once your class has established a sense of trust, concepts such as culture conflict, culture shock, and ethnocentrism would be helpful to explore. Be extremely cautious to avoid judgments that seem like put-downs.

Teachers are powerful models of affection in their interactions with students. Before good feelings can build between and among classmates, the teacher must establish the tone. The next paragraphs share what goes on in one teacher's room. In Lou's class, pep talks and incidental comments are woven into the discourse of lessons.

One day Lou introduces the language arts class period with interrogative lecturing, probing what students recall about literary vocabulary from the day before. Sprinkled throughout his words, and interjected into later class discussion are comments that speak to his students on a personal level. "Life is not that simple, is it? You have to make a lot of decisions as a teenager. Should you hang out with this person because he is cool? Or is that a bad idea because you know you might have to smoke?" And "That's okay. When I was your age I thought that, too" or "I would never relive being a teenager."

He gets the kids to reflect: "What you take into the book affects what you take away." He pays attention to his students, as in when he asks one girl, "Were you here? I didn't think so. I could see the puzzled look on your face." He gives them friendly advice: "I used to think that you *had* to read the whole book. If you didn't read it all, you'd be struck down by the gods of hardback binding. Then once I read to page 1,000 and I stopped."

Lou frequently relates to events in popular culture, "This is just like the guy in *Toy Story*!" He uses exaggeration: "I'll give you 7 minutes . . . and 21 seconds." He can be silly. When the morning announcements come on, the traditional opening is the Pledge of Allegiance. "Okay, let's say the pledge," Lou signals and off they go, saying the entire pledge before the girl on the loudspeaker can finish saying, "Ready. Begin." He has high expectations. During the morning announcements, the entire class is totally silent. Showing interest and respect to classmates, present or not, is what it is all about.

Activities with Action

Children tell us by their words and actions that they like to be active. They like to touch things, talk at times, and move about. As educators, we show that we are listening when we incorporate action into instruction. Classroom groups that engage in games, field trips, interactive projects, physical education, and the arts bring about emotional support and have the capacity to reduce anxiety if they are noncompetitive, win-win opportunities. In and of themselves they are valuable. When woven thematically into the curriculum, they provide threads of understanding and memorability to concepts as students engage multiple modalities.

These activities should be considered as "inlets" to learning, not "outlets" from the humdrum of academic information gathering. Because of the multitudes of specific opportunities that exist in all areas, I mention only representative group activities here. Teachers are sure to find excellent resources in catalogs and school supply stores that provide hundreds of paths to take. The rich array of tools such as books, posters, manipulatives, pictures, models, tapes, CDs, and videos available can enhance learning for all. The limiting factors include the "shallow pockets" of so many teachers and schools and the unfortunate personal techniques of teachers who do not permit hands-on access for students. Good teachers have access to "good stuff." They are known to become beggars, scroungers, and grant writers.

Games

Games of all sorts engage students in groups, and they certainly are springboards for conversation as they enhance learnings in literacy. In the best circumstances, competition is kept to a minimum. Teacher-made games may relate to specific vocabulary or themes from literature studies. They are always an outlet for teacher creativity. Student-made games challenge the *students'* critical thinking in the making and provide practice and metacognition in the playing. Rubrics for games are important, for they must make sense and provide meaningful activity.

Commercial games also play a useful part in bringing students together. Some commercial games intended for classroom use have specific purposes, such as practicing phonics or practicing vocabulary. They may be appropriate for some groups. Other commercial games are intended to provide fun for the general population. I recommend those as an investment, for students will be able to find willing players at home as well as school. They can be very useful for students, especially if the game-playing group includes an adult or well-qualified peer. The requirement might be to create words with tiles or cubes or explain words, define words, draw words, or guess words. Games do not have to be word games, however, to provide literacy support. Games that expect players to tell stories from their lives or react to situations serve to help participants know one another better and practice thinking and storytelling at the same time. Monopoly provides opportunities to read and understand a wide variety of words related to real estate.

Games can influence more formal literacy events when they become the focus of accounts or eventcasts. Some possibilities include the following:

Observation reports—A reporter watching a chess tournament or a sportscaster has plenty to say and write as an observer during and after the event. So can a classmate watching a game of any sort, whether it be a word game or a class kickball game.

Participation reports—Reports from players after the event can be descriptive and lively.

Invented games—Designing and describing a made-up game becomes a creative challenge. Possible themes include a piece of literature (The *Charlotte's Web* Game) or a class curricular topic (The Bears Game).

Chants and rhymes—Make up jumprope jingles or cheers for fans at a game. Try them out.

Field Trips

Class or group trips into new environments promote esprit de corps as well as build prior knowledge for future lessons. Teachers who capitalize on field trips not only plan ahead but provide lessons and create materials that enhance the trip experience and connect it for students in academic ways. Teachers who wait until the last week of school to drag the children through a steamy zoo and out for a sticky picnic may be promoting a celebration, but such an event does not rate full ranking as a field trip. Field trips are for field study. Many teachers provide miniature workbooks for their students, photocopied sheets that include cloze sentences and guides to highlights of the museum or locale. Students enjoy treasure hunt approaches as long as they are not at frustration level and are not too long.

Interactive Projects

Many activities fall in this category. As indicated earlier in Chapter 2, the best discussions tend to spring from circumstances that involve tangible objects. Examples include a sculpture, a tool, a photo, or a prop. Opportunities for literacy abound across the curriculum and projects with objects can influence reading/language arts classes. It takes a group.

Visual and Performing Arts. The artistic process and aesthetic response are integral to life. They are not "frills." Students may study illustrations from their literature selections to engage in dialogue or write scripts for the illustrations based on the language of the book. Various types of drums and interpretations of the music they make can be stimulating for students of all ages. The visit of a high school steel drum band to an elementary school had one group of students talking and writing for days. Literacy activities help prepare for a visit to a play, an opera, or a museum and can follow up such outings as well.

Math/Science.   Literacy events based on math and science activities are frequent parts of integrated curricular experiences. Manipulatives of all sorts bring people together, as long as their use is shared appropriately. Student groups may record in journals, prepare charts, and share through oral reports to interpret their work with everything from Cuisenaire rods, geoboards, and tools for measurement to building bridges, raising plants, or examining the habits of mealworms. Projects may be worthy of poster sessions afterward, allowing students to prepare organized accounts of their work in words and illustrations for presentation to the class or the school. Science fairs may serve as an example, although they sometimes have a way of becoming overdone when parents and money interfere. Adults in academic settings are familiar with posters as a good way to promote communication about project work.

History/Social Studies.   Project work comes naturally to the social studies. Manipulatives of all sorts enter daily lessons in effective classes. Models and globes, maps and photos, telephone books, surveys and interviews, and charts and graphs are just a few of the things that can enter in. Artifacts from long ago (a milk can, a butter churn, a carpet beater) or far away (a kimono, a saddle, a photo) can evoke questions surrounding "What was/is life like then/there?" Conducting surveys, then collecting, summarizing, and analyzing the data, reports, and analysis are pleasurable for all. Creating models of unique structures or building special modes of transportation can get students interacting. Collections of things (stamps, tools, dolls) can also inspire many literacy activities.

In one active fourth-grade class, students built an entire city from components that included Styrofoam, colored paper and cardboard, and assorted items gathered from homes across the neighborhood. Small groups were designated specific areas of the plan and were to provide certain community services. In another fourth grade, the students studied aspects of California history. They collaborated to create Mission Impossible, constructing a model mission and grounds on a scale of 1 inch to 1 foot. Groups were assigned parts of the mission or the grounds to furnish or equip, and, when class after class from the school walked through to take a tour, they gave speeches about "their" areas.

Physical Education.   Effective teachers include psychomotor activities from this realm in their instruction. Physical activity also lends to engagement in that a morning walk before class can activate sluggish students and tone down the "live wires." With the growing popularity of Tai Chi in Western settings, an early morning session can do good things, including build *esprit de corps*. Aspects of good practice (taking heart rates, counting calories, attending to the food pyramid) can become the focus of journals and other accounts.

Help

Students have a variety of ways to seek and deal with help, and teachers vary greatly in their ways of providing it. Often, teachers who remind students to ask for help if they need it will find that the students who need it the most do not ask. Knowing what to ask and when to ask it are challenging in and of themselves. Older students also find it more difficult to seek help because of the possible embarrassment. For help to be given and for it to make a difference, teachers must make sure that they present a warm and supportive context. Teachers do not have to provide all help themselves, although their consultation is one good source of assistance. Instead, they create situations that are helpful.

Girls prefer to ask girls for help and boys prefer to ask boys, but in studies of elementary students, girls will ask boys—far more than boys would ask girls, despite the fact that girls are the better students in the studied classes (Wigfield, Eccles, & Rodriguez, 1998).

Provide Help with Assignments

The students in Mary's room come from a variety of socioeconomic backgrounds. Some students walk to school from neighborhood homes, some come across the city on the bus from inner-city apartments that surround the downtown business center. At the start of the school year, she saw from the students' initial writing assessments that many of her fifth graders were struggling writers. Knowing that they would face writing proficiency tests in the spring, she initiated an action research project. She instituted a series of cloze story frames that she wrote to provide assistance to her fifth graders on directed writing assignments. Students continued to use flexible strategies during workshop times. Over time, the types of writing assignments changed, and the number of words that Mary typed in grew smaller. She emphasized that her help was only temporary and she encouraged students to throw away their frames. Some students were glad to be rid of the frames, others took longer, but they all wrote in their evaluations of the process that they were *so* glad to have the help.

Other teachers find ways to provide help for all their students by establishing group conversation times. Allowing students to work with others on a variety of assignments provides a sense of comfort for them. Making sure that they are on the right track, that they have not gone astray, is something that students can do for one another quite well.

Be Available at Times Outside Class
The school cafeteria at Lou's school is a crowded place. He is one of several teachers who open their rooms to student use during the lunch hour. Because his classroom is convenient for students with walkers and wheelchairs, many students find a safe haven there. Although an aide is there to supervise, kids with questions or problems know that Lou is usually available to talk to. Because students are in the room anyway, it makes it seem more casual to get help with questions that deal with assignments. No questions are dumb, he encourages students. So they ask, he listens, and they get to go on their way knowing that their concern, small or large, has had a hearing.

Hold Individual Conferences with All Students
A group of teachers in a college class were surprised when their instructor set up individual appointments for all of her students to chat about their action research projects. Many of them responded to the invitation with surprise: "This is the first time that I have *ever* met with a teacher about my work." All through school, when seeking help and asking questions are the only ways to interact with teachers outside class sessions, students from all types of backgrounds would probably have a similar experience. A chat with the teacher is not the usual; if it does happen, it happens for "high" students, not those in "low" groups. Structuring time to talk, partly with structure, partly just to talk, can pave the way for future conversations and make seeking help seem less "scary." One sixth-grade teacher makes a habit of calling homes to greet the parents and then *talk* to her students. They are shocked. They are pleased. It makes a difference.

Be Available to Help with Problems
If the problem is big or small, willingness to help makes a difference. Teachers often need just to listen to make a difference. The best solutions will come from the students themselves. Referring students to school counselors (or administrators) is a good way to help, remembering that students will find it hard to seek the help. Students and their parents must, of course, do the actual appointment making, but teachers who provide names, phone numbers, and say, "Let me know if you go," provide the necessary scaffolding.

In cases of school fights and violence, teachers are often afraid to help. Breaking up a fight is not easy, and disarming an individual is often outside the scope of teachers' abilities. However, standing by idle is not uncommon, and it is disturbing.

The message here is that educators must insist that their schools have action plans for a variety of contingencies. Areas in schools where someone "owns" the space (e.g., classrooms, offices, locker rooms) are seldom sites of trouble. The "unowned" areas (cafeterias, hallways, parking lots) are the potential sites of one-upsmanship and possible violence unless there is close, regular, consistent monitoring.

SPECIFYING GROUP NORMS AND EXPECTATIONS

Children make it clear that they know the teacher cares when she or he makes it safe and helps them. Kids need protection from bullies of all sorts (and from Babies and Bozos, as explained in Chapter 7). When guidelines are clear, groups have better opportunities to succeed. What must also, however, be clear is that "Rules are made to be broken . . . some of the time." Participants who are having a bad day, need to be silent, or have an off-topic incident to relate are not bad or wrong. Tolerance of imperfection allows educators to see that such human occurrences are part of normal adult life as well as normal child life. Yes, they are off task. They should not occur every day, but they do happen. The prevailing standards do not need to change when flexibility enters in. A day that goes without a hitch may bring true joy, for it is not the norm.

Class Handbook

Teachers and their students can coproduce a handbook of guidelines for their work together. The expectations for "how things go" can be based on typical experiences at that school and in that grade, and, those for "how things ought to go" can be based on notions of preventing breakdowns. The process of making explicit some of the unwritten rules can make a great difference to students new to the culture of the school. The participation of all students can assure that immigrants—from another school in the district or from another country—can question and influence the way things are done. The handbook can include pointers for parents, as long as teachers and students remember that they should consult with parents in the publication process. Books such as *Multicultural Manners* (Dresser, 1996) might serve as a resource for teachers and students alike.

Rules

Perhaps the only inflexible rules might be these: *Act safely* and *Have zero tolerance for put-downs*.

GIVING DISCUSSION REMINDERS

In General

1. Take turns talking.
2. Stick to the topic.
3. Be serious.
4. Do not interrupt.
5. Give comments, but be nice.
6. Help others out.
7. Encourage others.
8. Ask a question if something needs to be made clear for to be made clear for the group.
9. If you did not understand something, ask about it.
10. Comment on things others say.

With Literature

1. Refer to notes for ideas.
2. Tell about your likes and dislikes.
3. Compare characters.
4. Compare the story to things in your life.
5. Talk about or challenge the author's style.
6. Discuss why the author wrote the story.
7. Say whether you agree or disagree; tell why.
8. Check the story to back up your ideas.

Five Rules for Group Discussions

A more concise way of putting things might be these rules, adapted from Epstein (1972), Cohen (1986), and Robinson (1996) (see also Appendix K).

- Be concise. (Stick to the topic.)
- Listen. (Pay attention.)
- Reflect. (Repeat something from a previous person's comments.)
- Contribute. (Everyone is included.)
- Respect others. (Avoid blame, maintain confidentiality.)

A Place We Can Trust

Whether the context is a community organization, a corporation, or a classroom, the people want to trust their leaders and fellow group members.

Attributes that build trust include the following: She or he (a) listens to me/us, (b) respects what we have to say, (c) understands our concerns, (d) keeps promises, and (e) expects the best.

On the other hand, where trust is lost, the individual (a) is self-indulgent, (b) uses other people, (c) makes decisions without consultation, (d) does not listen, (e) does not consider our needs, and (f) hurts others.

Students can work in groups to discuss, design, and write procedures and expectations that will support trust building. Many people are familiar with activities such as "Trust Walks" in which partners navigate an area together, one blindfolded, the other serving as a trusted guide.

DEVELOPING SELF-AWARENESS AND PROMOTING INTRAPERSONAL STRENGTH

Howard Gardner (1983), in his work with the multiple intelligences, stresses the importance of both intra- and interpersonal intelligence. Many practices can support intrapersonal growth in the classroom. We learn from ancient Chinese philosophy, as well as from the thoughts of contemporary theorists, that an individual must know him- or herself before being able to know others. The activities described here are successful for individuals to think about their lives and the connections they have with other participants. Success will come when class members, including the teacher, come to hold self-knowledge and respect for other class members.

The ABC's of Cultural Understanding and Communication

To allow students to reflect on their own cultures and that of their classmates well, the activity sequence devised by Schmidt (1998, 1999) has had great success in many different school contexts. Not only is it a meaningful activity for elementary school–aged children, but it is the sort of opportunity that can work effectively with individuals in grades 9–16 and beyond as well. The process is composed of three broad activities. In the first step, the A activity, all members of the group write an autobiography, full of detail, including family, education, tradition, victories, recreation, and defeats. Step 2, the B activity, involves two partners interviewing each other and writing the biography of the other person. In step 3, the C activity, partners engage in a cross-cultural analysis of the differences and similarities between them. The amount of time and detail invested in each of the ABC activities will vary the benefits.

The ABC approach has been used effectively with fifth graders for a morning and for several weeks. It has been used with teacher preparation students for a year. It can be an activity for a lifetime for anyone.

Buddy Journals

In this type of dialogue journal, students write back and forth to someone from a different place. That "place" could even be in the same classroom, but, typically, distance adds to the interest of the project. Fourth graders can write to college students; second graders can write to sixth graders; students can write to other students in far-off places. Buddy journals are one way to bring a class together as a whole as individuals share their correspondence with partners from other locations. Written journals are fine if a regular delivery system is employed. E-mail also works.

Buddy journaling is a way for individuals to see life through the eyes of another person, and the written record allows review of past dialogue, something not automatically provided by pen pal letters. Journal entries inspire relationships that are not part of buddies' day-to-day lives. They also provide opportunity for personal reflection, self-expression, and building a knowledge base. The journals, and class conversations around them, can help build social skills and provide opportunities to combat prejudice and racism.

Findings from a fifth-grade/college student buddy project revealed what practices promoted longer entries from students at both ends of the project. Seen as Appendix M, "Advice to a Dialogue Journalist," the "rules" have more to do with relationships than with conventions of writing (Nagel & Kellerman, 1995). Such results make sense in view of the notion that KPA promotes discourse.

Literacy Autobiographies

Many individuals are also familiar with literacy autobiographies (e.g., Au, 1993). Teachers who develop their personal stories of early reading and writing can come to better understand their attitudes and abilities. In sharing their literacy memories with students, they help model, and they open channels for communication with students. Students, like their teachers, can complete literacy biographies. Teachers can also share their biographies with one another, for in doing so they build their bonds as a community of literacy learners and leaders.

Portfolio Reflections

Keeping notes and writing reflections for a teaching portfolio also helps. Each day is filled with lessons and projects. Some work; some do not. Every day is filled with achievements and foibles of students. Keeping track of the successes (and the flops) with artifacts (photos, tapes, notes, records) and annotations (titles, rationales, reflections) helps teachers reflect on the work of days and weeks. The process of writing about a given event can lead to insights that would never have emerged, especially if recollections about the details of the context and the conversation can be captured. When individuals share their teaching portfolios with others, they may capitalize further on reflections that arise in the dialogue (McLaughlin & Vogt, 1996).

Students, too, can maintain valuable portfolios. From the very earliest grades, children can select and reflect on the work that they accomplish and predict the tasks that they want to do. A portfolio is an ongoing project. It may contain assessments, both teacher and student prepared. It may share samples of reading (tapes, running records, voluntary reading logs) and writing (stories, poems, multiple drafts, along with rubrics) over time (Flood & Lapp, 1989; Valencia, 1990). Not only does a portfolio showcase key pieces, but it also communicates to families, promotes student reflection, and inspires plans for the future.

BEING A MODEL AND PRACTICING SELF-CONTROL

In a describing ways to work effectively with gang members, Hasan (1998) describes a teacher who is having difficult times with her students in a neighborhood that is considered to be gang territory. The woman scuffed around her classroom, wearing a too-tight white T-shirt and an old and tattered skirt with no stockings and rubber sandals. Wearing expensive clothes is not necessary, but looking professional is in the minds of students and their parents. Research tells us that students respond positively to "attractiveness," and it has little to do with beauty and a lot to do with being concerned. In other ways, actions speak more loudly than words.

Be fair. Good teachers develop eyes in the back of their heads. Not only are there benefits to knowing what goes on in the classroom, but the teacher helps the classroom climate by knowing who is responsible for what. Accusing the wrong person for misdeeds if sure to dampen spirits of children. Instead, effective teachers do not miss a step; they can keep focused on a lesson and correct a misbehaving child with subtle signals at the same time.

Finally, the best person to decide where you want to grow is you. A picture is worth a thousand words. Get a video camera. Use it. Watch it (alone, for the first time at least.) Reflect. Act.

DEVELOP MOTIVATION

Teachers can help students to find reasons for being at school, for engaging in lessons, and for doing well and sticking with it. What they say and do, as well as what they have the students say and do, all make a difference.

Classroom respect is enhanced by a teacher who holds solid standards, using language that is understandable and techniques that are memorable. The social organization of classrooms and group processes are all great influences on motivation (Wigfield et al., 1998). Because KPA is actually all about motivation, this section will merely provide a brief checklist as a reminder for teachers, remembering that students have a hand in motivation too.

To create interest, work on tasks that

- have personal relevance,
- have novelty,
- inspire activity, and
- have appropriate comprehensibility.

Not all tasks must have all qualities to be motivating, but the chart may help you to see why some opportunities do not work with students.

USING EMPATHY AND RESPECT; PROMOTING INTERPERSONAL GROWTH

Teachers need to examine their words. What they say and how they say it can make a big difference to others. The variables of voice tone, eye contact, and body language lend to the impact of words that are used in daily discourse. Put-downs of any sort, through either verbal or body language means, must not be tolerated. Educators must avoid the kinds of "teacher talk" that occur typically in low groups, such as criticisms, low-level questions, and an acceptance of interruptions to the group's activities (Allington, 1983; Grant & Rothenberg, 1986; Hiebert, 1983). They must avoid making ongoing negative comments that do not hold up in polite adult society, such as "You never have your book." "All you seem to do is argue." "Sit still." One upper-grade teacher had very different kinds of things to say to his low and high groups. To the first group of students, his talk was full of comments such as, "Can't you see that? Listen up. Why don't you pay attention? Give me a break. This isn't hard." To the latter, his comments included the following: "Come you guys. You need to do this. I know you are capable. This is the kind of work that makes a difference for college."

Opening Activities

Opening rituals can set the tone and promote a positive climate for the whole day. At the same time, everyone can participate in a literacy activity. One teacher's account:

In our classroom we have several activities to open each day. One thing that we are sure to do is have charts or overhead transparencies made for everything. The environmental print adds to the meaningfulness of our sung words and recitations and allows everyone to go back and read again. The transparencies are kept in a binder that anyone may look through. The charts are hung on a chart rack. Our class president leads us in the Pledge of Allegiance. Then the person who has chosen the song for the day gets up and leads the class in singing. That person points to the words and either sings or plays a recording. A few leaders play musical instruments. Robby is always willing to provide a drum accompaniment if the leader wants. Another student prepares the "Historical Fact about Today." The next student shares a "Poem for the Day." Then the class journalist for the previous day reads what he or she had written in the big book that is kept on the Daily Journal podium.

Conflict Resolution

Conflict is part of democratic life. It is going to happen. As a matter of fact, some authors remind us of the benefits. Conflict has its good points: it allows important issues to be aired, produces new, creative ideas, releases tension, strengthens relationships, helps groups to reevaluate and clarify goals, and stimulates social change to eliminate inequities and injustice (Folger, Poole, & Stutman, 1993). Conflicts, however, need to be resolved. One professor's favorite line makes sense: "They are not enemies; they are partners-in-conflict" (S. Rice, personal communication, 1998).

Schools across the United States have many fine programs of conflict resolution from projects and commercial materials of all sorts. They often include peer counseling. One of the key findings from research on programs in New York City was that the techniques worked, the results were great, but large numbers of teachers neglected to do the activities in the face of already-crowded teaching schedules (American Educational Research Association [AERA], 1998). In view of that, I shall not present a lengthy description of any particular program or process in this section. Instead, I will simply say, "Just do it."

Case Study Teams

Students have a conflict resolution "case" to read each week in one classroom. The narrative tells about a realistic situation that often emerges for elementary students. They then proceed to collaborate in preparing a document or talk that retells the facts, identify the problem(s), analyze the possible solutions, and decide on one, giving reasons as to why it is the best. Group members interact as they do their case analysis, and then groups can interact as they debate their decisions. Books of cases about authentic problems in students' lives are available and are done well in the spirit of promoting conflict resolution. Nevertheless, cases that are written by the students themselves are good to use.

Mini-Interviews

Many classes are familiar with the "Star of the Week" procedure in which one classmate is honored on a bulletin board. When their turns come, students bring in pictures and often submit compliments and sometimes acrostics of the person's name. Sara, for example, would be smart, active, reading, artistic.

Another way to honor students that does not leave any child waiting until the last week of school to be honored would be to post mini-interviews every other week, honoring all students. Students can do the interviewing and the writing. Topics may include those that seem to interest students of all ages: food, pets, favorite TV shows, favorite books, best place to go, and so forth. Students have a way of getting to know their classmates better on a regular basis, not just one week out of the year.

Time Lines and Shadow Boxes

Students, no matter how young or old, enjoy looking back at their lives so far. Two techniques are ways to represent key events in a child's existence. One approach takes a chronological look, with students labeling and drawing (or symbolizing) key events in their lives along a calibrated line. Dates for activities common to all (birth, first day at school) join with unique experiences to represent children's lives. Another approach that works well with upper-grade students is to construct a shadow box as a math project (e.g., a gift box with paper dividers that create 9 or 12 compartments) and then use cardboard, clay, and other materials to create 3-D representations of key events. The narratives (written and/or spoken) that accompany each shadow box allow students to know each other better and better.

PROMOTING SOCIAL SKILLS

In addition to gaining skill in conflict management, some typical areas for social growth include communication, cooperation, and perspective taking. They can be incorporated into lessons of all kinds, but they are important aspects of literacy learning. Lessons may directly focus on aspects of all.

Communication

Although people send and receive messages through a wide variety of techniques, the ways that impact group work are, basically, speaking and listening. Not that writings, drawings, gestures, and music do not communicate. They do. But I leave the task of exploring those media to other books. Speaking and listening are interactive within each individual. What you hear is what you get, and it does not always match perfectly what was said. Even when only one speaker interacts with one listener, distractions of all sorts enter in to prevent the audible signals from registering fully.

Listening

Being a good listener is not only good for students and teachers for academic reasons but also a fine way to cement relationships. To listen well also includes some attributes that have more to do with mind than with ears. One strategy is to appreciate others' appearances. Do not allow your own attributions about dress, skin, disability, and other outward signs color what you are hearing. Look as you listen, for the movements and gestures of the other individual will signal the meanings of some items. Do not, on the other hand, expect another person's gestures or eye contact to match your expectations. Cultural differences are prevalent, and you are best off not expecting direct eye contact from most students. Also, do not tune out if the other person does not get to the point or stick to the point in the fashion you like. Addition of background or side narratives is common to many cultures. Finally, take time and do not jump to conclusions. Ask for clarifications when you are not sure you have heard or understood (Cushner, McClelland, & Safford, 1992).

Speaking

The talk that teachers use with students can set the tone and make a difference (Garmston & Wellman, 1998; Ginott, 1972). Although talk is a key indicator of power in group settings, it is also a signal of affection. Speak slowly enough to be understood but quickly enough not to distract or bore listeners. Enunciate, especially if the listener knows your language as his or her second language. Put yourself in the listeners' shoes. Are there things going on in the context that would be distracting? Do you need to change the scene, close the door, or use different vocabulary? Ask how you are doing. A polite request for questions is one way to encourage feedback.

Cooperation

As Johnson and Johnson (1999) explain, cooperation is positive interdependence. The attributes of cooperation include a focus on achieving mutual goals and maintaining effective relationships. Frequent, complete, and accurate communication needs to be accomplished. Group members need to perceive each others' positions and motivations and search for ways to accommodate each person's needs and feelings. Conflicts are solved as mutual problems. Trust allows the members to respond helpfully to others' requests and needs. The ways to accomplish these attributes include the following:

- Do your fair share of the work.
- Support, encourage, and praise one another.
- Discuss how goals are being met.
- Enter into discussions of better decision making, communication, conflict management, and shared leadership.

Perspective Taking

> *Fear is what distances us from our colleagues, our students, our subjects, ourselves.—PARKER PALMER*

A question that parents and teachers find themselves asking young people is "How would you feel if someone did that to you?" It is part of the ongoing efforts of individuals to promote empathy. Teachers themselves must engage in taking perspectives to promote the idea with students. Looking at situation through students' eyes is good to do on a regular basis.

One of the most painful experiences for students in school is being the victims of name-calling. Girls, in particular, are subjected to harassment. Students definitely want adults to take charge on this issue. Making sure that there is no doubt about what words are hurtful is one technique (Shakeshaft et al., 1997). The explicit rejection of names and labels is necessary. Nobody wants to be called whore, Miss Piggy, cow, greasy, or joker. One girl's account of a boy who tells girls, "I want you now," makes a point. He purposely embarrasses unpopular girls and make them uncomfortable. The teacher only says, "Joey, calm down."

Teachers can also invite students to look at things through their eyes as instructors. A caring teacher certainly works hard, but the students must understand that hard work is a sign of affection. Sharing information about life as a teacher can help bridge the gap that does exist. Teachers like to joke about how they don't sleep overnight under their desks at school, but they do not always remember to dispel false notions about their lives.

Perspectives are always altered by personal thinking and experiences. In her review of psychological literature, Thompson (1998) concludes that perspectives of caring are different for individuals in nonwhite and/or poor cultures as compared to concepts held by those who are white and privileged. As opposed to a vision of care as promoting family-style warmth, a caring black woman teaches young people how to survive racism, for example. Recognizing that manners are multicultural and that civility can come in varied formats, teachers have a role in promoting caring for the classroom culture. Recognizing that promotion of competence and autonomy, knowledge and power, are a big part of caring or affection is important.

INVOLVING PARENTS

The following narrative is from an interview with Sophia, a first-grade teacher who works with Spanish speaking students, including many new children who are immigrants. Sophia is bilingual and has a reputation for being a strong, caring teacher. Many of her children's parents came out for Back to School Night, which pleases her because she wants them to be well informed. Although the parents do not play a major role in their in-class activities, she believes strongly in the accountability of the parent.

Like I mentioned before, many times it's difficult to get a whole lot of participation from [parents] because they see the teacher as she knows best, she knows what she's doing—you just respect her and listen to her. And unfortunately, in some of the other countries, parent involvement is not welcomed, so they know once the child crosses that door or gate, they belong practically to the teacher, and all that they have to worry about is homework, if anything. They don't have parent conferences. They only look at their report card, and if they see that their child is below grade level, they might not even ever have a chance to talk with the teacher and find out why or even if they can help. I mean, you have situations from parents not living together to children who might be abused, to parents who make sure their children eat well and do their homework. You do find yourself as a teacher having to play many different roles.

I think when they come here they are surprised by the fact that I have a letter that introduces myself and what I expect, and that I want to see them here and I want to see them at Back to School Night. . . . I let them know that this is going to be a team effort. I'm not the only one in charge of their child's education. At home, they are going to have to work as hard as I'm working here to get their child to succeed. . . . [m]ake sure that you help him and I help him and you will see that this child takes off . . . does really well. It goes with . . . coming across as both our work, and I need your help, and, if not,

I'm going to be calling you and writing you and letting you know that I'm not alone in this.

Sophia feels that students within her first-grade class are not particularly aware of their respective social positions. Children speak of fathers in jail, the houses or apartments they live in, the pleasant life with horses and cows that they had in Mexico, with no apparent concern to weigh their words in speaking and listening. She contends that differences do occur, as the students get older and more aware of socioeconomic status and status in terms of time in the country. Families who are new to the country are more careful to keep the girls in; sewing and ironing are taught and expected. They are not permitted to spend time on the street or go out with boys. Many mothers of girls in higher grade levels do not permit them to associate with other girls outside school hours or go to their houses if there is any thought that they are too free or associate with gangs. At this age, she feels that all of the children are protected and treated somewhat equally.

When I asked about whether two students, Cynthia and Maria, come from very different literacy backgrounds, she expressed her opinion:

For these two, no, I don't think literacy is the problem. I think both sets of parents write and read and are fluent. I think the difference is the concern they have with school, the difference in responsibility and what they teach their children. With Cynthia, the parents were very concerned that she was in my classroom because her brother had been with another teacher and she had been such a good teacher. I wanted them to know what my program was all about and what I was expecting from their child and after that "Oh, fine, she can stay with you then." The teacher was going to be doing her job, because they are going to be doing their job as parents at home. Where, with Maria's parents I've noticed more concern with how does she behave, does she get along, does she have friends, is she happy. You know, she's a cute little girl, but if I approached Mom with "She doesn't know this," or "She doesn't know that and we need to work on this or that," Mom just thinks, "Oh well," . . . you just didn't teach it to her and why should she do anything about it at home?" So I think it's a lot of the attitude that they have toward education—what the teachers need to do or not.

I think it would help a lot if Maria had a lot of reinforcement at home— if she practiced and did the homework, and the family was interested in her learning and not just completing it and bringing it back. She entered this classroom without knowing letters or numbers. Now I think she can distinguish between the two, but she still has a hard time learning the rest of the letters and knowing what their sounds are. I think what she has down is the vowels, and that's a good start, but we're going to have to work now with the consonants. So, I think she's capable. She is developmentally young also.

She can very easily start a conversation on anything that has to do with new foods or something else . . . she loves to talk and participate, but she's going to need a lot more of a modified curriculum teaching approach.

Sophia's experience is not unusual. Working with parents who hold a wide variety of perspectives is a challenge that comes with teaching in this era. Letters and newsletters are an important part of the communication process. Although neatly written, professional letters from the teacher are important every once in a while, another way to get information home that "works" is when the children prepare the letter or newsletter. Parents enjoy seeing the children's writing and drawing. The children benefit from preparing the authentic communication. The communication is apt to be more effective because the children can explain what the message is all about in addition to seeing that their parents read it. It is a win-win idea. Just have the children write their "articles" neatly on 3×5 cards with black pen. Add a masthead, paste them up, and photocopy your pages. Do it weekly if you can. Every other week works. Monthly is all right. But do it. The benefits will come back to you and your students in many ways.

OFFERING REWARDS

Recognize Effort and Hard Work

The kinds of certificates and words that you bestow on students will be best if they honor students' hard work. Ability-based awards are not particularly inspirational. Everyone knows who the top reader is. The person who read eight chapter books last month, on the other hand, may deserve a pat on the back. A job well done and a goal hard won deserve attention. Research and writing about extrinsic versus intrinsic motivation lets us know that there are times and places and individuals who will respond to certain types of extrinsic tokens of appreciation. They are not wrong in moderation. Most everyone would agree, on the other hand, that a self-regulated student who seeks opportunities and works with interest and persistence is our aim.

Everyone knows the dangers of talking behind other people's backs. But the negative connotation is about *bad* things that are said. Making a practice of saying *good* things behind others' backs can make a positive difference. Call students' homes with compliments. Say something nice about a seventh-period student in second period. Thank a student for helping someone else in a loud voice. Know that teachers' words are powerful, but understand that some compliments are dangerous. Don't label a "schoolboy" or "schoolgirl" in a setting that would make it dangerous. Do not create scapegoat students as teachers' pets. But do not avoid compliments, either. Just make sure that you study the context before you proceed. Ask the students. Listen to the students. Each child could probably do a good job of explaining what award she or he deserves and how it could be given.

Give Compliments That Do Not Hurt Other Students' Feelings

In attending to the context, make sure that in saying good things to one individual, you are not slighting another. If you say, "Good job on your newspaper article" to one writer and not to the surrounding writers, you have demoralized several individuals. Instead, compliment the specific attributes that made the story unique and effective. Then try to give a general compliment.

Provide Value and Respect

We do a lot of talking about how our answers, our participation, *everything* is valued and needs to be respected. Therefore, what can we do when something's incorrect? Well, help the person, not tease the person, because we would not like that to be done to us. And, if it is correct, praise them because they are doing a good job, and it is very nice to hear other people praising your work and value that. Students are pretty much secure in being able to participate whether they are right or wrong. I try to pull those children who are not going to participate, who are not going to raise their hand and probably do not have the answer, either. But I try to work at letting them know that it is okay; they are here to learn, first. Second, if they make a mistake, that is no problem; and, third, they do have some of the answer—it is just a matter of getting up there and trying. Sophia believes that positive reinforcement is so important. She feels that her control comes through simple things—a look, a question. She feels that the children are used to authority and respect.

A MINIVIGNETTE

The students know that Lou is always going to say something funny during the lesson. They just do not know exactly when, but when it does come up, it *is* funny. Everybody who does not laugh at first catches on by the second time their teacher uses a joke. Only a few kids really laugh the first time Lou mentions that it is March 32 today. By the second time, though, they get that it his corny way to wish them a happy April Fools Day. Another bit of humor for the day comes in the context of backgrounding for the day's task of discussing criteria for the four-point rubric that will guide their story writing. The topic is developing feeling for your character. What character did you really care for? Lou reminds the students that he is not talking about Mexican coins when he talks about *pathos*. He comments, "He must have Castillian Spanish." Students laugh with him and then answer, reminiscing about their characters. One boy mentions Bilbo. A girl mentions Johnny Tremaine. A boy mentions the hero of *Hatchet* but cannot recall his name. When one girl brings up *Bridge to Terabithia*, everyone sighs or comments softly in some way at the mention of each character. They nod. They smile. The feeling tone is positive. The class is feeling good. Lou reinforces the notion, the emotion: "We've all been there. You *care* what happens to them!"

> When I got to class I felt at home and my worries were over. Now I know it's not just the outside; it's the inside and the people. I'm growing to like it on the first day and later on I'll love it (maybe).
> —HECTOR, A STUDENT, QUOTED IN JERVIS

▶ 14

Moving Forward

There is nothing more practical than a good theory.
—LEV VYGOTSKY

Whether the group is the whole class, a temporary partnership, or anything in between, the attributes for success are the same: the health of group life depends on successful problem solving, effective leadership, high expectations, productive norms, and group cohesiveness (Schmuck & Schmuck, 1988). To accomplish their challenging tasks, teachers will want to use multiple types of groupings over time, knowing that they must also become capable diagnosticians, planners, and action researchers. As they work with KPA, they will be wise to expect adoption of new procedures to take time. For example, literature circles and student-empowering activities are well known, but not well used in many classrooms. Change is always accepted by some individuals with ease, while meeting some anxiety and resistance from others.

In addition, implementation of any new practice requires personal and technical support along the way. School districts across the United States provide varying degrees of learning time for their teachers. Beyond needing time for training, they need time for thinking, time for reading, time for discussion and dialogue. For practitioners to adopt something as basic to KPA as a positive view of children's abilities, instead of seeing each child as a collection of possible difficulties, takes time. It comes as no surprise that old habits seem right even though they are simply comfortable.

If we look at 30-year chunks of literacy history, we see that the more education changes, the more it stays the same. As we set to work in the 21st century, we are engaged in a pursuit of critical reading ability for our students, but a look into the past tells us that this is not a new effort. As a matter of fact, each decade since the 1930s has had its avid pursuers. Few would disagree that we want students who can think well, act with kindness, and feel energized by school. But so did John Dewey and, undoubtedly, others before him. He was passionate about the necessity for more active, expressive, and self-directing factors for schools if they are to have any meaning for life. Joining head, heart, hands, and health has been a motto for many North Americans, not just 4-H members, for decades.

As Fawcett (1998) reminds us, change is difficult not only for teachers and schools, but for students as well. Students want to be cool, not nice, in many instances. Many of us can recall being adolescents. I was a teenager who spent time with a group of girls whose motto was *"Anybody* can be nice," as if it were a cheap commodity. Perhaps, in a KPA environment, thinking and learning, reading and writing, listening and speaking can become cool. Students know when work applies to real dreams and real life. They are able to express their preferences in meaningful evaluations when they are given the opportunity.

In studies of incoming college freshmen over the years, Alexander Astin has tracked millions of students. He identifies the most disturbing trend at the start of the 21st century to be disengagement—disengagement from civic life and from academic work. Astin sees the lack of motivation as tied to materialism and reminds us that if Tocqueville was upset by materialism 150 years ago as he wrote "Democracy in America," he would be appalled today. When he says, "We're neglecting our spiritual side, our values, the things we care about," he calls us to action (1999). Within days of Astin's interview, the newspapers were faced with reporting the Littleton, Colorado, high school massacre in which two students killed and wounded classmates and teachers. Public response decried the negative influences of violence in television and movies as well as the availability of guns. But, as researchers have confirmed, school violence occurs in spaces that are not "owned" by teachers or monitors or students (1999), and the individuals who commit the atrocities are disaffected, even though they may appear to be "typical" students in that their grades are fine, their families are middle-class, and they have two parents with "decent" reputations. I hope that this book and its ideas can help educators in their efforts to combat the problems surrounding disengagement. Although the focus for these chapters has been kindergarten through eighth grade, the message is one that can certainly travel far beyond those years.

The more we can link the work of the university to the practice of public schools, the better we will be able to join forces of informational and procedural knowledge. One type of knowledge does not presuppose the other, and many educators do, indeed, possess both. Unfortunately, practitioners are often accused of not having enough appropriate content knowledge; researchers are accused of lacking practical sense in their ivory towers. Both town and gown educators must continue to work together in partnership to merge theory and practice. Solutions will come more readily and infuse practice when everyone meets in the "ivory garage" (L. Aceves, personal communication, March 8, 1990). We are all researchers. We can inform one another as long as we speak in understandable terms. Only when we probe through multiple perspectives can we begin to touch truth.

Status is based on many factors in our society and public schools. Individuals who have read my applications of Taoist philosophy to teaching and parenting (Nagel, 1994, 1998c, 1998d) will understand how 81 concepts from more than 2,500 years ago can influence current thought. Power relationships between adults and young people need not be combative. Calm and simplicity are to be valued. Paradoxes are the norm. If we see the yin and the yang as dynamic interactive forces, we can avoid dualistic thinking. Eastern philosophy can provide models for democratic teaching.

Regardless of the group size or age, a prevailing classroom motto could be "It all starts right here." Those teachers who see their role as preparing their first graders for second grade or preparing their sixth graders for seventh are not looking at the big picture. The best groups are preparing children for life, not just for the next grade. Not that education is not developmental. It is. But that is the point, for educational development flows along a lifelong continuum of multiple threads, not of chunks and bits and parts. In preparing for life, second grade or seventh grade can do the same things, just at different levels. Insights for all levels come from thinking about young children in ways such as those described in *All I Ever Need to Know I Learned in Kindergarten* (Fulghum, 1993) and the work of the National Association for the Education of Young Children (NAEYC).

Teachers will find it easier to improve classroom relationships when other relationships are in order. From the faculty lounge to the schoolyard to homes of faculty and students, good groups are needed for adults as well as students. The principles for adults and children in their interactions are not all that different. Not that children are little adults. Far from it—they are active and exploratory. But the most obvious thing about engaged individuals is that they can focus on the components of a project and work at something for a long, long time. They "own" the projects and have some say in the tasks that compose the activity. They enjoy mapping out strategies that help them to meet the challenges that arise. They enjoy thinking and solving problems.

This book has been based on many findings from research done both recently as well as long ago. I believe that it represent truths about grouping practices. I hope that it serves to inspire and reaffirm individuals who are working with students at all levels. They already work with many effective groups.

In closing, I would like to share just a few, brief recommendations. The hardest part of making change, of creating something new, is usually getting started. Many individuals get out paper and pen, only to stare at it day after day, and go about their other business. Writer's block and "doers" block hold much in common. Although your own personality style may make taking risks difficult, I recommend just doing it. I will assume here that you have already tried several types of grouping activities. It is probably rather simple to identify one thing about grouping that is bugging you. Therefore, first, focus on one observable problem, even though you may see several difficulties. For example, try to deal with "Students don't complete their assigned projects," not "Our project groups never work." Next, knowing that you will not be able to change anyone else's behavior but your own, think of one practice that you can alter to solve the problem. Avoid the temptation to say, "I've tried everything." You have not.

Next, consider whether you have clear purpose(s), clear norms, clear roles, clear tasks, clear deadlines, and clear procedures for individual and group assessment. Examine whether you have been a clear and consistent model, truly caring about the project and your students. Think about the ways in which you truly empower your students. Think about the combination of members in the group. Then implement your change, following your own set of prescribed directions with care. Perhaps your change will be to make standards clearer, posting them on a chart for all to see.

Then, listen and watch. If you are too busy to listen and watch, change what you are doing and saying. You must take the time to observe clearly. Empowering your students means that they do more and you do less. Use a tape recorder or a video camera if you are able.

Next, analyze your results. If students work diligently and get along but still do not complete projects, you may have expected too much to be done in the allotted time. Your lesson design for the tasks needs adaptation, so make another change in your procedure and repeat the previous steps.

In the meantime, continue to learn. The reference list at the end of this book is lengthy and full of interesting readings that are written from a variety of perspectives. It lists many journals and organizations that are devoted to providing information and research related to grouping excellence, community, and equity. In addition, I recommend the following resources, because educators at all levels have a need for ongoing information and support. These groups provide materials that communicate across public school and higher education cultures. Also, each group's publications recommend other materials that readers will find valuable.

Association for Supervision and Curriculum Development
1250 N. Pitt Street
Alexandria, Virginia 22314

Developmental Studies Center
2000 Embarcadero, Suite 305
Oakland, CA 94606-5300

International Reading Association
800 Barksdale Road
PO Box 8139
Newark, DE 19714

National Council of Teachers of English
1111 W. Kenyon Road
Urbana, IL 61801-1096

Rethinking Schools
1001 E. Keefe Avenue
Milwaukee, WI 53212

This nonprofit, independent urban education journal is published four times a year.

Teaching Tolerance
400 Washington Ave.
Montgomery, AL 36104

This classroom magazine shares strategies and current ideas in its efforts to fight intolerance. Schools are able to order excellent book/video sets that are developed along a special theme each year.

Teaching for Change Catalog
Network of Educator in the Americas
P.O. Box 73038
Washington, DC 20056-3038

U.S. Committee for UNICEF
Education Department
333 E. 38th Street
New York, NY 10016

This group offers materials to develop international perspectives.

A journey of a thousand miles begins with one step.
—LAO TZU

APPENDIX A

Some Ways in Which Students May Be Grouped for Language Arts

Teacher-Led Groups	*Peer-Led Groups*	*"Leaderless" Peer Groups*
Twos:		
Assistance; tutoring	Peer tutoring	Dyads (pairs)
	Helping	Think-pair-share
	Echo reading	Coteaching
		Reading buddies
		Turn to neighbor
		Paper checkers
		Drill partners
		Composition pairs
		Computer partners
Small Groups:		
(3–5)		
Focus on	Committee	Cooperative groups
• skills	Family groups	Jigsaw
• ability		STAD
• interest		TGT
• choice		Group retelling
• discussion		Writing response
• task		Group reports
• social		Reader's Theater
• random		Learning centers

(continues)

Teacher-Led Groups	*Peer-Led Groups*	*"Leaderless" Peer Groups*

Larger Groups:
(7–10)   Use only when absolutely necessary.

Large:

Half-class	Half-class	Readarounds
Whole-class	Whole-class talks	Popovers

Also:

School Groupings	*Individuals*
Early bird–late bird	SSR (DEAR, USSR, etc.)
Multigrade structure	Independent writing
Pullout programs	Learning centers
Gifted and talented	Computer work
	Seatwork

Categories influenced by Stodolsky (1984) and Manarino-Leggett and Salomon (1989).

The KPA Model

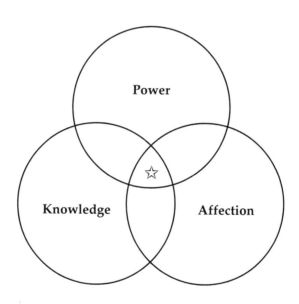

▶ APPENDIX C

Goals for Teaching

LEVEL 1: VISIONARY GOALS

People set instructional goals based on their value-based visions for what and how things should be. Individuals always act from their values, but those values may be hidden and unclear. If teachers work with their students, parents, and colleagues to develop a shared, clear vision of literate individuals, they will then be able set goals that are consistent with the vision and with one another.

Three possible broad categories envision students as becoming fulfilled adults:

1. Effective workers—Operational/workplace
2. Participants in a democratic society—Critical/political
3. Individuals who get along enjoy life—Cultural/daily life

LEVEL 2: BROAD GOALS FOR INSTRUCTION

1. The *social* family of models intend to expand students' ability to relate productivity to one another.
2. Models in the *information-processing* family seek to master information, retain it, organize it, and apply it as well as develop hypotheses and make inferences.
3. The *personal* family helps students learn about themselves, clarify their personal goals, and grow to contribute to their worlds.
4. In the *behavioral systems* family, models of direct instruction help students reach sequenced, organized behavioral objectives.

LEVEL 3: GROUP GOALS

Every group within the whole-class group also has its own goal(s). For example, when a class decides to write and perform a play for their parents, each group may carry out tasks to fulfill specific goals. Although the whole class is preparing a play for performance, one group may prepare scripts while another does costumes and others do staging, music, or acting. The composition and size of any group do relate to expectations for their work. Group goals connect to the tasks to be accomplished.

LEVEL 4: INDIVIDUAL GOALS

Good groups must have group goals but their members must also have explicit goals related to their work. Effective teachers recognize that not only do students have a variety of learning attributes, but they know that, as instructors, they have distinct styles and preferred approaches to instruction. Member goals can be set in collaboration with the teacher. Together, they can establish specialized outcomes within group learning situations. Good goal-setting with individual students can influence the ongoing dynamics of the class.

Characteristics of "Low" and "High" Groups

"LOW" GROUPS

- Differentiated status from labels that "stick"
- Inattentiveness of students
- Concentration on skills instruction
- Lack of access to the core curriculum
- Answering questions that require only low-level thinking
- Limited personal interaction with the teacher
- Overt criticism from the teacher
- Interruptions and distractions
- No self-selected silent reading

"HIGH" GROUPS

- Recognition of possessed talents and knowledge
- Intrinsically motivating instruction
- Wide assortment of good literature
- Seldom dwelling on skills
- Chance to enjoy and understand core pieces of literature
- Questions that require analytic and creative thinking
- Uncritical environment for the risks of speaking
- Treasured moments of literacy interactions
- Uninterrupted spans of silent reading in self-selected materials

High groups have problems too; their differentiated status mean that group members have limited physical and conversational access to other children and their ideas. That lack of proximity leads to lost opportunities for personal understanding and friendships. Flexible groups make a difference for high children in providing multiple opportunities for cross-status contacts.

Literacy programs need to offer multiple, flexible, heterogeneous grouping opportunities that

- recognize children for the talents and *knowledge* that they already posses;
- engage children through intrinsically *motivating* instruction;
- promote enjoyment of a wide *assortment* of good literature, including nonfiction, and not dwell on skill development;
- allow all children the opportunity to enjoy and understand *core* pieces of literature;
- engage students in thought about questions that require *analytic and creative thinking*;
- provide an *uncritical* environment that supports the risks of speaking;
- model for students that the moments of literacy *interactions are treasured*; and
- provide uninterrupted spans of time when *"silent" reading* in self-selected materials can take place.

APPENDIX E

Lesson Planning

Planning is a critical part of good teaching. Because good plans are designed with the situation (student and context) in mind, the process is usually time-consuming. Thoughtful planning considers lasting impact.

Teachers may select from many models of teaching to promote student growth in literacy. Indirect techniques evoke students' responses and are very important within motivating, meaningful education. However, one framework that is commonly used throughout classrooms in the United States is the Hunter model, named after educator Madeline Hunter. When students are expected to acquire explicit skills or information, direct instruction is called for. This model employs designated steps that assist in identifying and clarifying content for students to remember and apply. The model may be augmented with activities, questions, and expectations that also promote higher levels of thinking for the participating students.

1. ANTICIPATORY SET

How will you connect lesson content to students' prior knowledge and interest?

Many teachers combine questions ("Have you ever . . . ?" "What is . . . ?") with visual or tangible materials (overheads, photos, objects, etc.). The anticipatory set connects, but it also provides a shared experience for all of the involved students. Materials are ready, although not necessarily distributed at this stage.

Example: Teacher holds up the day's front page from the morning newspaper. "Boys and girls, many of you have seen newspapers at your home or for sale at a newsstand or a store. Have you ever read a newspaper article? (Elicit responses.) Today we are going to learn about an important guide that newspaper reporters use to write articles. You can use this handy guide to help you read and understand what you are reading as well. The guide we will learn about today is called 'The Five *W*s' I've brought newspapers from many days and places. You'll be able to cut your favorite article from the pages I give you today.

2. SET PURPOSES (OBJECTIVES)

What do you expect the students to achieve?

Direct lessons should be designed so that content is neither too easy nor too hard for the participating students. Teachers, over time, learn to expect certain outcomes from lessons that are tried and true. Good plans avoid elusive language or general outcomes such as "to understand." Teachers who invest time in careful decision making are able to write plans that make explicit what "understanding" really might mean.

Although most lessons can have objectives within all three domains of knowledge, power, and affection, the primary purpose should be clarified. Good lessons do not necessarily demand prior, measurable, behavioral objectives, but teachers are wise to clarify outcomes for themselves and their students. Well-designed experiences do promote changes in students and those changes may also be noted after the lessons.

Example: "At the end of today's lesson, I will expect you to know the Five *W*s—almost by heart—and identify where they are told in your news story."

3 / 4. INSTRUCTION

Ask yourself how you will provide access to information, through input or modeling.

Example, input: (List five letters on the overhead and fill in each word, giving a brief description of each.) "The Five *W*s stand for *Who? What? When? Where?* and *Why?* They are the common questions that every complete story must answer to convey the basic elements of a situation. When a reporter writes an article, the sentences flow as in a story. They don't just write answers, but they examine their writing to make sure they covered the important information."

Example, modeling: "First, we'll all read the same news story that I've copied for you. I'll read 'Killer Bees Here' aloud while you read silently. When I'm done, we'll all go back and hunt through our story to identify which sentence or sentences answer each *W*. I'll have you mark your article with a red pen. Remember, although we learn the Five *W*s in a certain order, that doesn't mean they appear in the story in that order."

5 / 6. CHECK FOR UNDERSTANDING WITH GUIDED PRACTICE

Monitor students' work as they begin to apply new skills and/or information. Coach individuals as to the techniques they employ. Use both complimentary and corrective talk.

Example: "We did a good job with that first story. Now, each of you needs to work alone on the story that I copied on the back of your page. Try to identify the Five Ws by yourself, but if you have a question you may ask your study buddy. I'll walk around to see how you're doing."

7. INDEPENDENT PRACTICE

Provide opportunity(-ies) for students to demonstrate their mastery of new learning. Although homework may be one typical way to get in practice, teachers want to make sure that students with difficulties or questions have a way to find appropriate answers.

Example: I think you've done a fine job with the sample articles. Now it's time to select an article from your newspaper. Take the first 5 minutes to choose your article, cut it out, and tape it to your writing paper. Then circle the sentences, draw arrows the way we did before, and write the Five Ws.

CLOSURE

Bring the lesson experience to an end; do not simply stop. One common way to come to closure is to elicit student responses to questions such as "What did we learn today?" This step allows students to reflect on their newly acquired knowledge.

Three Levels of Interdependence

INTERDEPENDENCE

Pooled

Sequential   O - O   O - O

Reciprocal   ⦿⦿   ⦿⦿

From Thompson (1967).

APPENDIX G

Using a Class Sociogram

All planning is time-consuming, but it is rewarding. Do not avoid this thoughtful process.

	Mary	Joe	Anh	Ceci	Tash
Mary		+		+	*
Joe	*				+
Anh		+		+	
Ceci	*	+	+		
Tash		+			

\--->

1. *In a private location;* write out a grid that lists all class members down the left side and again across the top. A portion of a class sociometric grid is shown above.
2. Announce that future classroom projects will require talking, listening, reading, and/or writing. Through interview or *confidential* survey, ask each child to name five classmates with whom he or she would like to work. Assure students that each will get to work with at least one of those friends during the various group times. Ask whether anyone would be difficult to work with.
3. Using the left-hand list, record each student's choices in the row for his or her name, marking a plus (+) under each name selected for positive reasons and an asterisk (*) to indicate a difficult match. Maintain *professional confidentiality* at all times.

    After you finish marking, note that the column beneath some students will have many marks of one sort or another; others may have few or none.

Note: The students' choices may be different from your predictions. This information will help you note which students are perceived very positively and could be leaders; some students are isolates and will need social assistance.

4. Establish groups.
   • Distribute leaders.
   • Distribute shy students and students who may be difficult to get along with.
   • Assure friendships.
   • Consider individual students' talents and prior knowledge. Use interest inventory information to inform your decisions.
5. Remind groups of norms:
   • Be concise.
   • Listen.
   • Reflect.
   • Contribute.
   • Respect others.
6. Work toward goals.

Adapted from Gibbs (1987).

Literacy Activities for a Democratic Classroom

Practices suggested here to help promote classroom democracy through student decision making and learning by doing. The list is not meant to be prescriptive, for in the hands of an authoritarian teacher, each and every practice could end up being quite UN-democratic. Each teacher's overall philosophy and day-to-day guiding beliefs allow for student voices to be heard—or not—and for their decisions to be ones that guide the process of task completion—or not.

Student Speaking / Listening

think-/pair-/share	councils	coaching
book groups	committees	student radio shows
literature circles	"Share & Stare"	book conferences
cooperative groups	peer tutoring	debates
inclusion opportunities	Speakers' Bureau	plays, Reader's Theater
class meetings	author's chair	guest speakers
book talks	student as teacher	student videos, TV shows
conflict resolution	"How To" talks	interviews

Student Writing

Daily News	job descriptions	photo essays
classroom newspaper	scripts	propositions
letters to the editor	constitutions	editorials
policies	class mission	consumer letters
critical essays	books	advertising/posters
prescriptions	Venn diagrams	charting
journals	"buddy" journals	e-mail
poetry	brainstorms	handbooks

Student Reading

student writings	book clubs	newspapers
self-select readings	class books	original documents
material on-line	pamphlets	research material
reader's theater	choral readings	poetry
cases		
teacher-selected readings		

Student Assessment

rubrics	self-correction	taping (audio, video)
peer editing	interviews	accomplishment lists
portfolios	letters	student-led conferencing

Strategies for Multicultural Teaching, A–Z

A *Asses* fairly in multiple ways.
B *Believe* in students.
C Appreciate *cultural* background of all.
D Understand language *development*.
E Provide *effective* feedback.
F Promote *family* participation.
G *Group* flexibly.
H *Help* develop social skills.
I Use *interactive* strategies.
J Teach *justice* and care.
K *Know* your students.
L Make *lessons* comprehensible.
M Promote *metacognition*.
N Have students *negotiate* meaning.
O Provide equal *opportunity* for access.
P Reduce *prejudice*. Understand *privilege*.
Q *Question* for high-level, critical thinking.
R *Read* multicultural literature.
S Elicit *student* goals and ideas.
T Align *texts* to children's needs.
U Promote *understanding* of others' ways.
V *View* the globe as our home.
W Provide a *win-win* atmosphere.
X Hold high *expectations*.
Y Reflect on *your* own culture.
Z Hold *zero* tolerance for put-downs.

Flanders Interaction Analysis—Categories to Consider

Teacher Talk

Indirect Influence

a. *Accepts feeling*—receives and clarifies student expressions of feeling, positive or negative, in a nonthreatening manner

b. *Encourages*—offers compliment or words of support for student actions, deeds; uses kind jokes (never at the expense of others) to release tension
"Go on. You can do it. That's all right."

c. *Accepts, uses student ideas*—develops or clarifies ideas suggested by a student; seldom used by ineffective teacher
"You mean. . . . Okay. . . . What else?"

d. *Asks questions*—Elicits answers from students about content or procedures; responses derived directly from lessons or based on inference or aesthetic response
"Why did that happen?"

Direct Influence

e. *Lectures*—gives facts, opinions about content or procedures; asks rhetorical questions
"Where do we go from here?"

f. *Gives directions*—orders students, who are expected to comply
"Set your pencils down and fold your hands."

g. *Criticizes or justifies*—makes statements intended to improve unacceptable student behavior; tells student what he or she has done wrong; tells why she or he (the teacher) is doing something
"I am preparing you for seventh grade."

Student Talk

h. *Responds*—student talk or contact that is initiated by teacher question or request
"It became the state of California."
i. *Initiates*—talk or action that comes from student without being directed; includes student questions and requests to talk
"May we go out to recess early if we're done?"

No Talk

j. *Silence or confusion*—pauses, short periods of quiet or confusion during which observer cannot detect oral communication

Five Rules for Group Discussions

- Be concise. (Stick to the topic or the task.)
- Listen. (Pay attention.)
- Reflect. (Repeat something from a previous person's comments.)
- Contribute. (Everyone is included.)
- Respect others. (Avoid blame, maintain confidentiality.)

Adapted from Cohen (1986), Epstein (1972), and Robinson et al. (1996).

Ways to Motivate and Promote Vocabulary Growth in Reluctant Learners

Edited by Delia Seligo Boehle, Margie Sauceda Curwen, and Greta Kallio Nagel

Thoughtful teachers know that all students, regardless of their socioeconomic backgrounds, are capable learners. Students' abilities to learn complicated new words have been proven time and again when teachers overhear the sophisticated language their students use when they discuss topics in which they are truly interested. For example, many children love to read and explain multisyllabic dinosaur names or discuss the character and scenarios portrayed in the Pokémon craze. Young children are able to articulate and manipulate many words and concepts efficiently and masterfully. They learn with ease because they are motivated by the subject and by the desire for connection with their peers.

Vocabulary learning is critical because students with limited knowledge of word meanings are at a great disadvantage for reading success, similar to those who have poor decoding skills. Rupley, Logan, and Nichols (1999) remind us "children's vocabulary knowledge closely reflects their breadth of real-life and vicarious experiences" (p. 337). Many students have not engaged in a wide variety of such experiences. In addition, students who have developed concepts in their first language may not possess the corresponding vocabulary in English. Garcia (1993) reminds us that "there is some evidence that the reading difficulties of limited English proficient students in the United States may be related directly to vocabulary knowledge (p. xx)."

Because personal interest is highly related to the amount and quality of learning that occurs, we share here a variety of learning experiences that our classmates in a graduate course in language study have used well over time with great success. We believe that the approaches all meet one or more of the following instructional criteria recommended by Nagy (1988): (a) integration, (b) repetition, and (c) meaningful use. Learning opportunities that incorporate *integration* access the students' prior knowledge about a particular concept before beginning study. By providing a foundation of understanding for the learners, teachers help their students attach new meanings to known words as well as acquire new words. *Repetition* provides students with numerous occasions to practice the word in a meaningful manner and use the word in multiple settings (Lapp, Jacobson, Fisher, & Flood, 2000). The third criterion, *meaningful use*, recommends that the learner be actively engaged in the learning process, hearing and speaking as well as reading and writing the word. Students will benefit from high levels of involvement. According to Nagy (1988), "Simply stated, the more deeply some information is processed, the more likely it is to be remembered" (p. 24). To develop students' English language acquisition, most activities include a verbal component to provide students with multiple speaking opportunities.

The contributors of the following activities are all practicing teachers with experience ranging from 3 to 20 years. The majority are employed in urban school districts that surround the university and serve students from lower-socioeconomic-status neighborhoods. Within their respective districts, more than 70% of the students receive free or reduced lunch, and English language learners exceed 50% of the student body.

MEANINGFUL "WORD USE IN THE COMMUNITY CIRCLE

MARGIE SAUCEDA CURWEN

This activity helps my primary grade students listen to one another and look for different ways to express themselves as they categorize and synthesize. I am pleased to have kindergartners and first graders become competent in speaking complete sentences and begin to rationalize their responses with reasons that incorporate key terms. Besides creating community, I see growth in student oral language, and student writing becomes more descriptive.

This activity is an enhanced version of the Daily Community Circle activity as described by Jeanne Gibbons in her book *Tribes*. Each morning, the students gather in a large circle on the floor. After I take care of housekeeping issues such as lunch count and attendance, we acknowledge and publicly celebrate individual student achievements. Each day we have a "question of the day." I model the technique and ask open-ended questions such as "How do you feel about the weather today?" or "In yesterday's science lesson, what was your favorite part about flying kites?" Each student has an opportunity to respond by using a complete sentence. I use rich vocabulary related to the topic and encourage the students who do. After a few weeks, I am able to turn over the responsibility of selecting the question of the day and the management of the Daily Community Circle to student volunteers.

VOCABULARY CARDS

DELIA SELIGO BOEHLE

Because this activity offers my students multiple opportunities to practice and discuss their words, I find that our class conversations often include target vocabulary words and students are able to use these words in context with speed and accuracy.

Each week, students write target vocabulary words on the front sides of 3×5 cards. The back side is divided into four sections. (See sample.) Students write a synonym for the target word in the first section, draw a picture of the word in the second section, use the word in a complete sentence in the third section, and write the part of speech in the fourth section. If a word has more than one part of speech, it is noted, and we are sure to talk about it in class.

The class uses these cards to practice. They quiz each other, or they may practice by themselves. The goal is to master all of the target words. Each child has a manila folder with an envelope glued onto each side, one labeled "Words I Know" and other "Words I Don't Know (Yet)." They are well used.

THE LOST ART OF LETTER WRITING

PEGGY RABE

Helping the students recognize their own and each other's strengths and having them draw on them in class helps define them as individuals and helps us build community in our room. Not only am I interested in what they have to say, but the students enjoy reading about each other, finding similarities and points of interest. Our letters have opened up channels of communication; students are able to go straight to the source (the author) to clarify meanings of words and broaden their own reading and writing vocabularies.

Each year I ask the students to write to me to give me a better understanding of who they are.

From just this one assignment, I was able to find out that one boy not only enjoys video games, but he even built a computer for his mom. His favorite game is "Boulder's Gate." He enjoys reading every night before his 10 o'clock bedtime too and was reading *Harry Potter in the Chamber of Ghosts.*

BEAT THE TIMER AND MAKE NEW WORDS

JENNIFER TOWNSEND

Lessons are more effective when my young students are active. It is wonderful to see my student's enthusiasm for arranging letters for words as they develop skills with sound and meaning. As we end the year, it is a great challenge to see how many different words students can make using letters from the day's lessons and see whether anyone can use all the letters to make one word. I can monitor to assess which students are using the correct letters.

The activity combines ideas that I have used over time with my second-language learners. When my students become familiar with the "Beat the Timer" routine, they rush to their seats to begin with just my mention of the activity. They all have bags in their desks containing cards with the letters of the alphabet. Their first job is to put the mixed up cards in alphabetical order on their desks and recheck them before the timer rings. Children who want help may ask other students if they finish early. Over time, the amount of time goes from 8 minutes to 3 minutes for my first graders.

Once the cards are in order on desks, I model words with large alphabet cards in a pocket chart in the front of the room. I tell them how many letters they need for the word and how many to exchange for a new word. Then students tell me what sounds (letters) they hear in the words, and I put them in the chart as they use the letters on their desks to make the words. We check my word and their words. They spell my word and their words. They say my word and their words. If everything matches, we define the word and move on to the next one.

VISUALIZING THE CHARACTER

BARBARA RUST

I am pleased by the interesting and appropriate vocabulary that emerges in my students' stories when we do visualization. The process of sharing along the way allows students to learn from one another and expand on their own ideas.

The activity is part of a sequence of visualizing activities I use to help my young students prepare for writing entire stories. After we brainstorm ideas about the term *character* during the prewriting stage, I model drawing a character on the overhead and think out loud, jotting down descriptive vocabulary words by my person. Students help me think of a name, age, color of hair and eyes, hairstyle, height and weight, and type of clothing, and decide the problem that needs to be resolved in the story. Then students draw pictures of the characters they want to write about, carefully labeling them. At the end of the planning session, we hold a modified author's chair time for students to share their characters and the words that will eventually appear in their stories. Then we repeat the process, adapting it to visualize the setting, visualize the plot with a flow map, and then pull it all together. We take several day to prepare.

WHAT IS IT?

MARY GIVENROD

My young children always respond enthusiastically to this guessing activity. They need to ask questions to figure out what object is hiding in a brown paper bag. Many teachers will recognize this game, but I add a written record of our questions and answers each time so that it allows practice in reading new vocabulary and helps with student's recall and reasoning. I put the secret object into a bag marked "What Is It?" Then as the children ask questions, I record their questions on chart paper. "Can you eat it?" I write my answers as well: "No you can't eat it."

Students attend to the print as I record our ideas. They learn that a question differs from a statement. Beginning readers feel successful reading along as I incorporate some of the same text in questions and answers. This activity is a good way to introduce a new theme that we are about to study; I also use it to share an object whose name contains a sound that we are studying.

CONTENT TEACHING

LINDA PHILLIPS

One of the ways I emphasize new vocabulary for my first graders is through content teaching. For example, science lessons allow us to enrich reading vocabulary as the children learn new concepts. I particularly enjoy teaching about the water cycle. I have my students notice the syllables in the long new words (evaporation, condensation, precipitation, etc.). We discuss their meanings, and they draw pictures to represent the various ideas. I have used preprinted materials that provide visuals for key vocabulary words. The children also read about the cycle in small books with tapes. Then we learn a water cycle song. The additions of rhythm, rhyme, and repetition help the children adopt the words. We also prepare a class bulletin board, and the students write about the water cycle in their journals. From then on, we expect our daily "weather person" to include new vocabulary in the class report each morning.

PARAPHRASING ELIZABETHAN ENGLISH INTO MODERN ENGLISH

CAROL MILLER

I have found a process that helps my adolescents deal with Shakespeare's diction, vocabulary, and rhyme scheme. It has been successful in my advanced English classes as well as with my new English language learners. I simply adapt the pace and level of assistance.

We begin by talking extensively about the changes in language since Shakespeare's day. For example, modern order is reversed as in Capulet's speech in Act I of *Romeo and Juliet:* "Why call you for a sword?" instead of "Why do you call for a sword?" Archaic forms of pronouns (*thou, thee,* or *thy*) are often used for *you* and *your.* Past tense forms do not always agree with modern usage as in *holp* for *helped* or *have spoke* for *have spoken.* I point out that linguists study a group of English speakers in an isolated area of the Appalachian Mountains whose speech is close to Elizabethan English.

Then students examine a Friar Lawrence speech that has been "translated" into modern English: "What early tongue so sweet saluteth me?" becomes "Who is talking to me so early this morning?" Each student chooses a monologue to translate into current English. Students put translated lines below the original words or put the old version in a column in the left, the new version to the right. We use the computer lab on campus, where students spell-check and print final copies. Their involvement with the language gets them to engage with the actual text; they deal with Shakespeare's poetry on a personally interpretive level, and they feel proud of themselves for accomplishing a difficult task. Those who choose to earn extra credit memorize their speeches for their classmates' enjoyment. One student's Romeo asked, "What's that soft light in that window?" ("But soft, what light through yonder window breaks?")

GAME SHOW

BEAU HEISS

The "Vocabulary Game Show" is a great way to review vocabulary words from a unit of study. It is similar to a popular television game show. All students interact with language and help each other understand vocabulary. It enhances the students' verbal skills, requires quick thinking, and develops new ways of describing a concept. Vocabulary words can be taken from any content area or unit of study. While students are having fun in this fast-paced (and sometimes quite noisy) activity, the teacher has the opportunity to observe and assess how well the subject matter has been understood.

The class prepares by lining up in two rows, with each student facing a partner. The object of the game is for students to quickly identify vocabulary words. Partner A has a stack of five vocabulary word cards (no definitions). He or she helps Partner B quickly identify a vocabulary word by providing them as many synonyms and descriptions as possible. When a pair successfully identifies all the vocabulary words in their stack, they raise their hands and wait. When every pair has finished, all Partner A students move to pair with a new partner and get a new stack of vocabulary words. After Partner A students have had the opportunity to describe their words, the game starts over. This time, however, Partner B students have the chance to describe the words.

FIVE SENSES POEMS

LINDA REABE

Searching for ways to combine social studies and poetry, I combined an old favorite, the "Five Senses Poem," with the fourth grade social studies topic of California regions. Students enjoyed collecting the words and constructing the phrases. They listened to the lyricism and playfulness of the words. They wrote marvelous poems that they enjoyed sharing with each other so much that they decided to make a class book. With the success of this activity, I plan to repeat it with Diane Siebert's book *Sierra* and compose diamante poems. The activity met our district standards in language arts, history/social sciences, and English language development.

First I read aloud the book *Mojave* by Diane Siebert. Our class brainstormed words and phrases for each of the senses. We constructed phrases that included descriptors such as "boom of thunder," "braying of donkeys," "hooting of owls," "grittiness of sand," "sweet smell of flowers," "colorful mustangs," and "sweet taste of fresh rain."

MORNING OPENING

VERONICA SULLIVAN

This activity empowers students and brings them into the classroom community as it generates participation. My students thoroughly enjoy having classroom jobs, and they learn to make announcements with confidence each day. This is demonstrated by the volume and clarity with which they begin to speak. I have noticed that second-language learners begin to feel more at ease in the classroom and are all able to join in. The confidence they gain from their verbal participation and their job responsibilities carries over into their academic areas and social interactions.

Each student in the class is assigned a job such as morning leader, calendar, poem of the month, and flag salute. For each job, the student has a specific sentence of introduction. For example, the morning leader may start with "Good morning, boys and girls! Will the monitors please take their positions?" Students must use complete sentences. To help shy students at first, the teacher may pair each one with another student. In the beginning, the students can follow the "teacher scripts." Once they become comfortable with the different jobs, they develop their own voice. As students finish their announcements, they can remain standing or take their seats. The teacher lists the different jobs and can rotate jobs weekly.

TRIPLE PHASE VOCABULARY STUDY

JERROD SAVALA

Noticing that my students were capable of learning word definitions but not always using the word correctly in context, I developed this three-part vocabulary study. Since using this method, I have seen my adolescent students gain a better understanding of their vocabulary words through their writing and test scores. I have observed the clarity and precision in their writing as they select and use words that have greater impact.

In phase 1, students work together to learn the definition of a word selected from their social studies and literature. They must learn how to use the word in context. In phase 2, students take a test on their vocabulary knowledge. They must show how to incorporate their new vocabulary words in their writing. In phase 3, we read passages aloud from a variety of books that incorporate new words. The students' vocabulary knowledge is reinforced, for as we read aloud from these books, they have opportunities to see words in a different setting, reinforcing the word's usage and their understanding.

ILLUSTRATED VOCABULARY

LORRI J. OLIVER

This intensified vocabulary instruction has increased my students' oral communication skills as well as improved written work. They begin to use new words in classroom interaction and daily written journals. This plan not only helps second-language learners, but is also easily adapted throughout all content areas. By increasing individual understanding of the English language, learners of all abilities and grade levels can expand their knowledge of words.

This activity is a modification of the vocabulary builder strategy from *Content Area Literacy* by Readence, Bean, and Baldwin (19xx). Students fold white paper into quarters. Then each student: (a) selects a new vocabulary word from a teacher-prepared list and writes it in the upper-left square, (b) writes the definition in the lower-left square, (c) draws a picture of what the new word means in the upper-right square, and (d) writes a synonym in the lower-right square. This technique encourages students to master dictionary and glossary skills, locate synonyms in a thesaurus, and create meaningful association to real life though personal illustrations of their newly learned vocabulary. A "Class Book of Vocabulary Words" may be created by binding pages together either alphabetically or by a specific content area.

We have learned that teachers must promote interesting instructional opportunities in order for students to develop rich vocabulary resources. In-depth word knowledge will increase readers' comprehension of texts and attentive reading of a wide array of understandable texts will increase vocabulary (Nagy, 1988; Rupley et al., 1999). Methods may be direct or indirect; both bring success. Therefore, in closing, we add that in addition to using guided activities and reading, all of us have our students participate in some form of self-selected reading. The most popular acronyms are still SSR (sustained silent reading) or DEAR (drop everything and read). Our students read for many minutes each day, adding to their vocabularies as they go.

APPENDIX M

Advice to a Dialogue Journalist

Writing back and forth with a "real" person is motivating. Length and detail in writing seem to be enhanced when the following conditions exist. These ideas stem from a longitudinal study of a cross-age journaling project (Nagel & Kellerman, 1995), but they should have carryover to a pen pal or e-mail correspondence as well.

1. Compliment your partner in *genuine* and specific ways. If your partner seems to be very different from you or even "difficult," try even harder to be complimentary.
2. Embed personal life stories within your regular conversations.
3. After modeling narratives, ask open-ended questions such as "Has anything like this happened to you?" "What are your plans for the summer?" "What was your spring vacation like?" "What is a day at your school like?"
4. Highlight your questions in such a way that you get your partner's attention; do not rattle on with a series of questions.
5. Make sure that your partner can understand your handwriting.
6. When your partner is new to English, do not use cursive writing; use printing. Use simple vocabulary and add pictures to your writing.
7. Share the books and poems you enjoy.
8. Teach your partner how to do something or about something.
9. Discuss your experiences at a level that your partner can understand.
10. If you do not understand something, ask. If your partner does not respond to your questions in a way that you understand, ask others (in your own class) to help you.
11. Notice how your partner signs off, such as "Yours truly" or "So long for now." Use that closing as a possible model,
12. Share photos and plan to meet your partner face to face, for what you think you know from the written word is not always the full reality.

APPENDIX N

Caring for Kids

- Know all of your students' names, and pronounce them correctly.
- Establish a comfortable climate; smile and chat.
- Listen to your students.
- Agree on classroom procedures, and teach explicitly.
- Teach social skills through role play, stories, and cases.
- Make sure that all students have appropriate academic challenges.
- Give authentic responsibilities beyond academic work.
- Clarify your high expectations.
- Arrange the classroom with purposes in mind.
- Avoid total emphasis on products; honor process.
- Display students' creative work, especially writing.
- Give prompt feedback, return papers quickly.
- Incorporate opportunities for peer feedback.
- Involve students in self-assessment.
- Appreciate the family obligations of students.
- Encourage them to reach out to others and honor classmates.
- Respect and enjoy your students.

Glossary

ability grouping   Procedure of placing students in materials and group meetings according to similar levels of intelligence or similar achievement test/assessment results. Also known as *homogeneous grouping*; usually refers to groups within a class. When whole classes are ability grouped, the procedure is usually known as *tracking* (or *streaming*).

affect   Emotion; may be positive or negative

affection   Belonging, care, and understanding; listening to someone else; an attitude of respect and high expectations for self and others; trust.

aliteracy   State of *choosing not to* read as compared to *not being capable* of reading as in illiteracy

"Babies"   Also known as *blockers* in group dynamics; characterized by attitude of noncooperation; may appear as laziness; along with "Bullies" and "Bozos," one of the types of individuals who damage positive group dynamics; one of the groups of "spoilers"

basal reader   Reading textbook designated for a certain grade level

behavioral objective   A stated, anticipated, specific outcome for a lesson; includes anticipated performance and degree of success; relates to specific behavior; contrasts with more general goals, purposes

book club   A group formed to read, discuss, and write about a common piece of literature

Bozos   Also known as *playboys*, characterized by irrelevant behavior or horseplay

Bullies   Also known as *aggressors*, characterized by dominance and lack of listening to others

choice group   Group membership of those who select the same option, such as the piece of literature, the activity, or the other partners

class   A group of students organized for instructional purposes, usually under the guidance of one teacher.

coercive power   Comes when someone has the authority to assign consequences of a negative nature.

cognitive flexibility   Addresses the need for multiple schemata to deal with
multiple perspectives and complex interrelationships

cohesion (cohesiveness)   Loyalty, ongoing membership, closeness, and trust
within a group; "sticking together" and "sticking it out"; builds on common interests, prestige, attractiveness of other group members

collaboration   Group interaction, discourse, to accomplish goals; goes beyond
side-by-side work completion; another way to describe reciprocal interdependence

committee   A group with three or more students assigned to work with a
leader to reach a specific goal(s)

community   Cohesiveness that develops when K, P, and A are strong for
members of a group.

competence   Internalized knowledge

cooperative learning   Any group pattern that permits students to interact,
working together to achieve group goals; best assessed with measures of
group and individual accountability

coteaching   Arranged instruction in which one partner learns thoroughly one
aspect or a procedure or a concept and then the two teach the pieces to
one another

cueing systems (multiple cueing systems)   Readers' interactive patterns in
using signals from word order, word meanings, and written symbols for
sounds (syntax, semantics, and graphophonics)

dame school   A private school for groups of young children; held in a
woman's home during colonial days in U.S. history

dialogue group   Members gathered to share ideas surrounding a concept, a
piece of literature, or a new idea

discourse   Oral or written communication; conversation

discussion group   Members gathered for purpose of responding to a piece of
writing through focused talk, usually through student answers to teacher's
questions requiring thought, but with student-to-student talk as well

drill partners   Two students who quiz one another on bits of information,
such as single words, for purposes of enhancing accuracy and speed of
recognition

dyad   One student with another individual, usually a student

early bird–late bird   Classroom scheduling pattern in which half of students
come at an early time and leave early and the other half arrive late and
stay late

echo reading   A strong reader reading with a less fluent partner in synchrony,
following the second student's gliding finger, ignoring words that are
skipped or mispronounced

empathy   In-depth understanding of another person's feeling and thinking in
groups of any size; the highest in the order of objectives for thinking.

empowerment In classroom contexts, authority of students to help select materials, ways of learning, arrangement of tools and time; within school contexts, similar authority of teachers

engagement Emotional involvement

esprit de corps Refers to the "team spirit" that can apply to feelings of group identification, regardless of the group size; builds morale by enhancing the attractiveness of members to one another; fosters uniformity of behavior and persistence of group membership

eu-stress Stress that is at a level to be motivating rather than debilitating; can vary from individual to individual

expert power Influence achieved by those who are knowledgeable and enthusiastic; bestowed on someone with informational and procedural knowledge that can be shared with others

family groups Three or more students of various ages and abilities working together, usually with the leadership of the eldest; common in multigrade-structure classrooms

flexible grouping The practice of designing multiple types of groups for multiple purposes with multiple memberships; groups that change over time

grade levels Ordered divisions within schools formed by students' ages or achievements; kindergarten, first grade, second grade, and so forth

grammar school In U.S. parlance, an elementary school for a large town; also British

group reports Oral or written nonfiction exploration of a topic, usually done as a pooled or sequential activity

group retellings Reciprocal responses to a piece of literature, re-creating the story through summary of key events

guided reading Instruction in which teacher provides structure, purposes, questions, and activities for lessons; directed reading

helping One student giving assistance to another on a temporary basis, usually with assignments involving written expression

heterogeneous grouping Forming clusters of students with a variety of skills and/or levels of intelligence

homogeneous grouping Forming clusters of students with similar levels of skills and/or intelligence

idiographic roles The variable parts played by individuals because of attributes that come with personal characteristics—for example, a motivator, a taskmaster. Also see *nomothetic roles.*

inclusion Placement of all individuals, regardless of abilities, within the same classroom

interest group Membership based on students' expressed or observed preferences and talents

jigsaw A type of cooperative group engaged in learning through a process whereby group members each learn an important part of the informational puzzle, usually in a study group, then gather to teach one another their respective key ideas

knowledge   The demonstration of expertise that is respected by the group and useful to the group's purpose(s); the possession of information or access to resources

KPA   Knowledge, power, and affection; three bases for group cohesiveness

KWL   Strategy first proposed by Ogle (1986) and used as a way to evoke prior knowledge, ask questions, and review: what I *know*, what I *want* to know, and what I *learned*

learning centers   Special areas established within the classroom for groups of students to do special activities related to a central theme or topic; may also be visited by individuals

legitimate power   Influence that is bestowed by an individual's designated title, rank

morale   When positive, allows group members to keep members going; characterizes any group with a sense of solidarity, seeing the glass as half-full instead of half-empty

multigrade structure   When students of two, three, four, or more traditional grades learn together in the same classroom; usually with emphasis on individual and group learning; also called *nongraded.*

nomothetic roles   Formalized, institutionalized duties. Also see *idiographic roles.*

open classroom   A style of teaching that uses space, grouping, and time flexibly with varieties of learning materials, integrated curriculum, and activities that permit student choice

paper checkers   Partners who examine one another's papers for correctness

peer tutoring   One student helping another, often to achieve academic goals; also known as cross-age tutoring when the tutor is from another grade; can be occasional or ongoing

pooled interdependence   A group situation in which all members can contribute to the whole, but like individual swimmers in a pool, do not necessarily interact; a form of cooperation, but individuals do separate parts of a larger project—for example, students writing separate sections of a newspaper that are combined into a final, published product

power   Having the opportunity to make decisions and have influence; having choice as well as a voice; having rights and responsibilities along with a vote; social justice; being listened to.

pullout programs   Special learning opportunities that require children to leave their regular classrooms; may be for purposes of learning English as a second language, help for children with learning disabilities, or Title I.

readarounds   Writing peer response activities in which all students' unidentified papers are shared around the class through a methodical passing procedure

reader response theory (Rosenblatt, 1994)   Distinguishes between responses to literature that are efferent (examining text-based facts such a plot, characterization, setting, climax) and responses that are aesthetic (going beyond the stated knowledge of the text to link personal evaluations and promote creative synthesis)

Reader's Theater Oral reading of a play, poem, or piece of literature done with dramatic expression but not with costumes or staging

reading buddies Two students who read to one another, taking turns in some prearranged way

reading level The ability to pronounce and understand words from written materials; include instructional (challenging, but appropriate), frustrational (too difficult), and independent or recreational (easy, fluent); accuracy often suggested for instructional level: word identification at 95%, comprehension at 75%

reciprocal interdependence A group situation in which all members interact, their work affecting the work of one another, collaboration

referent power Influence bestowed on individuals who are respected and liked because they are trustworthy, concerned, and fair and whose leadership is characterized by warmth and competence.

response group A group gathered to express reaction to writing through interpretive, creative expression

reward power Influence bestowed on an individual who has the ability to give awards and rewards and has the capacity, through words and actions, to enhance the power of others

scaffolding Support (activities such as questions, feedback, modeling, telling) provided by a knowledgeable adult or peer in an informal meeting with a student; provides a bridge of oral and/or written assistance in reaching next point of conceptual or procedural understanding; occurs within Vygotsky's (1978) zone of proximal development.

schema (e.g., Anderson, 1985) (plural: schemata) The structure that organizes long-term memories (prior knowledge) and is changed by adding new information through assimilation or replacing old ideas with new (accommodation); schemata grow and change as individuals acquire new knowledge

seatwork Other individual work, such as fill-in writing and worksheets

self-involvement Occurs when the norms of the group become internalized as the norms of the individual member

sequential interdependence A group situation in which one member must perform his or her task before the next person (writing, illustrating, presenting a poem). Members may interact during the process; their roles are more like those of relay teams in track and field events.

shared reading An instructional strategy, usually for early childhood education, in which the teacher shows a book and elicits response to print; interactive modeling, pointing, and explaining of reading strategies

sharing Presenting a written or oral story, often about an object or special event *skills group*   A temporary gathering of students to provide explicit instruction in a specific skill, such as using the question mark, choosing the right book, or finding words in a dictionary

sociopsychological   Involving social and psychological events; affected by both other people and the mind

SSR   The practice of reading quietly in self-selected materials through sustained silent reading; also known as DEAR (drop everything and read) or as USSR (uninterrupted sustained silent reading); typically occurs for 10 or 15 minutes to 30 minutes for older children

STAD   Student teams–achievement divisions; from the work of R. Slavin who states that heterogeneous groups work together to master material that has been presented by the teacher to increase their combined quiz scores through individual improvement, competing with other teams in the process

streaming   tracking (British)

talk (noun)   A speech to others about a specific topic

think-pair-share   Getting together to share ideas with one other person after both have had some time to think about their perspectives

tracking   Placing students in classes that are formed by ability

turn to neighbor   Using a nearby student to tell or do something in an informal manner

tutoring   Ongoing formal meetings with a student in sessions that are usually structured to promote academic growth

TGT   Teams, games, tournaments in which students gain similar mastery of material from a class presentation, but various contests of skill, not quizzes, test the individuals' achievements

writing groups   Based on the work of Peter Elbow, the process whereby group members read and listen to one another's writing and point out strong and interesting features to one another and suggest possible points for revision

zone of proximal development (Vygotsky, 1978)   The distance covered in going from what a student knows or can do independently to the point at which learning can expand through the assistance (scaffolding) of an adult or knowledgeable peer

References

Achilles, C. M. (1999). *Let's put kids first, finally: Getting class size right.* Thousand Oaks, CA: Corwin Press.

Adams, M. J. (1990). *Beginning to read: Thinking and learning about print.* Cambridge, MA: MIT Press.

Allington, R. (1998, December). *Exemplary Literacy Instruction in Fourth Grade.* An alternative format session at the 48th annual meeting of the National Reading Conference. Austin, TX.

Allington, R. L. (1983). The reading instruction provided readers of differing reading ability. *Elementary School Journal, 83,* 548–559.

Allington, R. L., & McGill-Franzen, A. (1989). School response to reading failure: Instruction for Chapter 1 and special education students in grades two, four, and eight. *Elementary School Journal, 89*(5), 529–542.

Allport, G. (1937). *Personality: A psychological interpretation.* New York: Holt.

Almasi, J. (1994). The effects of peer-lead and teacher-led discussions of literature on fourth graders' sociocognitive conflicts. In C. K. Kinzer & D. J. Leu (Eds.) *Multidimensional Aspects of Literacy Research, Theory, and Practice.* 43rd Yearbook of the National Reading Conference. Chicago: The National Reading Conference.

Almasi, J. (1995). The nature of fourth graders' sociocognitive conflicts in peer-led and teacher-led discussions of literature. *Reading Research Quarterly, 30*(3), 314–345.

Alvermann, D. E., & Dillon, D. R. (1991). Ways of knowing are ways of seeing. A response to Roller. *Reading Research Quarterly, 26,* 329–333.

Anderson, R. C., Hiebert, E. H., Scott, J. A., & Wilkinson, I. A. G. (1985). *Becoming a nation of readers: The report of the Commission on Reading.* Washington, DC: National Institute of Education.

Anzaldua, G. (1987). *Borderlands/La frontera.* San Francisco: Spinster/Aunt Lute.

Au, K. (1980). Participation structures in a reading lesson with Hawaiian children: Analysis of a culturally appropriate instructional event. *Anthropology and Education Quarterly, 11*(2), 91–115.

Au, K. (1993). *Literacy instruction in multicultural settings.* San Diego: Harcourt Brace Jovanovich.

Bachofer, K. V. (1990). *An alternative assessment sourcebook.* Unpublished manuscript, Claremont Graduate School.

Back, K. (1951). Influence through social communication. *Journal of Abnormal and Social Psychology, 46,* 9–23.

Bandura, A. (1977). Self-efficacy: Toward a unifying theory of behavioral change. *Psychological Review, 84,* 18–38.

Banks, J. (1995). Multicultural education: Historical development, dimensions, and practice. In J. A. Banks & C. A. McGee Banks (Eds.), *Handbook of research on multicultural education* (pp. 3–24). New York: Macmillan.

Banks, J. A., & Banks, C. A. M. (1993). *Multicultural education: Issues and perspectives* (2nd ed.). Boston: Allyn & Bacon.

Barr, M. (1995). Who's going to interpret performance standards? A case for teacher judgment. In *Claremont Reading Conference 59th Yearbook* (pp. 22–45). Claremont, CA: Claremont Reading Conference.

Barr, R. (1989). The social organization of literacy instruction. In *Cognitive and social perspectives for literacy research and instruction: The 38th yearbook of the National Reading Conference* (pp. 19–33). Chicago: The National Reading Conference.

Barr, R. (1995). What research says about grouping in the past and present and what it suggests about the future. In M. C. Radencich & L. J. McKay (Eds.), *Flexible grouping for literacy in the elementary grades* (pp. 1–24). Boston: Allyn & Bacon.

Barr, R., & Dreeben, R. (1983). *How schools work.* Chicago: University of Chicago Press.

Battistich, V., Solomon, D., & Delucchi, K. (1993). Interaction processes and student outcomes in cooperative learning groups. *Elementary School Journal, 94*(1), 19–32.

Battistich, V., Solomon, D., Kim, Watson, M., & Schaps, E. (1995). Schools as communities, poverty levels of student populations, and students' attitudes, motives, and performance: A multi-level analysis. *American Educational Research Journal, 32*(3), 627–658.

Bellah, R. N., Madsen, R., Sullivan, W. M., Swidler, A., & Tipton, S. M. (1985). *Habits of the heart.* San Francisco: Harper & Row.

Benne, K. D., & Sheats, P. (1948). Functional roles of group members. *Journal of Social Issues, 4,* 41–49.

Berger, J., Rosenholtz, S. J., & Zelditch, M. Z., Jr. (1980). Status organizing processes. *Annual Review of Sociology, 6,* 479–508.

Berk, L. E., & Winslert, A. (1995). *Scaffolding children's learning: Vygotsky and early childhood education.* Washington, DC: National Association for the Education of Young Children.

Berliner, D., Fisher, C., Filby, N., Marliave, R., Cahen, L., Dishaw, M., & Moore, J. (1978). *Beginning teacher evaluation study—teaching behaviors, academic learning time and student achievement: Final report of phase 11-B.* San Francisco, CA: Far West Laboratory.

Bernstein, B. (1972). A critique of the concept "compensatory education." In C. B. Cazden, B. John, & D. Hymes (Eds.), *Functions of language in the classroom* (pp. 135–151). New York: Teachers College Press.

Beyer, B. K. (1987). *Practical strategies for the teaching of thinking.* Boston: Allyn & Bacon.

Bloom, B. S., Engelhart, M. D., Furst, E. J., Hill, W. H., & Krathwohl, D. R. (1956). *Taxonomy of educational objectives.* New York: David McKay Company, Inc.

Bonner, H. (1959). *Group dynamics, principles and applications.* New York: Ronald.

Borich, G. D., & Tombari, M. L. (1995). *Educational psychology: A contemporary approach.* New York: HarperCollins College Publishers.

Bradford, L. P. (1978). Group formation and development. In L. P. Bradford (Ed.), *Group development* (pp. 62–78). San Diego, CA: University Associates.

Bristow, P. S. (1985). Are poor readers passive readers? Some evidence, possible explanations, and potential solutions. *The Reading Teacher, 39*, 318–325.

Bruner, J. (1983). *In search of mind: Essays in autobiography.* New York: Harper & Row.

Burns, R. B., & Mason, D. A. (1998). Class formation and composition in elementary schools. *American Educational Research Journal, 35*, 739–772.

Caine, R. N., & G. Caine (1994). *Making connections: Teaching and the human brain.* Menlo Park, CA: Addison-Wesley.

California State Department of Education. (1987). *English-language arts framework for California public schools.* Sacramento, CA: Author.

California Teachers Association. (1998). Making the case. *California Educator, 2*(8) 28–29.

Campbell, J. R., Voelkl, K. E., & Donahue, P. L. (1998). *Report in brief: NAEP 1996 trends in academic progress* (Publication No. 98-530). Washington, DC: National Center for Education Statistics.

Cherniss, C. (1998). Social and emotional learning for leaders. *Educational Leadership, 55*(7), 26–29.

Clay, M. (1985). *The early detection of reading difficulties.* Portsmouth, NH: Heinemann.

Cochran-Smith, M., & Lytle, S. (1993). *Inside/outside: Teacher research and knowledge.* New York: Teachers College Press.

Cohen, E. G. (1972). *Designing groupwork: Strategies for the heterogeneous classroom.* New York: Teachers College Press.

Cohen, E. G. (1982). Expectation states and interracial interaction in school settings. *Annual Review of Sociology, 8*, 209–235.

Cohen, E. G. (1986). *Designing groupwork: Strategies for the heterogeneous classroom* (2nd ed.). New York: Teachers College Press.

Cohen, E. G. (1994). Restructuring the classroom: Conditions for productive small groups. *Review of Educational Research, 64*(1), 1–35.

Coie, J. D., & Krehbiel, G. (1984). Effects of academic tutoring on the social status of low-achieving, socially rejected children. *Child Development, 55*, 1465–1478.

Cole, M. (1985). The zone of proximal development: Where culture and cognition create each other. In J. V. Wertsch (Ed.), *Culture, communication and cognition: Vygotskian perspectives.* New York: Cambridge University Press.

Coleman, A. D., & Bexton, W. H. (1975). *Group relations reader.* Sausalito, CA: GREX.

Collins, M. (1992). *"Ordinary" children, extraordinary teachers.* Norfolk, VA: Hampton Roads.

Connell, J. P., & Wellborn, J. G. (1991). Competence, autonomy, and relatedness: A motivational analysis self-esteem processes. In R. Gunnar & L. A Stroufe (Eds.), *Minnesota symposia on child psychology* (Vol. 23, pp. 43–77). Hillsdale, NJ: Erlbaum.

Cook-Gumperz, J., (1986). *The social construction of literacy.* New York: Cambridge University Press.

Cooper, H. B. (1989, November). Synthesis of research on homework. *Educational Leadership, 46*(3), 85–91.

Countryman, L. L., & Shroeder, M. (1996). When students lead parent–teacher conferences. *Educational Leadership, 53*(7), 64–68.

Csikszentmihalyi, M. (1990). *Flow: The psychology of optimal experience.* New York: HarperCollins.

Cummins, J. (1986). Empowering minority students: A framework for intervention. *Harvard Educational Review, 56,* 18–36.

Cummins, J. (1989). *Empowering minority students.* Sacramento: California Association for Bilingual Education.

Cunningham, P. M., Hall, D. P., & Defee, M. (1998). Nonability-grouped multilevel instruction: Eighty years later. *The Reading Teacher, 51,* 652–664.

Cushner, K., McClelland, A., & Safford, P. (1992). *Human diversity in education: An integrative approach.* San Francisco: McGraw-Hill.

Dahl, R. (1985). *A preface to economic democracy.* Berkeley: University of California Press.

D'Arcangelo, M. (1998). The brains behind the brain. *Educational Leadership, 56*(3), 20–25.

Darder, A. (1991a). *Culture and power in the classroom: A critical foundation for bicultural education.* New York: Bergin & Garvey.

Darder, A. (1991b). *What do Latino children need to survive in school? A study of four Boston public schools.* Boston: Mauricio Gaston Institute.

Deci, E. L., & Ryan, R. M. (1985). *Intrinsic motivations and self-determination in human behavior.* New York: Plenum..

Deci, E. L., & Ryan, R. M. (1990). A motivational approach to self: Integration in personality. In R. Dienstbier (Ed.), *Nebraska symposium on motivation,* (Vol. 38). Lincoln: University of Nebraska Press.

Delpit, L. (1995). *Other people's children.* New York: New Press.

Derry, S. J., & Potts, M. K. (1998). How tutors model students: A study of personal constructs in adaptive tutoring. *American Educational Research Journal, 35,* 65–99.

Dewey, J. (1966). *The school and society.* Chicago: University of Chicago Press. (Originally published 1900.)

Dewey, J. (1916). *Democracy and education.* New York: Macmillan.

Diamond, B., & Moore, M. (1995). *Multicultural literacy: Mirroring the reality of the classroom.* New York: Longman.

Dodge, B. (1989). *Interestingness.* Unpublished manuscript.

Dooley, N. (1991a). *Everybody bakes bread.* Minneapolis: Carolrhoda.

Dooley, N. (1991b). *Everybody cooks rice.* Minneapolis: Carolrhoda.

Dresser, N. (1996). *Multicultural manners: New rules of etiquette for a changing society.* New York: Wiley.

Eash, M. J. (1961). Grouping: What have we learned? *Educational Leadership, 18,* 429–434.

Edelsky, C. (1991). *With literacy and justice for all.* Bristol, PA: Falmer.

Eder, D., & Felmlee, D. (1984). The development of attention norms in ability groups. In P. L. Peterson, L. C. Wilkinson, & M. Hallinan (Eds.), *The social context of instruction: Group organization and group processes* (pp. 189–208). Orlando, FL: Academic Press.

Educational Research Service (1980). *Class size research: A critique of recent meta-analyses.* Arlington, VA: Author.

Edwards, P. A. (1995). Empowering low-income mothers and fathers to share books with young children. *The Reading Teacher, 48,* 558–564.

Epstein, C. (1972). *Affective subjects in the classroom: Exploring race, sex and drugs.* Scranton, PA: Intext Educational Publications.

Erlbaum, B. E., Schumm, J. S., & Vaughn, S. (1997). Urban middle-elementary students' perceptions of grouping formats for reading instruction. *Elementary School Journal, 97,* 481–500.

Fader, D. N., & McNeil, E. B. (1968). *Hooked on books: Program and proof.* New York: Berkley Pub.

Faltis, C. J. (1997). *Joinfostering: Adapting teaching strategies for the multilingual classroom.* Upper Saddle River, NJ: Prentice Hall.

Farnham-Diggory, S. (1994). Paradigms of knowledge and instruction. *Review of Educational Research, 64*(3), 463–477.

Fawcett, G. (1998). Curricular innovations in literacy instruction: How students respond to change. *Journal of Literacy Research, 30,* 489–514.

Fearn, L., & Farnan, N. (1998). *Writing effectively: Helping children master the conventions of writing.* Boston: Allyn & Bacon.

Felmlee, D., & Eder, D. (1983). Contextual effects in the classroom: The impact of ability groups on student attention. *Sociology of Education, 54,* 151–161.

Finn, J. D. (1989). Withdrawing from school. *Review of Educational Research, 59,* 117–142.

Flanders, N. A. (1970). *Analyzing teacher behavior.* Reading, MA: Addison-Wesley.

Flood, J., Lapp, D., Flood, S., & Nagel, G. (1992). Am I allowed to group? Using flexible patterns for effective instruction. *The Reading Teacher, 45,* 608–616.

Flood, J., Lapp, D., & Nagel, G. (1991). An analysis of the array of literature in district core selections. In J. Zutell & S. McCormick (Eds.), *Learner factors/teacher factors: Issues in literacy research and instruction: The 40th yearbook of the National Reading Conference* (pp. 269–276). Chicago: National Reading Conference.

Flood, J., Lapp, D., & Nagel, G. (1993, February). Assessing critical action beyond reflection. *Journal of Reading, 36,* 420–423.

Folger, J. P., Poole, M. S., & Stutman, R. K. (1993). *Working through conflict: Strategies for relationships, groups, and organizations.* New York: HarperCollins College Publishers.

Ford, M. (1992). *Motivating humans.* Newbury Park, CA: Sage.

Foucalt, M. (1980). *Power/knowledge.* New York: Pantheon.

Freire, P. (1993). *Pedagogy of the oppressed.* New York: Continuum.

Fulghum, R. (1993). *All I really need to know I learned in kindergarten: Uncommon thoughts on common things.* New York: Ballentine.

Galton, M., & Williamson, J. (1992). *Group work in the primary classroom.* New York: Routledge.

Gamoran, A. (1992). Is ability grouping equitable? *Educational Leadership, 50*(2), 11–17.

Garcia, G. (1993). Spanish-English bilingual students use of cognates in English reading. *Journal of Reading Behavior, 25,* 241–254.

Gardner, H. (1983). *Frames of mind.* New York: Basic Books.

Garmston, R., & Wellman, B. (1998). Teacher talk that makes a difference. *Educational Leadership, 55*(7), 30–34.

Gee, J. P., & Green, J. L. (1998). Discourse analysis, learning, and social practice: A methodological study. In P. D. Pearson & A. Iran-Nejad (Eds.), *Review of Research in Education, 23,* 119–169.

Get Along (1995, Aug. 3). *The Los Angeles Times,* p. A1.

Getzels, J. W., & Thelen, H. A. (1960). The classroom group as a unique social system. In N. Henry (Ed.), *The dynamics of instructional groups* (pp. 52–82). Chicago: National Society for the Study of Education.

Gibbs, J. (1987). *Tribes: A process for social development and cooperative learning.* Santa Rosa, CA: Center Source Publications.

Gilligan, C. (1982). *In a different voice: Psychological theory and women's development.* Cambridge, MA: Harvard University Press.

Ginott, H. (1972). *Teacher and child: A book for parents and teachers.* New York: Avon.

Glass, G. V., Cahen, L. S., Smith, M. L., & Filby, N. N. (1982). *School class size: Research and policy.* Beverly Hills: Sage.

Goldenberg, C. N. (1989). Parents' effects on academic grouping for reading: Three case studies. *American Educational Research Journal, 26,* 329–352.

Goleman, D. (1995). *Emotional intelligence.* New York: Bantam.

Good, T. L., & Brophy, J. E. (1973). *Looking in classrooms.* New York: Harper & Row.

Good, T. L., & Marshall, S. (1984). Do students learn more in heterogeneous or homogeneous groups? In P. L. Peterson, L. C. Wilkinson, & M. Hallinan (Eds.), *The social context of instruction: Group organization and group processes* (pp. 15–38). Orlando, FL: Academic Press.

Good, T. L., & Stipek, D. (1983). Individual differences in the classroom: A psychological perspective. In M. Fernstermacher & J. Goodlad (Eds.), *NSSE yearbook.*

Goodman, Y. (1985). Kidwatching: Observing children in the classroom. In A. Jaggar & M. T. Smith-Burke (Eds.), *Observing the language learner* (pp. 9–18). Urbana, IL: National Council of Teachers of English.

Gordon, J. (1966). Grouping and human values. In A. Morgenstern (Ed.), *Grouping in the elementary school* (pp. 103–112). New York: Pitman.

Gordon, R. (1997). How novice teachers can succeed with adolescents. *Educational Leadership, 54*(7), 56–58.

Graden, J. L., Thurlow, M. L., Ysseldyke, K. E., & Algozzine, B. (1982). *Instructional ecology and academic responding time for students in reading groups.* Ann Arbor: University of Michigan Institute for Research on Learning Disabilities.

Grant, C., & Sleeter, C. (1986). *After the schoolbell rings.* Philadelphia: Falmer Press.

Grant, L., & Rothenberg, J. (1986). The social enhancement of ability differences: Teacher–student interactions in first and second grade reading groups. *Elementary School Journal, 87,* 2–49.

Graves, M. F,. Graves, B. B. & Braaten, S. (1994). Scaffolded reading experiences for inclusive classes. *Educational Leadership, 53*(5), 14–17.

Gross, J. (1989). *Activities of the help-line.* Los Angeles: Milken Family Foundation.

Gudykunst, W. B. (1991). *Bridging differences: Effective intergroup communication.* Newbury Park, CA: Sage.

Haller, E. J., & Waterman, M. (1985). *The criteria of reading group assignments. The Reading Teacher, 38,* 772–781.

Hallinan, M. T. (1984). Summary and implications. In P. L. Peterson, L. C. Wilkinson, & M. Hallinan (Eds.), *The social context of instruction: Group organization and group processes* (pp. 229–240). Orlando, FL: Academic Press.

Hallinan, M. T., & Sorensen, A. B. (1985). Ability grouping and student friendships. *American Educational Research Journal, 22,* 485–499.

Hare, A. P. (1962). *Handbook of small group research.* New York: Free Press.

Hare, A. P. (1976). *Handbook of small group research* (2nd ed.). New York: Free Press.

Haskins, R., Walden, T., & Ramey, C. T. (1983). Teachers and student behavior in high- and low-ability groups. *Journal of Educational Psychology, 75,* 865–876.

Hatch, J. A. (1987). Status and social power in a kindergarten peer group. *Elementary School Journal, 88,* 79–92.

Heath, S. B. (1983). *Ways with words: Ethnography of communication in communities and classrooms.* New York: Cambridge University Press.

Heath, S. B. (1986). Sociocultural contexts of language development. In *Beyond Language: Social & Cultural Factors in Schooling Language Minority Students* (pp. 143–186). Los Angeles: Evaluation, Dissemination and Assessment Center.

Heath, S. B. (1993, December). *Cross-age tutoring and research: Before or after policy?* Plenary address at the 43rd Annual Meeting of the National Reading Conference, Charleston, SC.

Hickerson, N. (1966). *Education for alienation.* Englewood, NJ: Prentice Hall.

Hiebert, E. H. (1983). An examination of ability grouping for reading instruction. *Reading Research Quarterly, 18,* 231–255.

Hiebert, E. H. (Ed.). (1991). *Literacy for a diverse society: Perspectives, practices, and policies.* New York: Teachers College Press.

Hirsch, E. D., Jr. (1996). *The schools we need: Why we don't have them.* New York: Doubleday.

Hobbes, T. (1991). *The leviathan,* R. Tuck (Ed.) New York: Cambridge University Press.

Hughes, L. (1962). *Motto.* Available: http://home.uchicago.edu/~noneal/writings/poetry/hughes.html#motto. Internet Langston Hughes.

Hunter, M. (1982). *Mastery teaching.* El Segundo, CA: TIP.

Hyman, H. H. (1942). The psychology of status. *Arch Psychology,* 269.

Ichheiser, G. (1970). Appearances & realities: Misunderstandings in human relations. San Francisco: Jossey-Bass.

Indrisano, R., & Paratore, J. R. (1991). Organizing and managing instruction. In J. Flood, J. Jensen, D. Lapp, & J. Squire (Eds.), *Handbook of research on teaching the English language arts.* New York: Macmillan.

Jackson, P. (1968). *Life in classrooms.* New York: Holt, Rinehart & Winston.

Jaich-Yokley, G. (1990). *Investigating first-grade pupils' exploratory behaviors.* Unpublished doctoral dissertation, University of Cincinnati.

Jensen, E. (1998). *Teaching with the brain in mind.* Alexandria, VA: Association for Supervision and Curriculum Development.

Joe, S. (1993). Rethinking power. In M. Cochran-Smith & S. Lytle (Ed.), *Inside/outside: Teacher research and knowledge.* New York: Teachers College Press.

Johnson, D. W., & Johnson, R. T. (1972). *Learning together and alone: Cooperation, competition, and individualization.* Englewood Cliffs, NJ: Prentice Hall.

Johnson, D. W., & Johnson, R. T. (1999). The three Cs of school and classroom management. In J. Freiberg (Ed.), *Beyond behaviorism* (pp. 119–144). Boston: Allyn & Bacon.

Joyce, B., & Weil, M. (1992). *Models of teaching* (4th ed.). Boston: Allyn & Bacon.

Juel, C. (1990). The effects of reading group assignment on reading development in first and second grade. *Journal of Reading Behavior, 22,* 233–254.

Kamil, M. L., & Rauscher, W. C. (1990). Effects of grouping and difficulty of materials on reading achievement. In J. Zutell & S. McCormick (Eds.), *Literacy theory and research: Analyses from multiple paradigms: The 39th yearbook of the National Reading Conference* (pp. 121–127). Chicago: National Reading Conference.

Kaplan, J. (1980). *Walt Whitman a life* (p. 187). New York: Simon and Schuster.

Keene, E. O., & Zimmerman, S. (1997). *Mosaic of thought*. Portsmouth, NH: Heinemann.

Kerns, L. (1999). *Portfolio days at Hill Middle School*. Unpublished manuscript.

Kierstead, J. (1999). *Yes, A balanced approach—but let's get it right this time*. Paper presented at the 66th Annual Claremont Reading Conference, Claremont, CA.

Kirshner, D., & Whitson, J. A. (1997). *Situated cognition: Social, semiotic and psychological perspectives*. Mahwah, NJ: Erlbaum.

Kirst (1998, March). *Effects of small class size*. A symposium at the Annual Meeting of the American Education Research Association, San Diego, CA.

Klassen, C. (1993). *Teacher education that is multicultural: Expanding preservice teachers' orientation toward learning through children's literature*. Unpublished doctoral dissertation, University of Arizona, Tucson.

Klingner, J. K., & Vaughn, S. (1999). Promoting reading comprehension, content learning, and English acquisition through Collaborative Strategic Reading (CSR). *The Reading Teacher, 52,* 738–747.

Koch, A., & Peden, W. (Eds.). (1944). *The life and selected writings of Thomas Jefferson*. New York: Random House.

Koch, K. (1990). *Rose, where did you get that red? Teaching great poetry to children*. New York: Vintage.

Koch, K. (2000). *Wishes, lies and dreams: Teaching children to write poetry*. New York: HarperPerennial.

Kohn, A. (1996). *Beyond discipline: From compliance to community*. Alexandria, VA: Association for Supervision and Curriculum Development.

Kolb, D. A., Rubin, I. M., & McIntyre, J. M. (1979). *Organizational psychology: An experiential approach*. Englewood Cliffs, NJ: Prentice Hall, Inc.

Korostoff, M. (1998). Implementing class size reduction: With equity and access for all? *Issues in Teacher Education, 7*(2) 15–20.

Kovalik, S. (1994). *ITI: The model-integrated thematic instruction*. Kent, WA: Books for Educators.

Krashen, S. D. (1982). *Principles and practice in second language acquisition*. Oxford: Pergamon.

Krashen, S., & Terrell, T. (1983). *The natural approach: Language acquisition in the classroom*. Haywood, CA: Alemany.

Labaree, D. F. (1997). Public goods, private goods: The American struggle over educational goals. *American Educational Research Journal, 34,* 39–81.

Ladson-Billings, G. (1994). *The dreamkeepers: Successful teachers of African American children*. San Francisco: Jossey-Bass.

Lankshear, C., & O'Connor, P. (1999). Response to "Adult literacy: The next generation." *Educational Researcher, 28*(1), 30–36.

Lapp, D., Jacobson, J., Fisher, D., & Flood, J. (2000). Tried and true word study and vocabulary practices. *California Reader, 33*(2), 25–30.

Lave, J. (1997). *Cognition in practice: Mind, mathematics, and culture in everyday life*. Cambridge, UK: Cambridge University Press.

Leaver, B. (1997). *Teaching the whole class*. Thousand Oaks, CA: Corwin.

Lenney, E. (1977). Women's self-confidence in achievement settings. *Psychological Bulletin, 84,* 1–13.

Lewis, C. (1998). Literary interpretation as a social act. *Journal of Adolescent & Adult Literacy, 42,* 168–177.

Lieberman, S. (1956). The effects of changes in roles on the attitudes of role occupants. *Human Relations, 9,* 385–402.

Lincoln, A. (1995). *The Gettysburg address*. Boston: Houghton Mifflin.

Lloyd, C. V. (1998). Engaging students at the top (without leaving the rest behind). *Journal of Adolescent & Adult Literacy, 42,* 184–191.

Ly, P. N. (1998, September). Challenges. In A. DePaul (Ed.), *What to expect your first year of teaching*. Washington, DC: Office of Educational Research and Improvement, U.S. Department of Education.

Madden, L. E. (1997). Motivating students to learn better through own goal setting. *Education, 117*(3), 411–414.

Mager, R. (1970). *Goal analysis*. Belmont, CA: Fearon.

Manarino-Leggett, P., & Salomon, P. A. (1989, April). *Cooperation vs. competition: Techniques for keeping your classroom alive but not endangered*. Paper presented at the International Reading Association, New Orleans, LA.

Manke, M. P. (1997). *Classroom power relations*. London: Erlbaum.

Marshall, J. D., Smagorinsky, P., & Smith, M. W. (1995). *The language of interpretation: Patterns of discourse in discussions of literature*. Urbana, IL: National Council of Teachers of English.

McCracken, R. A., & McCracken, M. J. (1978). Modeling is the key to sustained silent reading. *The Reading Teacher, 31,* 406–408.

McKenna, B. (1982). Policy implications of research on class size: View from the NEA. In G. V. Glass, L. S. Cahen, M. L. Smith, & N. N. Filby (1982). *School class size: Research and policy* (pp. 93–102). Beverly Hills: Sage.

McLaughlin, M., & Vogt, M. (1996). *Portfolios in teacher education*. Newark, DE: International Reading Association.

Mehan, H. (1989, August). *Understanding inequality in schools: The contribution of interpretive studies*. Paper presented at the annual meeting of the American Sociological Association.

Menninger, K. www.listen.org.

Merriam-Webster's collegiate dictionary (10th ed.). (1993). Springfield, MA: Merriam-Webster.

Miller, E. H. (1989). *Walt Whitman's song of myself: A mosaic of interpretations*.

Miller, W. (1974). *Reading diagnosis kit*. New York: Center for Applied Research in Education.

Moll, L. (March 1992). Bilingual classroom studies and community analysis: Some recent trends. *Educational Researcher, 21*(2), 20–24.

Monaghen, E. J. (1989). Literacy instruction and gender in colonial New England. In C. Davidson (Ed.), *Reading in America*. Baltimore: Johns Hopkins University Press.

Morrow, L. M., & Smith, J. K. (1990). The effect of group setting on interactive storybook reading. *Reading Research Quarterly, 25,* 213–231.

Morrow, L. M. (1995). *Family literacy: Connections in schools and communities*. Newark, DE: International Reading Association.

Mosenthal, P. (1987). Relating taxonomies of reading methods to taxonomies of reading goals. *The Reading Teacher, 40,* 610–613.

Murray, H. A. (1938). *Explorations in personality.* New York: Oxford University Press.

Nagel, G. (1991). Four pedagogies for teaching reading. In P. H. Dreyer & M. S. Poplin (Eds.), *Knowing: The power of stories: The Claremont reading conference 55th yearbook* (pp. 322–342). Claremont, CA: Claremont Reading Conference Center for Developmental Studies.

Nagel, G. (1992). *Good groups: The search for social equity and instructional excellence through first-grade literacy groupings.* Unpublished doctoral dissertation, Claremont Graduate School, Claremont, CA.

Nagel, G. (1994). *The tao of teaching.* New York: Donald I. Fine/Penguin.

Nagel, G. (1996). How to do "How To." In C. B. Olson (Ed.), *Elementary ideas for teaching writing as a process* (rev. ed.). Sacramento: California Department of Education.

Nagel, G. (1998a). Looking for multicultural education: What could be done and why it isn't. In J. Houck (Ed.), *Education, 119*(2), 253–262.

Nagel, G., with Tsao, M. (1998b). *Multiple intelligences: Ways to know.* A paper presented as part of a symposium organized by Willis & Diamond.

Nagel, G. (1998c). *The tao of parenting.* New York: Penguin.

Nagel, G. (1998d). *The tao of teaching* (2nd ed.). New York: Dutton-Plume.

Nagel, G. (1998e). Using the *ABC* strategy in fifth grade. In A. Willis, B. Diamond, et al. (Eds.), *Know thyself and understand others.* National Reading Conference, 48th Annual Meeting. Austin, TX.

Nagel, G., & Flood, J. (1995, November). The language of interpretation: Patterns of discourse in discussions of literature, a review. *Journal of Reading Behavior: A Journal of Literacy, 27*(5), 245–247.

Nagel, G., & Kellerman, K. (1995). Advice to a dialogue journalist. In P. H. Dreyer (Ed.), *Toward multiple perspectives on literacy: The Claremont reading conference 59th yearbook* (pp. 137–139). Claremont, CA: Claremont Reading Conference Center for Developmental Studies.

Nagel, G., & Thicksten, M. (1997). Democratic literacy classrooms. In P. H. Dreyer (Ed.), *Literacy: Building on what we know: The Claremont reading conference 61st yearbook* (pp. 132–144). Claremont, CA: Center for Developmental Studies.

Nagy, W. E. (1988). *Teaching vocabulary to improve reading comprehension.* Urbana, IL: ERIC Clearinghouse on Reading and Communication Skills and the National Council of Teachers of English and the International Reading Association.

National Association for the Education of Young Children. (1988). *Appropriate education in the primary grades.* Washington, DC: Author.

National Governors Association. (1993). *Ability grouping and tracking: Current issues and concerns.* Washington, DC: Author.

Nelsen, J. (1996). *Positive discipline.* New York: Ballantine.

Nieto, S. (1996). *Affirming diversity: The sociopolitical context of multicultural education.* New York: Longman.

Noddings, N. (1986). Fidelity in teaching, teacher education, and research for teaching. *Harvard Educational Review, 566*(4), 496–510.

Noddings, N. (1992). *The challenge to care in schools: An alternative approach to education.* New York: Teachers College Press.

Oakes, J. (1985). *How schools structure inequality.* New Haven, CT: Yale University Press.

Ogaki, L., & Frensch, P. A. (1998). Parenting and children's school achievement: A multiethnic perspective. *American Educational Research Journal, 35,* 123–144.

Ogbu, J., & Matute-Bianchi, M. E. (1989). Understanding sociocultural factors: Knowledge, identity, and school adjustment. In Bilingual Education Office, *Beyond language: Social and cultural factors in schooling language minority students* (pp. 73–142). Los Angeles: Evaluation, Dissemination, and Assessment Center.

Ogbu, J. (1987). Variability in minority school performance: A problem in search of an explanation. *Anthropology and Education Quarterly, 18,* 312–334.

Ogle, D. M. (1986). KWL: A teaching model that develops active reading of expository text. *The Reading Teacher, 39,* 364–370.

Okagaki, L. & Frensch, P. A. (1998). Parenting and children's school achievement: A multiethnic perspective. *American Educational Research Journal, 35,* 123–144.

Oldfather, P., & Thomas, S. (1991). Researcher, classroom teacher, and student co-researchers jointly present perspectives on a qualitative study of student motivation. In P. H. Dreyer & M. S. Poplin (Eds.), *Knowing: The power of stories. The Claremont reading conference 55th yearbook* (pp. 106–128). Claremont, CA: Claremont Reading Conference Center for Developmental Studies.

O'Neil, J. (1990). New curriculum agenda emerges for '90's. *ASCD Curriculum Update, 32,* 1, 8.

Otto, H. J. (1950). Elementary education III: Organization and administration. In W. S. Monroe (Ed.). *Encyclopedia of educational research* (pp. 376–388). New York: Macmillan.

Palincsar, A. S. (1986). The role of dialogue in providing scaffolded instruction. *Educational Psychologist, 21*(1, 2), 73–98.

Palincsar, A. S., & Brown, A. L. (1984). Reciprocal teaching of comprehension-fostering and comprehension-monitoring activities. *Cognition and Instruction, 1,* 117–135.

Palmer, P. J. (1998). *The courage to teach.* San Francisco: Jossey-Bass.

Peterson, H. A. (1963). *Teacher and student reactions to overt work and work-avoidant behavior in secondary school classrooms.* Unpublished Ph.D. dissertation, University of Chicago.

Peterson, P. D. (1998). Why do educational research: Rethinking our roles and identities, our texts and contexts. *Educational Researcher, 27,* 4–10.

Peterson, P. L., Wilkinson, L. C., Spinelli, F., & Swing, S. R. (1984). Merging the process-product and sociolinguistic paradigms: Research on small-group processes. In P. L. Peterson, L. C. Wilkinson & M. Hallinan (Eds.), *The social context of instruction: Group organization and group processes* (pp. 125–152). Orlando, FL: Academic Press.

Pogrow, S. (1989, November). *Do general thinking skills and transfer exist for at-risk students?* Paper presented at the annual meeting of the National Reading conference, Austin, TX.

Poplin, M. (1992). Educating in diversity. *American School Board Journal, 179,* A18–A24.

Poplin, M., & Weeres, J. (1992). *Voices from the inside: A report on schooling from inside the classroom.* Claremont, CA: Institute for Education in Transformation at the Claremont Graduate School.

Radencich, M. C., & McKay, L. J. (1995). *Flexible grouping for literacy in the elementary grades.* Boston: Allyn & Bacon.

Reeves, S. (1999, October). Factors associated with NAEP assessment. Keynote address at the Fall Conference of the California Council on the Education of Teachers.

Renzulli, J. S. (Ed.) (1986). *Systems and models for developing programs for the gifted and talented.* Mansfield Center, CT: Creative Learning Press.

Rico, G. (1983). Writing the natural way: Using right-brain techniques to release your expressive powers. Los Angeles: J. P. Tarcher.

Rist, R. (1970). Student social class and teacher expectations: The self-fulfilling prophecy in ghetto education. *Harvard Educational Review, 40,* 411–451.

Rogers, C. (1983). *Freedom to learn for the 80s.* Columbus, OH: Merrill Publishing Co.

Rogers, K. (1991). The relationship of grouping practices to the education of the gifted and talented. *Grouping Practices, Researched-Based Decision Making Series,* pp. 1–9.

Rosenblatt, L. M. (1938). *Literature as exploration.* New York: Appleton-Century.

Rosenblatt, L. M. (1994). The transactional theory of reading and writing. In R. B. Ruddell, M. R. Ruddell, & H. Singer (Eds.), *Theoretical models and processes of reading* (4th ed., pp. 1057–1092). Newark, DE: International Reading Association.

Rosenholtz, S. J., & Cohen, E. G. (1983). Back to basics and the desegregated school. *Elementary School Journal, 83,* 515–527.

Rupley, W. H., Logan, J. W., & Nichols, D. (1998–99). Vocabulary instruction in a balanced reading program. *The Reading Teacher, 52*(4), 336–346.

Sagor, R. (1992). *How to conduct collaborative action research.* Alexandria, VA: Association for Supervision and Curriculum Development.

Salomon, G., & Perkins, D. N. (1998). Individual and social aspects of learning. In P. D. Pearson & A. Iran-Nejad (Eds.), *Review of Research in Education, 23,* 1–24.

Salvino, D. N. (1989). The word in black and white: Ideologies of race and literacy in antebellum America. In C. Davidson (Ed.), *Reading in America.* Baltimore: Johns Hopkins University Press.

Scarcella, R. (1990). *Teaching language minority students in the multicultural classroom.* Englewood Cliffs, NJ: Prentice Hall.

Schell, L. M., & Rouch, R. L. (1988). The low reading group: An instructional and social dilemma. *Journal of Reading Education, 14,* 18–23.

Scherer, M. (1997). A conversation with Mike Rose. *Educational Leadership, 54*(7), 7–11.

Schmidt, P. R. (1998). The ABC's model: Teachers connect home and school. In T. Shanahan & F. V. Rodriguez-Brown (Eds.), *47th Yearbook of the National Reading Conference,* 194–208.

Schmidt, P. R. (1999). Know thyself and understand others. *Language Arts, 76,* 332–340.

Schmuck, R. A., & Schmuck, P. A. (1979). *Group processes in the classroom.* Dubuque, IA: Brown.

Schmuck, R. A., & Schmuck, P. A. (1988). *Group processes in the classroom* (2nd ed.). Dubuque, IA: Brown.

Schon, D. (1983). *The reflective practitioner: How professionals think in action.* New York: Basic Books.

Schon, D. (1987). *Educating the reflective practitioner.* San Francisco: Jossey-Bass.

Schwartz, E. (1995). Crossing borders/shifting paradigms: Multiculturalism and children's literature. *Harvard Educational Review, 65,* 634–650.

Scribner, S., & Cole, M. (1981). *The psychology of literacy.* Cambridge, MA: Harvard University Press.

Shake, M., & Allington, R. (1985). Where do teachers' questions come from? *The Reading Teacher, 38,* 432–37.

Shakeshaft, C., Mandel, L., Johnson, Y. M., Sawyer, J., Hergenrother, M. A., & Barber, E. (1997). Boys call me cow. *Educational Leadership, 55*(2), 22–25.

Sharan, S., & Sharan, Y. (1976). *Small-group teaching.* Englewood Cliffs, NJ: Educational Technology Publications.

Sheldon, G. W. (1991). *The political philosophy of Thomas Jefferson* (p. 46). Baltimore: Johns Hopkins University Press.

Shor, I., & Freire, P. (1987). *A pedagogy for liberation.* Granby, MA: Bergin & Garvey.

Short, K., Kaufman, G., Kaser, S., Kahn, L. H., & Crawford, K. M. (1999). "Teacher-watching": Examining teacher talk in literature circles. *Language Arts, 76*(5), 377–385.

Short, K., & Klassen, C. (1993). Literature circles: Hearing children's voices. In B. R. Cullinan (Ed.), *Children's voices: Talk in the classroom* (pp. 66–85). Newark, DE: International Reading Association.

Shulman, L. (January 28, 1989). Teaching the disciplines liberally. Paper presented at the third annual meeting of The Holmes Group, Atlanta.

Simmons, D. C., Fuchs, L. S., Fuchs, P., Mathes, P., and Hodge, J. P. (1995). Effects of explicit teaching and peer tutoring on the reading achievement of learning-disabled and low-performance students in regular classrooms. *Elementary School Journal, 95*(5), 387–408.

Slavin, R. E. (1980). Cooperative learning: Review of educational research. *SO,* 315–42.

Slavin, R. E. (1983). *Cooperative learning.* New York: Longman.

Slavin, R. E. (1986). *Education psychology: Theory and practice.* New York: Allyn & Bacon.

Slavin, R. E. (1987). Ability grouping and achievement in elementary schools: A best-evidence synthesis. *Review of Educational Research, 57,* 2993–3336.

Slavin, R. E. (1997). Educational psychology: Theory and practice. Boston: Allyn & Bacon.

Sleeter, C. E., & Grant, C. A. (1993). *Making choices for multicultural education: Five approaches to race, class, and gender* (2nd ed.). Englewood Cliffs, NJ: Merrill/Prentice Hall.

Sleeter, C. E., & McLaren, P. (Eds.). (1996). *Multicultural education, critical pedagogy and the politics of difference.* Albany: State University of New York Press.

Sorenson, A. B., & Hallinan, M. (1984). Effects of race on assignment to ability groups. In P. L. Peterson, L. C. Wilkinson, & M. Hallinan (Eds.), *The social context of instruction: Group organization and group processes* (pp. 85–103). Orlando, FL: Academic Press.

Spinoza, B. (1968). Quote from "A Political Treatise," 1670. In J. Bartlett (Ed.), *Bartlett's familiar quotations* (14th ed., p. 373). Boston: Little, Brown.

Spiro, R. M., Coulson, R. L., Feltovich, P. J., & Anderson, D. K. (1994). Cognitive flexibility theory: Advanced knowledge acquisition in ill-structured domains. In R. B. Ruddell, M. R. Ruddell, & H. Singer (Eds.), *Theoretical models and processes of reading* (4th ed., pp. 1057–1092). Newark, DE: International Reading Association.

Sprenger, M. (1999). *Learning and memory: The brain in action.* Alexandria, VA: Association for Supervision and Curriculum Development.

Staff (1990, September). Purposes. *PTA Magazine, 32,* 1.

Stanovich, K. E. (1986). Matthew effects in reading: Some consequences of individual differences in the acquisition of literacy. *Reading Research Quarterly, 21,* 360–407.

Stephan, W. G. (1985). Intergroup relations. In G. Lindzey & E. Aronson (Eds.), *Handbook of social psychology* (3rd ed., Vol. 2, pp. 599–658). New York: Random House.

Sternberg, R. (1998). Abilities are forms of developing expertise. *Educational Researcher, 27*(3), 11–20.

Stodolsky, S. (1984). Frameworks for studying instructional processes in peer work groups. In P. L. Peterson, L. C. Wilkinson, & M. Hallinan (Eds.), *The social context of instruction: Group organization and group processes* (pp. 107–124). Orlando, FL: Academic Press.

Sylwester, R. (1994). How emotions affect learning. *Educational Leadership, 52*(2), 60–65.

Tennyson, A. L. (1968). Quote from "Locksley Hall," 1842. In J. Bartlett (Ed.), *Bartlett's familiar quotations* (14th ed., p. 647b) Boston: Little, Brown.

Thelen, H. A. (1967). *Classroom grouping for teachability.* New York: Wiley.

Thomas, J. A., & Montgomery, P. (1998). On becoming a good teacher: Reflective practice with regard to children's voices. *Journal of Teacher Education, 49,* 372–380.

Thompson, A. (1998). Not the color purple: Black feminist lessons for educational caring. *Harvard Educational Review, 68,* 522–554.

Thompson, J. D. (1967). *Organizations in action.* New York: McGraw-Hill.

Thoreau, H. D. (1854). Quote from *Walden.* In J. Barlett, Ed. (1968) *Bartlett's familiar quotations* (14th ed.). Boston: Little, Brown.

Tinajero, J. V., Nagel, G., Flood, J., & Lapp, D. (1995). I never knew I was needed until you called! Promoting parent involvement in schools. *The Reading Teacher, 48,* 614–617.

Tobias, S. (1994). Interest, prior knowledge, and learning. *Review of Educational Research, 64* (1) 37–54.

Tocqueville, A. (1955). *Democracy in America* (vol. II, pp. 142–143). New York: Vintage Books.

Tomlinson, C. A., & Kalbfleisch, M. L. (1998). Teach me, teach my brain. A call for differentiated classrooms. *Educational Leadership, 56*(3), 52–55.

Topping, K. (1989). Peer tutoring and paired reading: Combining two powerful techniques. *The Reading Teacher, 42,* 488–494.

Torres, C. A. (1998). *Democracy, education, and multiculturalism.* Lanham, MD: Rowman & Littlefield.

Turner, J. C. (1995). The influence of classroom contexts on young children's motivation for literacy. *Reading Research Quarterly, 30,* 410–441.

Tway, E. (1991). The elementary school classroom. In J. Flood, J. Jensen, D. Lapp, & J. Squire (Eds.), *Handbook of research on teaching the English language arts* (pp. 425–437). New York: Macmillan.

Ueland, B. (1999). In *The Art of Listening.* http://www.igc.org/traubman/listenfa.htm.

Urdan, T., Midgley, C., & Anderman, E. M. (1998). The role of the classroom goal structure in students' use of self-handicapping strategies. *American Educational Research Journal, 35,* 101–122.

Valencia, S. (1990). A portfolio approach to classroom reading assessment: The whys, whats, and hows. *Reading Teacher, 43,* 338–340.

Vygotsky, L. S. (1962). *Thought and language.* Cambridge, MA: MIT Press.

Vygotsky, L. S. (1978). *Mind in society: The development of higher psychological processes.* Cambridge, MA: Harvard University Press.

Wales, C. E., Nardi, A. H., & Stager, R. A. (1986). Decision making: A new paradigm for education. *Educational Leadership, 43* (8), 37–42.

Webb, N. M., Nemer, K. M., Chizhik, A. W., & Sugrue, B. (1998). Equity issues in collaborative group assessment: Group composition and performance. *American Educational Research Journal, 35,* 607–651.

Webster's new collegiate dictionary (11th ed.). (1959). Springfield, MA: Merriam-Webster.

Weinstein, C. S. (1991). The classroom as a social context for learning. *Annual Review of Psychology, 42,* 493–525.

Weinstein, C. S., & Valenti, K. (1995). *I want to be nice, but I have to be mean: Exploring prospective teachers' conceptions of caring and order.* Paper presented at the Annual Meeting of the American Educational Research Association, San Francisco. APRIL

Weinstein, R. (1976). Reading group membership in first grade: Teacher behaviors and pupil experience over time. *Journal of Educational Psychology, 68,* 103–116.

Welner, K. G., & Oakes, J. (1996). (Li)Ability grouping: The new susceptibility of school tracking systems to legal challenges. *Harvard Educational Review, 66,* 451–470.

Wenger, E. (1998). Communities of practice: Learning, meaning, and identity. London: Cambridge University Press.

Wesson, C., Vierthaler, J., & Haubrich, P. (1989). The discriminative validity of curriculum-based measures for establishing reading groups. *Reading Research and Instruction, 29,* 23–32.

Wigfield, A., Eccles, J. S., & Rodriguez, D. (1998). The development of children's motivation in school contexts. In P. D. Pearson & Iran-A. Nejad (Eds.), *Review of Research in Education, 23,* 73–118.

Wilkinson, I. A. G., & Anderson, R. B. (1995). Sociocognitive processes in guided silent reading: A microanalysis of small-group lessons. *Reading Research Quarterly, 30*(4), 710–741.

Williams, B. (1999). Diversity and education for the 21st century. In D. D. Marsh (Ed.), *1999 ASCD yearbook: Preparing our schools for the 21st century* (pp. 89–116). Alexandria, VA: Association for Supervision and Curriculum Development.

Williams, B., & Newcombe, E. (1994, May). Building on the strengths of urban learners. *Educational Leadership, 51*(7), 75–78.

Wolf, D. (1989). Portfolio assessment: Sampling student work. *Educational Leadership, 46*(7), 73–81.

Woolfolk, A. (1998). *Educational psychology.* Boston: Allyn & Bacon.

Young, L. D., & Allin, J. M. (1986). Persistence of learned helplessness in humans. *Journal of General Psychology, 113,* 81–88.

Index